Take

Take

*Your Guide to Creating
Happy Endings
and New Beginnings*

LEEZA GIBBONS

HAY HOUSE, INC.
Carlsbad, California • New York City
London • Sydney • Johannesburg
Vancouver • Hong Kong • New Delhi

Published and distributed in the United States by: Hay House, Inc.: www.hay house.com® • **Published and distributed in Australia by:** Hay House Australia Pty. Ltd.: www.hayhouse.com.au • **Published and distributed in the United Kingdom by:** Hay House UK, Ltd.: www.hayhouse.co.uk • **Published and distributed in the Republic of South Africa by:** Hay House SA (Pty), Ltd.: www.hayhouse.co.za • **Distributed in Canada by:** Raincoast: www.raincoast.com • **Published in India by:** Hay House Publishers India: www.hayhouse.co.in

Cover design: Christy Salinas
Interior design: www.doghaus.net and Tricia Breidenthal
Interior photos: Courtesy of the author, except where noted

Library of Congress Cataloging-in-Publication Data

Gibbons, Leeza.
  Take 2 : your guide to creating happy endings and new beginnings / Leeza Gibbons. -- 1st ed.
    p. cm.
  ISBN 978-1-4019-3981-6 (hardcover : alk. paper) -- ISBN 978-1-4019-3983-0 (ebk)
1. Self-management (Psychology) 2. Self-actualization (Psychology) 3. Self-help techniques. I. Title. II. Title: Take two.
  BF632.G483 2013
  158.1--dc23
                                    2012040565

Hardcover ISBN: 978-1-4019-3981-6
Digital ISBN: 978-1-4019-3983-0

16 15 14 13   4 3 2 1
1st edition, February 2013

Printed in the United States of America

This book is lovingly dedicated
to my children—Lexi, Troy, and Nathan—
who are the best part of the story of my life.
You inspire me, challenge me, forgive me,
encourage me, and dare me to try harder and
love more every day. A journey to find myself
without you would take me nowhere.

And to my husband, Steven: I wished for you,
and there you were, the best plot twist in
my second take! Thank you for helping me
rewrite the pages of my story to create a fulfilling,
meaningful, and loving new beginning.

I love you all, always and forever.
No matter what.

Yep, it's in here. The inspiration, motivation, gentle nudge, or *kick in the ass . . .* whatever it is you think you need to change the energy or direction of your life, you're gonna find it in this book. How do I know? *Because you just told me by picking it up.* You said it all loud and clear. See, when someone is ready to really get into the **"better business,"** it's not so much about the right words, the perfect lessons, or the top teachers; it's all timing, and yours is impeccable!

So, if you've been waiting for a sign, *this is it!* You know what you want to feel like, look like, and how you want to live. *You've got this!* Turn the page and get on with it. Welcome to *Take 2!*

CONTENTS

INTRODUCTION

THE DOOR MARKED *CHANGE*

*"You can't reach for anything new if your
hands are still full of yesterday's junk."*

— LOUISE SMITH

Okay, my friends—are you ready for change? Is it time to shake
things up, start over, and hit the reset button on your life? Congratulations on having the guts and the wisdom to call for Take 2.
No matter where you were for the first take or who you were before, that was then and this is *now*—this is your moment. There's
nothing more important.

They say that our life's work is finding our life's work, but I
was lucky. Early in the sixth grade, I discovered my calling was to
be a conduit of information. It didn't matter to me the medium or
the message. Just give me a microphone, and I'm rarin' to go. I'm
a storyteller—it's all I've ever really wanted to be, and I've never
looked back.

In storytelling and journalism, we use the term *sagging middle.* (Horrifying image, right?) This refers to the point in the story
that seems dull and boring due to a lack of action. You've probably seen movies or read books that you described as being "slow."

Well, as a reporter, I can't be slow. Viewers will change the channel in a nanosecond. And nobody wants a saggy middle! Authors, bloggers, journalists, and storytellers of all kinds avoid it at all costs. So should you!

It has been said that life is analogous to an epic journey, a hero's tale. So I guess you could say that sometimes the story gets a little . . . saggy. Can you relate? If you're in the middle of building your career or growing your family, what did you think life would look like or feel like at this point? If you're farther down the road (like me), have you ever felt that somewhere between menstruation and menopause, things became a little too predictable? Have you ever woken up and said, "This is not the life I ordered"?

It may be time to take a deep breath and survey your situation. Look at your decisions, career, relationships, and physical and mental health. If the story is boring and not worth reading or reporting, it's time for some creative writing, baby! Call for a do-over and reset yourself *now* in the direction you want to go. It doesn't matter if it's not where you thought you were headed—in fact, that's the point.

Interviewing people for a living, I've heard a solid cross section of what I call "life interrupted" stories from people who spent a lot of time figuring out who they were and what they should do when change came along and reshuffled the deck. They were divorced or separated, grew older or were fired. Someone they loved became ill or died. I've heard from many who have danced with the devils called depression and addiction. Some just forgot their steps once the music of their lives changed.

Life changes on the way to happily ever after, doesn't it? I mean, sometimes you don't even see it coming until one day you wake up and say, "Wait—this is not where I was supposed to end up!" It doesn't matter if you got divorced, got fat, got fired, got sick, or just got stuck—you can always call for a "redo."

See, you're the author of your own book and it's time for a dramatic plot twist, so let's get working on that. This is not the end of your story; this is where you learn about second acts, second chances, and new beginnings.

The Story Within Your Story

Have you ever noticed that the evenly split weight of the first and second halves of a story naturally cause a book to open at its midpoint? This is where the hero's trial occurs—in other words, the good stuff. I'm telling you: Your middle doesn't have to be saggy (proverbially or literally!) if you recognize that this is where the real lessons lie, where the valuable experiences happen, and where you deliver re-creation and transformation in a bold second take!

I've been the writer and editor of my own story for some time now. Over and over, I've had to strip away the dysfunctional and out-of-date definitions of myself in order to achieve reinvention. I know that may sound lofty—*to achieve reinvention*—but isn't it better than *succumbing to sameness?* Sometimes the process was daunting and the introspection humbling. But other times, shedding the old notions of who I was and where I wanted to go was liberating. It helped me focus and reminded me that I needed to call for another take, or I'd risk becoming a minor character in someone else's story.

The idea of life being under construction can be thrilling. We get to decide how it's going to happen and who's going to come along as we create our new self. Most of us edit our dreams and cut out our passion because we either don't feel we deserve it, are waiting for permission, or don't know how to eliminate risk. At some point, we have to figure out what our dreams really are *now* and what they're worth to us.

We can start by identifying how we want to live—in terms of our relationships, career, financial life, and family—and asking one important question.

Now that I've grown up, who do I really want to be?

We give a lot of respect to loyalty in our society, and it has always been one of my core values. But why are we devoted to the people around us, and does that dedication still serve us? What about a love relationship that has just worn us to a frazzle? Friendships that no longer support our vision of who we want to be? Jobs that are suffocating our souls? We stay because we've been taught to do so and because society rewards commitment. It may be helpful to suspend that notion of loyalty while taking a life inventory.

The re-creation process can seem incredibly self-indulgent to those were taught to go out there and climb mountain after mountain without asking why *this* mountain—or even why climb at all. But I don't think we can even start the process of giving back, which I know motivates a lot of us, until we find our center, the best version of ourselves. The closer we get, the better it is for everyone else.

So despite the fact that I don't fancy myself to be anybody's guru, and my attempts at self-help have been erratic at best, I still think there are some basics that have helped me stand tall, buck up, transition, and transform—and I'm happier and more fulfilled than at any other time in my life. This book is a compendium of what I know now. I hope you find it helpful.

MY TAKE: LEEZA'S LENS

Still Climbing

It's a long way from grits to glitz for this small-town girl from Irmo, South Carolina, who became a Hollywood businesswoman; and the biggest distance has nothing to do with the 3,000-plus miles between the locations. Being queen of the Irmo Okra Strut festival did little to prepare

me for hanging on to my self-esteem in a city where perfection seems to be a basic requirement for acceptance. Still, I plowed forward, gathering up experiences quicker than I could put peanuts in a bottle of Coke. And you know what? I've had some great ones.

It's interesting that when I look back, I see a lot of climbing. I've climbed the Brooklyn Bridge in New York and the Sydney Harbour Bridge in Australia. I've climbed Machu Picchu and Mount Washington. Then there are my many leaps of faith, including hang gliding off the cliffs in Rio, parasailing over the Sacred Valley in Peru, hot-air ballooning into wine country in France, parachuting over oil refineries in Texas, and flying the Goodyear blimp. I've raced cars with Tom Cruise, danced the tango with Arnold Schwarzenegger, and gone scuba diving with Mickey Mouse. I've shot a Beretta and learned to fly a helicopter and drive a terrorist-proof getaway car. (Truthfully, I haven't had much use for those last skills, but you never know!)

I've also dated the stars, interviewed political leaders, and been a guest in the homes of royalty. I have brushed shoulders with legends and losers and observed the neuroses and paranoia that make up the epidermis of the magical place called Hollywood. Along the way, I've also spent the night with the homeless, seen children die in a hospice, and sat

with drug addicts and drunks as they went cold turkey. Television guests have told me their most personal stories. They've trusted me with their secrets
and allowed me to touch their lives. Somewhere along
the line, I realized that I was living the life of my dreams.

But I've also been fabulous and a flop in the same week.
I divorced and found love again, fudged the delicate balance
between participating in the corporate world and being a
mother of three, and had enough red-carpet catastrophes to
keep the fashion police on alert full-time. My mistakes have
become my greatest lessons and have helped prevent me
from getting too full of myself.

Through the stories of my life—my "lens"—I'll share
some of the most important lessons I've learned. Some were
bitter pills to choke down, and some I wear as visibly as bum-
per stickers. Some I had to devise on my own, and others I
learned from those who have walked this path with me. No
matter what the lesson (or the source), each one built on
what came before and helped me realize that life is one big
story of reinvention.

In this book, I'll share with you what I've learned about
calling for a second take in my own life. I'll tell you how I've
done it in a very public business and managed to come out
the other side with my heart intact and my feet on the ground.

I'm assuming that you and I might actually have a lot
in common—well, unless you're one of those astonishingly
lucky women who married the right guy (the first time), got
the job you wanted making the money you wanted while
brilliantly parenting the children you imagined, and living it
all in your size-2 body, perfectly happy and serene. Now, if
you *do* happen to be one of those women, please put down
this book and go write one of your own! As for the rest of us,
I've always thought we reach our highest "goddess quotient"

when we share our paths, especially the detours, bumps, and potholes that help us find who we really are.

My greatest hope is that through this book you'll find inspiration to get more honest with yourself than ever before and to celebrate who you are and where you are today—regardless of whether it reaches your expectations. To move on, you first have to make peace with your starting point.

I hope that sharing some of my experiences will help you learn how to identify the areas in your life where you're fearful or resistant to change. **The point is simply to help you find and follow your story, understanding that it's the rewrites and second takes along the way that make it sizzle.** If it doesn't feel like you're starring in your own show, it's time to move on, establish new roots, stop living on the sidelines, take on fresh challenges, or just have a different attitude. I like to think of it as getting into the "Better Business."

Re-creation means determining what resources you need to execute your new plan—what physical, spiritual, financial, educational, or therapeutic support do you need? Get your team together, keeping in mind that *you* are the quarterback, the coach, and the owner, so you call the shots. If you're smart, you'll know when to recruit others, recognizing that true strength comes from knowing your limits. If you want to be in the Better Business, it also means that no matter who is on your side you have to accept sole custody of your life, knowing that you are enough and that your opinion about yourself is the only one that truly counts.

At the end of this book, I hope you'll go for it! The new job, the new relationship, the new body—the new *you*—just put it out there and make it happen. Celebrate your victories and understand (and be grateful for) your defeats. You can't have one without the other.

Get Real about Your Reality

When I was 12 years old, I came home from school in tears because auditions were being held for the school talent show, and I had no talent. Nothing. Everyone else sure seemed to be brilliantly gifted. Kids were playing piano, twirling batons, and turning pirouettes. One girl was spinning a hula hoop and another was crocheting! Me? Epic fail. No singing, dancing, piano playing, harmonica blowing, humming—nothing.

"Mom, I can't even whistle," I sulked.

Then in that way that mothers do, my mom (out of thin air and desperation) came up with the profound wisdom that changed the course of my life. "Shush up, Leeza Kim! You *do* have a talent," she told me. "You're a storyteller, so I want you to go stand up in front of that room and tell the best story of your life."

I believed her, and that's the moment when I became a journalist. It's also been a reminder to me as a mom to be very aware of what I say to my children about who they are and what they can do.

When my mother was in the early stages of Alzheimer's disease, my life was a flurry of on-camera appearances. I was hosting, reporting, and contributing to everything from my own talk show to *Larry King Live, Entertainment Tonight (ET)*, E!, and half a dozen others. I knew how to gather facts and communicate them— and goodness knows I could talk! I decided to ask my mother for her permission to talk publicly about her condition, and again she told me, "Honey, you're a storyteller. Now this is your story. Tell it, and make it count." My mom always wanted her life to matter. We all do. So she appeared on my talk show, *Leeza,* and encouraged others to find the courage to face their reality and get a diagnosis. "Don't hide it," she said, like the steel magnolia she was. I was never more proud to be her daughter than at that moment when she got real about her new reality. That's what we all should do.

You don't have to face a health crisis or a disease to step out of the shadows of fear, denial, or shame and show up for a new take. If you want to be better, happier, stronger, more loving, or more fulfilled, don't hide it. *Re-create yourself by rewriting the rules, reorchestrating the music, or recasting your role in your own life. That's the really cool thing: You get to make it up.*

Mom's disease forced everyone in our family to get real about our feelings and fears and face our own truths. I'd never realized how much I'd been walking around in a fog until then. My life had become a series of systems and programs on autopilot. I knew all the steps to my very predictable dance until the thief called Alzheimer's broke in and changed the music.

If your life's music has changed, take custody right now and claim this reality. That's the first step in preparing for Take 2. It's an important part of your story. Throughout this book, I hope that you will be inspired to complete your story on your terms—courageous, fulfilled, strong, and unapologetic for who you are. Right now it's time to get started on your next act. Go ahead and walk through the door marked *change.*

Make a Promise to Yourself

If they held midterm elections for your life, what would your platform be? Would there be a referendum for change or maybe even a recall? Re-creation, reinvention, transformation—whatever you choose to call it, you're ready to accept it, embrace it, and use it to your advantage. This entire journey is transformative, isn't it? The person you were yesterday is not who you have to be today or tomorrow. You have the power, the will, the tools, and the energy to transform yourself into whatever you want.

With this in mind, I've written what I call a "Transformation Proclamation." Think of it as your daily mantra. I hope it helps remind you of who you are and where you're going. If you like, tear this page out and stick it to your fridge or the front of your computer. Fold it up and tuck it in your purse. In any case, read it often and make it your own until the words and meanings imprint themselves in your mind.

TRANSFORMATION PROCLAMATION

I proclaim that this and every day is a blank page—a new chance to see things the way I want to. I choose to see possibilities. It is choice, not chance, that creates fate in life.

I proclaim that I will always try. If I fail, I know failure is a teacher. It's a delay, not a defeat. Effort is my goal.

I proclaim victory over the circumstances that show up in my life themselves; and I will look for a way through, under, around, or over the mountains that seem to stand in my way.

I proclaim that I can move ever forward. I can forgive and forget. My rearview mirror is a perfectly nice place for all things in life that I passed over, passed by, or rejected.

I proclaim that I will seek out opportunities and turn down the negative noise in my life. I will focus on abundance. I see myself as strong physically, financially, spiritually, and emotionally. I will not sabotage my success with self-doubt and fear of rejection.

I proclaim that I will own my power to effect change in my life and in the world. I have sole custody of my thoughts and myself. People who can't be supportive of that will be kicked to the curb!

I proclaim that I am perfect in my imperfection. I will not be afraid to open up and show my vulnerabilities.

I proclaim that at times I will stop achieving and start receiving. I will allow myself to breathe and believe, quieting my mind so I can welcome the answers the universe may be trying to deliver.

I proclaim that when I am frustrated, unfulfilled, distracted, or negative, I will become the queen of change and simply select another emotional state.

I proclaim that it is never too late to start over and redo, rewrite, or reclaim my life. I can call for Take 2 and be shamelessly committed to my own happiness.

Ever forward –

Fun fact: Whatever you say aloud with passion and energy embeds in your "emotional DNA" more effectively. You also receive an extra boost when you're physically active, so I recite my proclamation on my exercise bike or while I'm walking.

You're at the starting line of the rest of your life, and you can come out of the gate strong. Ready, set, transform!

Your proclamation should be *your* pledge—your promise to yourself about the things that you want to guide your life, your limits, your lines in the sand, your list of nonnegotiables. I hope you're inspired to write your own, and I'd love to see it! Please send me your own Transformation Proclamation through **www.leezagibbons.com**, or connect with me at **facebook.com/ officialleezagibbons**. Let's share the words, philosophies, and life lessons that inspire us all in strengthening our reinvention process.

MAKE IT
ALL ABOUT *YOU*

"You are unique, and if that is not fulfilled,
then something has been lost."

— MARTHA GRAHAM

If life is one big, epic story, who's writing your narrative? If you go back to your personal Chapter 1, is this how you thought the plot would unfold?

I believe we attract everything that comes into our lives, and it always shows up to serve our best interest—even those perplexing episodes of drama, piercing moments of pain, disappointments, and defeats. Nothing happens *to* you. Your story is revealed *through* you, and you're writing it. Through it all, you're the central character. So how come we don't always see it that way? Why do we think things happen *to* us and around us without realizing that we're always center stage in our own productions? I believe we are often waiting to be backed into a corner and forced into action, or we just think no one really runs their own show. The reality is, we are always writing new chapters in our story. We can always call for another take, claim the starring role, and put our name above the title.

Every good story needs a main character. For reporters, it's all about *who, what, when, where, why,* and *how*—and *who* always comes first. Journalists can't report without a subject or a source; television pundits can't pontificate without a politician or public figure; and let's face it, *Harry Potter* just wouldn't be the same if it weren't for, well, Harry Potter. When I dished up the entertainment news for *ET* and *Extra*, the leads usually focused on the celebrity—the character we all wanted to know about. Today, as an advocate for Alzheimer's research, education, and resources, I wouldn't be able to raise awareness without the people I meet. They're the main characters in their struggle against the insidious disease.

You get the point. In *your* story, the main character should be *you*. The person you should be most curious about and invested in and should want the latest news on is you! But I'm going to tell you something you already know: Sometimes you skim through your lines, hoping to get through your day on a wing and a prayer. You give your power away by not showing up, standing up, or following up.

Why are we inclined to believe that there's something wrong with being—and acting like—the main character in our own story? Maybe we just don't feel deserving or don't want to rock the boat. But until we realize that this is a dangerous form of personal neglect, we'll always be chasing our tails. *Come on and either buckle yourself into your driver's seat or stop whining and complaining when you don't get to where you want to go.*

I don't mean to sound harsh—okay, maybe I do a little bit. But it's because I'm concerned for women, including myself, who take so much focus off of their needs that they wind up causing heartache for themselves and others.

Vote for Yourself

Each day needs to begin and end with a focus on *you,* a lesson I first learned at a young age. When I was a teenager, I got the message that it was unladylike and ungracious to consider myself first in anything. Being raised in the South, a propensity for good manners and being neighborly were practically built into my genetic coding. I didn't ever want to come off as stuck up or "too big for my britches," as Mom always said. So around age 12, I unofficially enrolled in the Society of Perpetual People Pleasers and began a pattern of putting everyone else ahead of me. Of course this created a huge conflict because I didn't really *want* it that way—in fact, I resented the hell out of it, although I always tried to be a "lady" and a class act.

It may have started as false modesty, but the brain doesn't know the difference between what's real and what's not. If we back a message with actions, those become the habits of head and heart that create our reality. In other words, we become exactly who we think we should be and who we tell ourselves we are. Every time I undervalued myself, I was signaling to my brain that I wasn't worth much.

Do you ever feel like you're a horrible, selfish person for so much as thinking that you might deserve something before someone else? Well, I'll tell you what my mother had to say about that: "Honey, it's a poor frog who doesn't praise his own pond." If you don't vote for yourself, how can you expect others to think you're worth it, she always wanted to know.

At my alma mater, Irmo High School, after the team of cheerleaders had been voted on by the student body, the elected girls then selected a head cheerleader. There was nothing I liked better than being in charge, but rather than owning that, when we all cast secret ballots for which girl would call the shots, I voted for someone else. Who was I kidding?

I really wanted the job (which I ultimately got anyway), but as I wrote down another girl's name, I remember thinking, *What if it all comes down to* one *vote, and I cost myself this election?*

It's that way in life. It will often come down to your believing that you're the best one for the job, for the role, for the boyfriend, to adopt the baby, or to reinvent your life. *One* vote makes a difference. This is not a "nice-off." There will be plenty of times for you to show your humility, graciousness, and desire to help others, so don't give up the lead and let your understudy step in. You are uniquely qualified to run your life.

Take Stock, So You Don't Stew

Each morning ask yourself how you feel mentally, emotionally, and physically. I like to take the first five minutes of the day doing a check-in on how things feel—during my "first five," I scan my mind, body, and spirit. Taking stock of how you're doing is a selfless act because when you're good to yourself, everyone and everything reaps the benefits.

Many women act as if they're the caregivers of the entire world, not just their little piece of it. Giving selflessly to others is a wonderful thing, but not at the expense of neglecting our own needs. Too often when we don't get what we need, we stew about it and pout. "Nothing's wrong," we say indignantly, even though we're standing there on a chair with a noose around our neck, and then we withhold sex or huff around the house. It's not fair to us or to the poor person who just asked, "What's wrong?"

They say that in relationships—romantic or otherwise—if you don't have it, you can't give it away. If you don't value yourself first, you won't attract someone of value into your life. With all due respect to that great line in the movie *Jerry Maguire*, no one completes you. If you're incomplete, you'll just attract other people in your life who aren't whole.

So here are three quick and easy, relatively painless things you can do right now to get started making yourself the main character in your story as you call for a second take.

1. Pay Attention to How You Feel

This means being in tune with your physical and emotional self at all times. As women, we're practically incapable of turning off both the mind and the body, especially at the same time. C'mon, we have to keep something revved, or the world might collapse—right? Here's a simple system to follow: When your body is tired, exercise your mind; when your mind is tired, exercise your body. If you've been working on a project at your computer for hours, leave it and pump some oxygen through your heart—climb the stairs, take a walk, and switch your setting. That will directly benefit your brain as well, so when you return to work, you'll feel better about it. I tend to zone in on responding to texts and e-mails, writing, paying bills, organizing, and anything else on my computer that sucks me in. I stay at it till I get that familiar sense of overwhelm. That's when I know I need to change the environment and the energy.

It's the same with physical overexertion. If you've been on your feet, driving, running errands, working out, or anything else that leaves you physically depleted, tune in to that feeling. Before I go on to the next thing on the list, I like to soak in a tub, put my feet up, or do gentle stretching and think about my mental space opening up. I usually find that I have great clarity and focus after physical exertion.

2. No, No, a Thousand Times No!

I realize this is a basic idea here, but we still seem to be mastering it! Mothering three children through the toddler years taught me the art of saying no. If you ever need lessons, listen to two-year-olds. They say this word with conviction and don't think about providing an explanation why. They don't seem to really care how you feel about their refusal to go potty, eat their broccoli, or put their toys away. In my business, every good diva intrinsically knows how to say no. It's often followed by "Call my agent," but there's still a definite refusal. "No" is a complete sentence all by itself. Be brave enough to let it stand alone.

Even knowing this, are you like me in feeling you might need a 12-step program for yes-aholics? Who hasn't talked herself into thinking she could say yes to going on the business trip, making cupcakes for the school bake sale, serving on a committee, and watching a friend's child—all in the same week? Who hasn't had a meltdown as a result? Okay, you can put your hand down now.

Yes just feels good. People like you when you say yes. You feel capable and responsible and helpful. Yeah, till you watch it all come tumbling down, and then you feel put out—like a doormat —when in fact, you're the martyr who created the avalanche that's about to do you in. Some women can go from their latte in the morning to their chardonnay at night and still not see how they're piling one more rock on the mountain with every yes they utter.

If you think about women's natural inclination to say yes to things they either don't want to do or simply can't do, saying no isn't actually the thing that worries me the most. It's the desperate need to come up with or own up to excuses that I find so upsetting. That's what shows a basic lack of value for our own time and desires. Think back to the last time you agreed to do something you didn't want to. When you were thinking, *I can't do this. Say no. Absolutely not,* chances are you were troubled by your lack of a justifiable reason to say no. If you didn't have an excuse ready, you probably took the bait. Maybe you'd be okay responding with something like, "Oh I wish I could, but I have to take my son to a doctor's appointment to see about his asthma." That seems more understandable than saying, "No, I'm creating boundaries in my life, valuing and honoring my time. Leeza's mom said I have to vote for myself, and committing to this task would just add to my daily stress."

Look, I love to be involved, and I say yes as often as I can; but I've learned that for me, a well-placed no translates to more sanity.

Here's what I now know and keep in the front of my mind when people come at me with 300 different tasks to accomplish in three days: No one needs an explanation when you decline something. Just say you aren't available. You're unable to participate because you have other plans. *You do.* Valuing your time and your health is reason enough. Instead of committing to someone else's priorities and buying into their emergency, plan on *not* being stressed and overwhelmed. Otherwise, when you take on too much, you not only become a victim of stress, you're a full-blown carrier and spread that anxiety wherever you go. Saying no to things means you say yes to yourself more often.

This is an emerging skill of mine. Every time I tell someone, "I wish I could help, but I can't this time," I smile and feel proud of standing up for myself. Whenever I say, "No, sorry, I'm unavailable," I know I'm saying yes to making sure I *am* available for my family and the things that matter most.

YES *"Your Empowerment System"*

Before you say yes to anything make sure it fits into Your Empowerment System. *In other words, make sure it's really a "YES" for you! If the request fits in, feel good about saying yes, but if not, do what I do: shake your head and walk away without giving it a second thought or any hesitation.*

To say yes to yourself, make a list of the things you need to feel strong. Include what you need in order to feel in control and know you're running your life. Put these items on a checklist to consult before you make decisions about the people you let into your life and the projects you take on. Many times, what you need to feel strong is confidence and self-worth, but you may do things that erode your self-esteem, especially when you take on something out of guilt, obligation, or just to avoid saying no.

3. Fight to Be Heard

Just because I'm a nice girl from the South doesn't mean that I haven't had to stand up for myself and run the risk of (yikes!) not being liked. Don't ever confuse a people pleaser with a pushover.

It's always easier to cave. Your kids want a later bedtime or more allowance, your husband wants to skip the trip home to see your parents, or your boss wants you to work another weekend with no extra pay. Whatever it is that challenges your values and beliefs, it's worth the struggle to take it on and find your voice. I think being heard is one of the most basic human needs. If you don't fight for it, you passively confirm that you have nothing meaningful to say and relinquish your right to sail your own ship. When you allow others to bulldoze their ideas or opinions over your own, you can lose respect for yourself, and that's one of the first signs that you've given up on yourself.

I worked at Paramount studios for a couple of decades, and let me tell you, I loved it! Those were some of the best years of my professional life, and while I was growing from strength to strength in the business, my kids were growing up right alongside me. Lexi and Troy went to preschool on the lot, and we worked our show-taping schedule around my nursing schedule when Nathan arrived.

Mary Ann Halpin Photography

On my set, I had a little playroom for my kids, a suite of offices that housed my production company, a drop-dead-diva dressing room, my own parking space, and my name on the awning and door. When I drove through the fabled arched gates in my snazzy convertible with two car seats strapped in the back, I couldn't help but smile. In every sense, I felt it was my home. Still, it *is* business, and I was in business with Paramount when it all hit the fan.

While I was the executive producer and host of the *Leeza* show, I was also working on *ET* and *Entertainment Tonight* Radio, and developing shows at Leeza Gibbons Enterprises through an overall deal at Paramount. My home studio and I were heavily invested in each other, which is why it was a dark day for me when they sued me, claiming breach of contract. I disagreed. Think about it— the people who wrote my paycheck had also written a legal complaint about me. All my

"stuff" about not being liked started to bubble up. All my fears about not being heard and not being enough began to resurface.

At issue was my on-camera interview with Tony Robbins for his *Get the Edge* infomercial, selling his motivational tapes and DVDs. Paramount said I was violating the non-compete clause in my contract by doing another competing entertainment program. I said it was a commercial, which was allowed in my agreement. So I spent the mornings facing an audience at my talk show and the afternoons facing a team of lawyers in court. The bottom line? I was at the end of a contract cycle, and Paramount leveraged this dispute to try to get me to re-up.

My litigator was Joe Taylor, already a young hotshot at the time and now a legal superstar. Joe did a great job representing me and later became my friend. Still, even he couldn't prepare me for what it felt like for the two of us to walk into the courtroom and see over a dozen of *them*—the opposing side—full of black suits and stern expressions.

Now, as you know, I'm a big supporter of the Law of Attraction. Remember when I said that everything shows up in our lives for our best interest, even when we can't see it? This was a prime example. I learned grace under fire. I learned how strong I was and how much I could take. I saw that no matter how far I went to avoid conflict, it was still waiting for me until I faced it down. I discovered that even the best legal advice money could buy was no substitute for my own gut feelings, my own heart, and knowing my own limits. I still have boxes of hard copies of depositions and a few articles in *The Hollywood Reporter* to remind me of what a powerful course in "bucking up" this really was.

Was it hard? Yes, but it was necessary for me to stand up for myself. I knew it was a David and Goliath situation. I remember sitting in the office of Kerry McCluggage (he was chairman of Paramount Television then) and saying, "Look, I know you are a great big 747 jet and I'm this little Cessna prop plane, and you can shoot me out of the sky, but I believe I have a case and I have to defend my position." The studio leveraged its weight and power to make it uncomfortable for me not to settle, but I hung in as long as I could. It was important for my personal integrity that I be heard. It was a brutal few months. In the end, I ran out of energy, time, and money. We settled, I (happily) signed a new contract with Paramount, and life went on.

Throughout the entire ordeal, I held my head high and did my job, refusing to take it personally. (It wasn't personal.) I would do it all again the same way in a heartbeat. I still have great respect and appreciation for being part of a team, a family, where we could honor each other through a dispute with our core relationship intact. I maintained my self-respect and integrity, and they retained an employee and probably used my case as precedent to squash future lawsuits.

But more important, I was heard. I had a chance to state my case, and that means everything. I've interviewed tens of thousands of people, and I don't care if the issue is losing weight, battling addiction, fighting for justice, or winning a trivial argument with a spouse—we *all* want to be heard. If any situation or person is silencing your voice, that's a red flag warning that it's time to refocus and call for a second take.

MY TAKE: LEEZA'S LENS

Don't Flinch; Make the Change

I used all of the strategies I just talked about when I made a big shift in my career. As is often the case with change, there was really no way to prepare for this, no way to see it coming. While the unplanned detour turned out to affect my professional life, it had an even bigger impact on my personal life and gave me solid guideposts for what mattered most.

I will always be grateful for the people who held my hand through the initial few months after my mother was diagnosed with Alzheimer's disease. I was so lost, so sad, and so uncomfortable with not having answers. I felt like the walls of my world were crashing down. My colleagues, friends, and family members all helped me see that I would survive only by running straight toward the crisis. I did that big-time by going public with our struggles and creating a 501(c)(3) non-profit to offer help to others in our situation.

My entire family was on board, but I was the captain of the ship that would sail us into the world of health advocacy through the Leeza Gibbons Memory Foundation (LGMF). In 2002, I had just begun the charity, and I was in Florida for one of my first official appearances on behalf of our foundation. We were very excited about our efforts to support those newly diagnosed with a memory disorder and their family caregivers. I was on the way to make a speech when I took a call from one of the executives at *Extra,* where I was the host and managing editor at the time. I was told that I needed to go back to Los Angeles immediately. I don't remember what the explanation was, but I do remember the certainty of the moment. I was requested to return to the set, and I said no. The call was unexpected, and I'd received permission to be away—but the outcome was even more unexpected.

I didn't feel compelled to justify my answer. It was clear: I'd committed to something important for a cause close to my heart, and I wasn't going to head back to the studio without first completing what I'd set out to do for my foundation.

"Either come back now, or you might not have a job to come back to," is basically what I heard on the other end of the line as I was riding in the backseat of a cab.

I didn't hesitate, didn't flinch. In that moment, I walked through the door marked *change* and didn't even know it. I took stock of my feelings and weighed my priorities. Saying no to *Extra* meant saying yes to an opportunity to create something that has given me and so many others more satisfaction than any job ever could. I am still friends with my wonderful colleagues at *Extra,* and I am still certain I made the right move.

Today, the LGMF is celebrating its ten-year anniversary and remains a foundation of strength and purpose in connecting caregivers to one another and to much-needed community resources. Our free support centers, Leeza's Place and Leeza's Care Connection, are my mother's legacy and a source of great pride for me. I grew up that day in Florida. I owned my life, I created a change, and I was changed.

A Gentle Nudge

All right. Time for some energy shifting. I'd like you to take out your PDA, smartphone, or old-fashioned planner and put in at least *one* thing a week that you're going to do for yourself. Maybe it's something as simple as a manicure or as extravagant as a day trip to the spa. Of course, it doesn't necessarily have to do with physical pampering. Maybe you'll recite a serenity prayer silently or make a call to a friend you've been out of touch with.

I really believe in what happens when you make one small change in the way you do, think about, or approach things. For example, I'm guilty of "overproducing" things in my life. My husband, kids, assistant, and friends know that I habitually subscribe to the idea that more is more—except for more time for me. Well, a few years ago I shifted the energy in my life and began carving out time exclusively for myself. This was part of what I changed when I decided to Take 2. I didn't explain myself to my office assistant who keeps the calendar, nor did I justify it to my children. I simply started taking the time I needed to feel sane.

"I have the morning blocked out on that day," I would say when a request came in, or "I'm afraid I can't do that; I have prior commitments." "No, I'm sorry I can't" is a complete sentence, yet we feel the need to explain and elaborate, which just makes us feel guilty. For me, making this change was a process and included tutoring others in my life in how to treat me differently. I had to build a new emotional muscle in order to find harmony. I had only myself to blame for all the pressure and stress I'd been feeling because I'd set things up that way. But since it was my own passive creation, I knew I could create another story based on my newfound awareness.

My dear friend Bobby, who took care of me and ran my office for a long time, really helped me build up some emotional walls and protective barriers in this space. I knew he always had my back, and his loyalty and friendship has been a big part of my reinvention story. I hope you can find someone like that as you call for a second take. This is the time to have people around who want to see you win.

Sometimes you have to see yourself in a fresh light in order for others to see you differently. Following are some ideas to shift your energy in your day-to-day life. I hope they inspire you to take stock, find your voice, and open up time in your schedule to round out your experience of *you*. Get acquainted with the part of yourself who rarely comes out to play.

• **Check out local architecture.** The next time you go by that building you've always admired, try walking in. Spending a little quiet time admiring beautiful or intricate surroundings can be soothing and inspiring.

• **Go on a gratitude hike.** You don't have to have an actual mountain to climb or a wilderness trail to follow. Walk around your neighborhood or the streets outside your office. Get some real-life vitamin D to improve your mood while you work on your hips, legs, and heart. This is a soul-satisfying way to focus on only the things that fill up your well of gratefulness.

• **Take a class:** cooking, dancing, yoga, language, whatever. Maybe you want to learn how to organize your closet or grow an herb garden. What matters is that you find something to do with new people while concentrating on something that's not yet in your skill set.

• **Write.** Don't think too much about it; just pour out your heart. Dream big and don't edit. Compose a letter to yourself and save it.

• **Create your own Angel Alert:** Anonymously pay for lunch, coffee, or parking for someone—the person behind you at the parking garage or someone in line at the coffee shop. There will be no honor, no glory, no list of "friends and contributors" with your name on it. You'll just feel the natural high that comes from knowing you made life better for someone else.

• **Care for yourself.** When was the last time you had a physical, full blood work, a stress test, or a mammogram? Once in a while you need to check in with yourself and ask: *Am I getting enough sleep? Do I drink enough water, and take any necessary supplements? Do I exercise enough or get enough sunlight?* These questions, when answered honestly, lead to better overall health. And a healthy woman is a strong woman.

The Search for Meaning

I often visualize my life as a long hallway. There are doors and archways and portals and gates all along the way. Each of the openings represents a meaningful experience or an expression of who I am. Some of them are open and the lights are on, while others are closed tight, shut off. But they all symbolize moments in time. At night especially, I mentally roam around the hall and recall the sights and sounds of my life. Sometimes I peer through an archway and smile at the scene; other times I open a door and go in, still trying to figure out what went on during that time. I see who was there with me, what we did, and why it mattered.

One way or another, that's what we all do. We search for meaning. I think you can always find it by examining what you love, whom you love, and how you spend your time. But you have to look. That's what this chapter has been encouraging you to do: Turn inward, notice yourself, and make yourself number one in your life. My time has been spent as a storyteller. That's how I've made my living, working in radio and television as a TV host, an interviewer, a reporter, a producer, a CEO, and a philanthropist—but I am more than that. I'm a caregiver, mother, wife, sister, and friend. And I know that I am even better at being all of these things when I take care of myself first.

Who do you think you are beneath the layers? Go ahead and ask yourself. Mentally roam the hallways, secrets entries, portals, and gates of your life and your *self*. Spend some time nurturing you. It will come naturally, if you let it.

Chapter 2

LET CHANGE BE AS NATURAL AS BREATH

"If you do what you've always done,
you'll get what you've always gotten."

— TONY ROBBINS

I work pretty well under pressure. I suppose it comes from 30-plus years of having a stage manager count me down to a live event. I'd hear, "In three . . . two . . . one . . . ," and I always had to be on. I had no choice—and neither do you, not when it comes to being the person you want to be and having the life you imagine. When you get the cue for your life's second take, don't hesitate and don't let anyone's voice be louder than your own.

With my work on television, I'm constantly researching, making assessments on the fly, and asking questions of news makers and celebrities. On any given shoot, I deal with a dizzying array of "handlers"—publicists, agents, and managers—who are fiercely guarding their clients. Everyone has an opinion and wants in on the action, from the limo driver to the celebrity's pet pig! My role is to listen; assess; and either react, respond, or stand my ground.

I've had to size up the subject, build consensus, and cut to the chase all in the first five seconds of the report. It's a kind of entertainment triage. While this certainly isn't brain surgery, it's given me some useful skills, particularly in the areas of flexibility and willingness to change. I can change a script, an angle, or a point of view, all under the gun of the countdown cue.

Dealing with people who aren't under your control is a humbling experience. You have to be ready to react to anything. In the business of live television, you learn quickly that it's more important to be ready for the unexpected than to waste time and energy trying to avoid or deny it. So I learned to be a champion of change, to love it and look for it. That doesn't mean it's easy, though. The first shift is always internal, and for me, the biggest transformation has been letting go of my need to be in control most of the time. Now, I'm not necessarily saying I'm good at this, but I am trying. If you ask my kids, they'll tell you I'm beyond an epic failure at relinquishing control, but even they have to admit that I'm pretty good at change. In fact, I think most women are in some ways.

We change our clothes and hair color, change our minds, and have a change of heart—all without batting an eye or breaking a nail. But sometimes escape is easier than switching it up, and many of us are pretty good escape artists. Where do you hide to resist change? Too much time on Facebook or eBay, overeating, shopping sprees, sleeping a lot, or gambling—I'll bet these are signs that you're avoiding facing change in your life by indulging somewhere else. But everything new comes with some pain, so you may as well bring it on and do the heavy lifting!

Change is coming for you, no matter what. It's either gonna break into your life, or you can open the door and invite it in.

Heck, I now set a place at the table and ask it directly, "What have you come to teach me?" The way you react to change is what makes the difference. Many of us fear it. Loathe it. Run to the hills to avoid it. The smart ones consider themselves more like the wind, blowing where it may and adjusting course in a natural synchronicity with the universe. But getting in the flow takes a new perspective. If you look up the word *change,* you'll see it defined as, "To make the form, content, future course, nature of (something) different from what it is or from what it would be if left alone." Do you know what I see as the scariest part of that definition? *"Different from what it is . . ."*

Why is different so terrifying? Why do we get so afraid when we don't know what's coming next? I think we're timid when we think we aren't going to know enough to be successful. *It helps me to remember that amateurs built the ark, but professionals built the Titanic.* We must be confident that we have what it takes; let's set new rules for our life that says we won't be afraid of something different or new. Change doesn't have to be the villain in our story, if we could learn to shift the way we perceive it.

Think about people who have been catalysts for transformation: Martin Luther King, Jr.; Twitter creator Jack Dorsey; Starbucks guru Howard Schultz; Bill Gates; and the list goes on. People like this are no different from you and me—they just have a different way of experiencing change. I believe they've been able to either face it or create it because they stood for something; they believed in something and had the courage to back it up. They had a unique vision for their lives that kept them in forward motion, and without that, life is in rewind. Did they mess up? Big time! Did they fail? Over and over again! Yes . . . and? You can be smarter, stronger, sexier, and happier than ever before; but you need to hold on to your goal mentally, take action physically, and know emotionally that you're the only one who can put the change into action.

When you're committed to something and your life serves as a living record of that value, you have to serve it with integrity, not fear. So if you stand for honesty or hard work or effort, that's the fuel you run on to face change. That's what this book is all about. I want to help you discover what you stand for and reintroduce you to who you are today and what your rules or values are. Establish how you'd like to live them, with all the courage of a warrior and zero apologies for your choices. Author Christopher Morley spoke directly to this point when he wrote, "There is only one success . . . to be able to spend your life in your own way, and not to give others absurd maddening claims upon it."

MY TAKE: LEEZA'S LENS

One of My Sheroes

Maria Shriver is one of my "sheroes." I'm not ashamed to admit she's on my list of girl crushes because of my respect for the way she has chosen to play her cards. Maybe it has something to do with the fact that she's never shied away from anything, and she always navigates her way through the twists and turns of change. Maria comes from a family that knows a lot about change. Her mother, Eunice Kennedy Shriver, created the Special Olympics; and her father, Sargent Shriver, served as founding director of the Peace Corps. If there's a need in the world, this family knows how to fill it!

Ronald Reagan said that "All great change in America begins at the dinner table," and I guess Maria's family believed it. She once told me that her family had conversations at dinner like most of us do, but if you were in Maria's family, you sure as heck better bring something to the table. My own kids were often quizzed on vocabulary words and current events, but the Shriver family took it much further than that when the children were asked, "What did you do today to change the world?" They didn't hear, "How was school today?" or "What did you get on that math test?" but had to answer how they'd made this a better place for everyone.

So Maria knew she had to find some way to make a difference. She did, and she was good at it. As a TV journalist at NBC, audiences loved her and so did the network. She got bigger and better assignments and more attention. When she married Arnold Schwarzenegger, having her own identity as a newswoman was more important than ever. But things change. Arnold ran for governor, and Maria had to leave the news business during the election so she didn't give the appearance of favoritism or partisan politics.

After their victory, she went back to reporting—but that changed, too. Anna Nicole Smith caused Maria to leave her job. She didn't quit because of anything Anna Nicole did; rather, Maria walked away from the career she loved because of the way her industry, the news media, had handled the story of Anna Nicole's passing. At that time, Maria chose not to be part of a business that would exploit and sensationalize such a tragic story. She made a change. Then more recently, when her famous husband betrayed her, she faced upheaval again. She showed enormous grace in dealing with the public scandal, staring it square in the face and allowing herself time to walk with the pain before moving forward on her way to reinventing her life.

I've always been proud to call Maria my friend, but never more than seeing her respond so powerfully to her father's diagnosis of Alzheimer's disease. She is poised to be one of the most influential voices of change in the world to make things better for those who are diagnosed with this heinous disease and their families.

If you make a list of anyone you admire and pin down what their lives stand for, I bet you'd find change at the base of it all. I love

Maria's story because so many aspects of her life revolve around shifting positions, varying perspectives, and reacting with flexibility. Maria isn't immune to the deafening sound of change knocking at her door. Every time she has answered the call. Not because she is fearless, but because she chooses to move toward the fear rather than away from it. That always makes us better. The same is true for you.

The Paradox of Change

While we might find it hard to be different or alter the status quo, we often crave it. We have a natural desire to be better, reinvent ourselves, and undo bad habits or acquire healthy new ones because change is a part of life, as natural as breathing. We see this in the turning seasons, planetary positions, and patterns of nature, which are all examples of necessary change. This is the paradox: We need change, but we often fear it.

I've learned that how I manage change is the key. Early on in my career, there were times when I thought things were great and I was hot stuff, only to have it all crash and burn. I saw that *"success is not final, failure is not fatal. It's the courage to continue that counts."* Winston Churchill is reported to have said that, and I've borrowed it many times.

When you have to continue or give in, what do you do? If you find that you most often give up, take inventory of those moments. Was there a turning point—a threshold when you threw in the towel—or was it a slow build, a gradual acceptance of the futility of running your own life? I'm not talking about control; I'm talking about knowing what you want and going after it. They say that those are two characteristics of happy people, and you can do it. You just need a playbook, a set of standards, and a mission statement for your life. No one can write these for you—not your husband, teachers, children, or employers, or even your mother. No one else has your operating system.

At the end of the day or the decade, have you let out a sigh and thought, *How did I get here*? Well, you get to be your own master programmer in this thing called life. If you find a virus in your life operating system, then approach it as you would one on your computer. You have to examine all the files and programming to see what needs to be deleted, what needs to be wiped clean, and what you can reinstall. That's stuff to be decided by you and you alone.

So why might you let others run your life? Maybe you think somehow that they know you better than you know yourself. If that has indeed been true for you, realize you're moving past it because you've just called for another take. Order of business number one: deal with your stuff and choose to embrace change.

Surviving and even thriving through change depends on your ability to search out the good and work with what you have. How well you do that depends on how you view shifts in your life. I grew up in an idyllic family, in a *Father Knows Best* neighborhood (or at least I thought it was at the time). My parents encouraged me to believe in the power of my dreams. It worked. I took my energy, enthusiasm, and talent out into the world; and I found jobs and created a career that I loved. I found romance, too, and gave birth to healthy babies. I surely didn't want change. I was comfortable in my safe, predictable little bubble. The bubble might have become thin at times, with a few leaks here and there, but I considered myself lucky.

Then the changes came for me as they do for each of us, ready or not. I got divorced. I got older. My image of happily ever after didn't fit into this new reality, and then the bubble burst when my mom got Alzheimer's disease. That forced a change in me, which I shared with you in the last chapter.

Change like this is an introduction to my higher self—at least that's how I've come to perceive it. I used to try to avoid it, but now I ride the wave as calmly and with as much faith as I can. It's hard, but it's not until life kicks you to the curb that you learn how to kick back, right? I agree with British philosopher Alan Watts, who said, *"The only way to make sense out of change is to plunge into it, move with it, and join the dance."*

Here's something to think about: Without overusing the "life is like a story" metaphor, let's consider change as nothing more or less than a plot twist. Aren't the best-written novels, movies, or miniseries the ones with the unexpected twists? "I didn't see that coming!" we exclaim. A good narrative with some real monkey wrenches thrown in gets our adrenaline going, and we want more—maybe even a sequel. Why would this be any different when it comes to our lives?

Don't Be a Victim of Predictability

I've come to the conclusion that change is difficult for many of us because we've become seduced by the idea of predictability. It gives us a sense of security. After all, what is there to be scared of when you can predict the future? But the majority of us can't see what's going to happen as a result of our actions or inaction. We don't know what the boss will think of the presentation, what the guy at the singles' event thinks of our smile, or what the doctor is going to say about our next mammogram. But this doesn't give us permission to suspend our lives until we can be sure.

So gear up for it and give the presentation, put on your best outfit and head out to that speed-dating event, or take a deep breath and take the exam. Outcomes aren't your responsibility. *Your* work is the process as well as the approach and the intention you bring.

If you've created a life that's so routine you feel insanely stuck, fidgety, unfulfilled, or afraid, maybe you're ready to let go of your false sense of security—but how? *Try setting a place for change at your emotional table and spend some time getting to know it.* Once you do, you'll see that change isn't your enemy. Your real power to navigate the flow of life is found in the present moment, not borrowing problems from the future or stressing over the past, but recognizing that right now is the apex of possibilities. Honestly, I grapple with this myself, but I'm happy to share what I try to keep in mind all the time about living in the moment.

Life can change in an instant, and I'm not talking about winning the lottery. How long does it take to say "I do," or "No more"? What about when we say "I quit"? We can start over or stop in an instant. The only thing in the way is the safety and security that we think we need. Of course those are both good things on many levels, but not if they prevent us from going after a secret dream, making a healthy change, or offering an olive branch to an old friend.

MY TAKE: LEEZA'S LENS

A Moment of Truth

One of my favorite stories about life-changing moments happened on Stage 27 at Paramount, where my talk show was taped for years. We were profiling controversial moments of truth, and I was interviewing a panel of abused women who faced their fears and walked away from their dangerous lives. They'd been threatened at knifepoint, spit on, burned with cigarettes, and called worthless whores. Their abusers told them that if they left, they would be killed and their children would be harmed. In fact, the time when a woman is at the greatest risk of being killed in an abusive relationship is when she leaves. It's like walking out of a burning building into a tsunami.

There was a woman in the audience who'd asked to sit in on this show. She was thinking of leaving her abuser but wasn't sure where she'd find the courage. Her kids were in our greenroom backstage, each with a little packed bag—just in case. We had a car outside with the motor running to take them to a safe house. This woman had no money and no job and would have to face starting over with a new identity to protect her from her husband, who had a criminal record and a history of assault.

She told me that she didn't want to be seen on camera, but she knew this could be her moment of truth. I looked at her during a commercial break and could see a shift in her energy. When we returned from break, I walked over in her direction, and she grabbed the microphone from me and said, "I've had enough. Thank you to the women on the stage for helping me find my courage. I'm leaving with my children."

One of our producers got her children, we walked her out, and she was given a wig and a hug before she got into a car and drove through the gates. She faced the pain of change because her desire for a new life was stronger than her fear. We never heard from her again. She and her kids started their lives over at that point with new identities. My fondest dream is that she continues to get stronger and stronger, that the children learned to feel safe, and that every day she celebrates her everlasting change. Some of you may relate to this woman and feel trapped in an abusive relationship. If so, leaving is a change you shouldn't try on your own. I encourage you to face your fear and contact a local or national hotline and begin your journey to safety today.

Even if we don't live each day in danger, all of us can benefit from making new choices right in the present moment. We think that we'll have tomorrow to live our dreams, make our mark, and change the world—or at least ourselves—so we lull ourselves into a false sense of the value of keeping things static. We think, *Oh, just a little bit more time in the safety zone where I know my way around the who, what, where, why, and how of it all. I'll make a move when I'm ready.* And the next thing we know, we're doing nothing.

I'm asking you to reframe that habit. *Call of the Wild* author Jack London said, "You can't wait for inspiration. You have to go after it with a club!" You can predict till the cows come home, stay where you are, and never do a thing to move forward, but it's not going to stop change from pitching a tent in your yard. The only certainty is that you have this moment right now and you're closer than you ever imagined to wherever you want to be.

Be Unpredictable Today!

It's probably best not to go from zero to a hundred on the change-ometer, so let's take it slow and make sure you have some fun on the rev-up.

• **Break your routine.** Something as simple as driving a different route to work (or changing your mode of transportation altogether) can enhance your mood and help you get out of a rut. The daily grind doesn't have to be such a . . . grind if you remember that you have choices to help you breathe new life into your day.

This reminds me of the summer that my friend Holly and I decided to take an adult dance class at my daughter's dance academy. We dutifully strapped on our tap shoes and laced up our jazz shoes so we could totally humiliate ourselves amid a group of middle-aged ladies, all of whom had the same idea as we did: *Wouldn't it be fun to have our own moment to share the love of dance with our daughters?* At the end of summer, we had a featured spot in the recital, complete with costumes and trophies. I loved being onstage in front of an audience, even if most people were offering us pity applause. I got so carried away that I forgot the steps and was the only one up there shuffling off to Buffalo when I should have been doing a flap ball change. It is still one of my fondest memories. (Wanna see the video? You'll find it at **www.leezagibbons.com**)

• **Be silly.** Catching someone off guard can be so much fun. Shoot off a rubber band or throw a ball of paper into your office mate's cubicle. (Just don't tell your boss I told you to!) Have an unexpected pillow fight with your kids or jump on your husband when he comes through the door from work. Notice their reactions to your sudden burst of childishness. If you're doing these kinds of spontaneous things already, great, but most of us become so *serious* as we age. Doing something goofy and unexpected will surprise your friends and family, and remind you of the laughter you are capable of spreading.

And how about releasing yourself from the closet trap, while we're at it? Do you find yourself wearing the same two pairs of jeans or work pants with the same blouses or sweaters week after week? This is one of the ironies of being a woman. While we love to shop (and maybe have a slight fixation on shoes), we tend to revert into some sort of cycle when it comes to our clothes. Sure, we all have our favorite jeans that fit just right or our comfy shoes, but seeing ourselves in something different can open us up to sides of ourselves that have been dormant. Invite a friend over, try on your outfits from the back of the closet, and shake it up.

• **Play.** There has been so much recent research telling us to play more. In fact, playful couples experience more frequent intimacy and stay together longer than their "grown-up" counterparts. At first it might seem too off the wall to have a tickle fight with your boyfriend or play hopscotch with your best friend, but it's like riding a bike—you know how to do it, so take your hands off the handlebars!

When my son Nathan was about seven, we'd been going through a lot as a family and I knew he was stressed. He told me that he never got to play with me. It didn't take long for me to realize that he was right, so I picked him up from school early one day, and we came home and had a water fight with the hose in our front yard! We both felt better.

I often find meaning and value in quotes from best-selling inspirational author Marianne Williamson. I especially love this statement: "Our deepest fear is not that we are inadequate. Our deepest fear is that we are powerful beyond measure." Did you catch that? Is she saying there's a possibility that we reject change because at the heart of it, we're actually afraid we might succeed? If we break it down, it makes sense. I'll talk more in the next chapter about how we have to let go of fear, because I know as well as anyone, it's easier said than done.

A Mind-set for Success

Successful people know that you need to focus on growth to get where you want to be, and in order to do that, you have to be real about where you've been. In order to grow you'll have to see all those defeats and failures as precursors to success, allowing your power to emerge. Not until you get into the right "headspace" will you really move forward. Henry Ford said, "Before everything else, getting ready is the secret of success." So, let's get you ready with some tips to help you value what got you here as you plan your lift-off.

1. Past Perfect

Build your future on the failures of your past. I know, I know! Everyone talks about this, and there's a reason: Nothing is truer. This mind-set is possibly one of the single greatest things to master in your personal database of skills, and it can make the biggest difference in your life. Whether it's things you wish you'd never done, jobs at which you failed, men you shouldn't have married, or abandoned attempts to learn something, all of the misfires can keep you right on target in your current moment of discovery. Think of the past failures as practice. If practice makes perfect, then you're just one mistake closer to getting it right the next time. As Thomas Edison said, "I have not failed. I've just found 10,000 ways that won't work."

2. Look for Role Models

If you're stunted because of the fear of making a change, consider other women who have throttled forward regardless of how big or small the obstacle. Some of my favorite role models thrived in the court of public opinion, in wars, and in the quiet rooms of their own homes. I think about the battered woman who dared to start over when I'm feeling vulnerable to fear and can't make a change.

As an interviewer, it's always more revealing to focus on a person's failure because those are the moments that define us. You really only get to know a person's character through how she acts when she's down, so I focus on the inspiration that comes from failures instead of notable victorious moments. And do you know what I found? The biggest successes, the best role models, failed a thousand times. That's what winners do—they fall flat on their faces. It's what they do when they pick themselves up and dust themselves off that matters. Want examples? I'm glad you asked:

- JK Rowling was a single mom without much hope— broke, depressed, and living on welfare—when Harry Potter made her one of the richest women in the world. She now encourages others to stop living so timidly and to risk failure to get what they want.

- After just one performance, Elvis Presley was told by staff at the Grand Ole Opry, "You ain't going nowhere, son. You ought to go back to driving a truck."

- Vincent van Gogh had a brief career as a painter and sold only one painting when he was alive. Now he's revered as one of the most influential artists of all time, with more than 800 known works in museums or private collections.

- Lucille Ball was considered to be a "B" movie star at best. She had pretty much failed at acting when her drama teacher told her to find another profession.

- "You lack imagination and have no good ideas," were the words Walt Disney reportedly heard when he was fired from a newspaper job. After that he had several failed attempts at entrepreneurship.

- Thomas Edison was told by teachers that he was "too stupid to learn anything."

- Oprah Winfrey was once fired from her job as an on-camera reporter because she was "unfit for TV." Need I say more?

3. Don't Shy from the Try

I like to think of my mistakes—and I've had a bunch—as training sessions. When I work out a new muscle, I get sore and initially can't lift that much weight. With change, I'm just using heavier weights than usual, tearing up muscles I rarely use so that I can make them stronger. Sure, maybe I'll need to layer on something soothing, like arnica cream after a workout, but the soreness reminds me that I'm breaking something down in order to build it up. Once a muscle gets stripped, it can get ripped. The key is to start small and train on a regular basis, just like at the gym. You can build your change muscle and become great at all things new!

Think about the last time you were in pain, whether from a toothache, a broken bone, or childbirth. It's hard to conjure up exactly what that felt like, isn't it? Our brains protect us that way, and it's the same with emotional anguish. These are temporary states. Even the heartbreak of all time is worth the risk because while it hurts (no doubt, it can hurt like hell), the pain diminishes over time and the reward gets stronger.

What I'm saying is, don't shut yourself down because of the fear of being hurt. ***Don't keep from trying because you're afraid you'll fail, and don't stop dreaming because you can't imagine that dream coming true.***

Losing, hurting, and doubting are just like scheduled stops on a bus. They're necessary markers along the way, required chapters in our stories—but temporary. The benefits that come from these moments or events, however, are lasting.

If you fail at love, if you miss the mark, if you get hurt, you still get the rewards. But if you "shy from the try" and sit out your turn, you get smaller and smaller; and your respect for yourself will diminish with each moment you choose not to step up to the plate. In my view of life, there is no limit to your times at bat, so strike, foul, or ball—it doesn't matter. The point is to *swing*.

The Bigger Picture

Being discouraged about failure and holding on to that emotional state just doesn't work. I mean, you can give yourself a bit of time to be pissed off, sad, and disappointed, but then you've got to find a better space and move there. It's something I talked about while walking along the shore in South Carolina with one of my best friends, Zaidee. Having known each other since before we were in training bras, we drop into conversations effortlessly, and this past July we were fixated on the good stuff that comes at the halfway point of life.

"I think one of the things I like best," I told Z, "is that I can move on past things more easily now."

"It's all about letting go of disappointment and failures," she said. "I can really see how those served me, though. I've finally learned who I am, and that is the thing that changed everything."

As we walked, we reminisced about how we obsessed about pretty much everything in our 20s while trying to appear as though we didn't. Anything that went wrong was the end of the world, and we beat ourselves up for not "getting it." Now we see that the answers were always inside us, but we were afraid to look within—or feared we didn't have the code or the key because we didn't know ourselves well enough.

Well, we knew ourselves well enough now that, for our beach-walk, we had skillfully positioned wraps over our bathing suits to hide our hips; but we both decided that while we might like to get back our 27-year-old bodies, we wouldn't trade this time for anything else. We'd finally arrived at a place in our lives where our wounds had turned into wisdom, and the insight we valued most was about failure.

Failing is a way to learn the things that don't work, so take that knowledge and transition from discouragement to curiosity. Find your personal victories in every lap, look to others for examples of going from "flop to fabulous," celebrate your successes along the way as much as you harp on your defeats. You're not likely to change the world in one shot. However, awareness of your little triumphs creates a ripple effect of subsequent achievement. And a life filled with numerous small victories is certainly more fulfilling than one giant win and then nothing else. Sometimes your life is just a millimeter away from working—you know, the difference between water and steam is one degree, that's it. So value all those small steps toward your goal. That's how you create change.

When you can make change as natural as your next breath (it is), you can move it out of your "uncomfort zone" and into your daily rhythms. Once you're no longer afraid of it, it can start to work for you. Fear is like that. If you can strip it of its uniform and take away its sword, it's almost always masquerading as something else. In my opinion, it is never your enemy, but let's talk now about how to make it your friend.

Chapter 3

FACE DOWN FEAR

*"Be the kind of woman who, when her feet hit the floor
in the morning, the devil says, 'Oh crap, she's up!'"*

— AUTHOR UNKNOWN

However we feel about war, most of us agree that soldiers at home and abroad are heroes. I see their faces and wonder what goes on beneath the helmets and behind the sandstorm goggles. We have no way of knowing, of course, but I suspect they all wonder how they'll react in the moment. The training, equipment, camaraderie, and sense of duty are in place, but the questions remain: *How will I react when the time comes? Will I do my job, complete my mission, fulfill my destiny, and do my duty? Will I be brave?* I imagine they pray, *Oh, Lord, above all else, let me be brave. Give me courage.*

PUSH PAST YOUR NORMAL. HERE'S THE WAY TO DO IT:

Change your point of view. Step outside of your comfort zone to get a new perspective on yourself. I like the way Bill Cosby put it, "Decide you want it more than you're afraid of it."

In order to find your fearlessness, you'll have to begin to see yourself through a different lens. Here's how: Courage (like change) is a muscle that needs exercising, and it requires action, so take the risk. If jumping out of a plane—or even jumping on a phone call with your boss—is what scares you, push past your "normal" and watch your opinion of yourself transform. When you see yourself differently, you can begin to sustain the differences you want to create. I'm all about moving mountains and slaying dragons, and that's great; but the real growth comes when you can step back and see that most of those obstacles are your own creations. In my own life, it took me some time

How many times have you prayed the same thing? We think these heroes are made from better stuff than we are. They must be inherently superior with high self-esteem—that's why they can face such extraordinary things. While they don't seem to feel fear, our assumptions about heroes may not be accurate at all.

Think about this quote that is attributed to Franklin P. Jones: *"Bravery is being the only one who knows you are afraid."* As you call for a second take, you will no doubt discover the hero within you. Standing up for yourself and owning who you are takes courage, this much I know for sure.

We've already talked about fear, and besides being the subject of this chapter, it will definitely come up again throughout the rest of the book. Fear and courage are feuding cousins, present in everything you do and every choice you make. Big things like fighting for your country take courage; but it's also brave to get out of bed in the morning and take care of your children, your parents, your clients, and yourself. It takes guts to teach your children right from wrong, to not take the easy way out, or to try to run an extra mile on the treadmill.

Give yourself credit for all the daily acts of courage you show. You grow your fearlessness that way.

The Courage to Follow Through

Making the decision to reinvent yourself, your situation, or even just your outlook or attitude is a great beginning, but it isn't going to amount to much without the follow-through. And *that* takes courage. As I mentioned in the last chapter, I see so many women (myself included) who allow fear to be at the heart of their failure to make changes, as well as their inability to believe in themselves enough to know they can do it—whatever "it" is. This reminds me of a great quote by Albert Einstein: *"The world as we have created it is a process of our thinking. It cannot be changed without changing our thinking."*

Every year on their birthdays, I write letters to my children. These are part wisdom, part lectures, and part snapshots of a time in life that will never come again. When my daughter, Lexi, turned 16, much of what I wrote in her letter was about fear: "You will face fear many times in your life. Acknowledge it, for fear is the only way for your courage to grow." I really needed to hear those words myself, as I confronted my anxiety that my children would see me as a failure as a parent when I couldn't keep our family together under one roof. Until I was broadsided by the devastation of my marriage ending, I don't think my kids had ever really seen me lose it. I'd been the rock, the steady force in their lives, and I do think that's

to realize that when I felt insecure about something, I would just take myself out of the race. I mean, if I didn't compete, I couldn't fail—right?

By avoiding opportunities to stand and deliver, I lost my best shots at building self-esteem. I withdrew and let inertia take over. Nothing was holding me back except my own fear, and the more I tried to hide, the worse I felt about myself. Be aware of what stories you're creating about why you can't have what you want or become who you'd like to be.

Look at your life and see if you have a wheel of excuses. Chances are that the wheel spins around, and when a moment of truth arrives, it always stops on the same cop-outs: "I don't have time," "I'm shy," "Every time I've tried before, it hasn't worked out," "I'm not the kind of person who does well with change," or maybe "The ship has sailed—I'm too old to start something new." If you stop creating excuses, then you can start making changes.

as it should be. A parent's job is to keep his or her children safe emotionally as well as physically, which includes showing them that hurting is unavoidable, but survivable.

I hadn't done that very well, and I wasn't able to get in front of the hurt that was speeding straight for us like a bullet train. There was no stepping off the track, until at one point, the four of us were huddled on the stairs at home, sobbing. No one was crying harder or louder than I was. I can see now that because my kids rarely saw me mess up or get hurt, I had in essence not given them permission to be vulnerable in their own lives. With this experience, they could see that I was getting strong by showing my weakness—and our family was growing stronger, too.

My fear that my kids would think I failed them never came true. They knew that their father and I had tried to keep our marriage together, and they wanted a better situation for everyone: I then had the courage to begin to rebuild.

MY TAKE: LEEZA'S LENS

How I Grew My Courage

Fear is courage dialing your number, waiting for you to answer. As is usually the case when you're dishing out great advice, it took me longer than necessary to learn this for myself, despite being raised by the greatest role model for courage anyone could ask for.

My mother, Jean, was a vivacious, beautiful woman; she was quick to laugh and loved to dance. She parented my brother and sister and me with wit and wisdom and was never afraid to admit when she got it wrong. She was finally headed into the calm waters of her life, where she'd learned to adjust her sails and enjoy the ride, when her boat began to take on water. Sadly, none of us could stop it.

Mom, me, and Granny

Mom was 63 when she was official-
ly diagnosed with Alzheimer's disease
in the spring of 1999. Yet long before
that, in our darkest moments, our family suspected that this might be her fate.
We never dared to give those thoughts
enough oxygen to live on their own,
though—whenever they came to the sur-
face, we suffocated them and sent them back to the corners
of our souls. My grandmother had struggled with the illness
for many years, and it was unbearable to think that Mom
would disappear that way, too.

In fact, I first learned about courage from watching my
mother care for her own mother. "She needs her music," Mom
would say, and she made sure the sounds of her mother's
youth surrounded her. She fixed Granny's hair and bought
her pretty nightgowns. Mom changed soiled linens and ar-
gued with her sister about whether decisions were right or
wrong. She struggled to get Granny to take her medications
and often closed the door behind her to cry it all out when
she thought no one was looking.

When Granny died, it was shortly after my mother received her own diagnosis. I was beginning to strengthen my
muscle of change, making friends with fear, and I really needed it. The day we buried Granny, my mother knew that she
would eventually die of the same disease. At the funeral, she
gazed into the face of the woman who had given birth to her,
while I stood back looking at my mom. Over my shoulder,
my children were looking at me. I knew I'd moved up a place
in line, and it was chilling.

My mother just kept moving forward. The courage it took for her to look head-on at her future,
knowing what it held, is unfathomable to me
even to this day. Mom displayed other acts of
courage throughout the early stages of her
diagnosis, which are gifts to her family because

they're reminders of how naturally we can make friends with fear when it really matters—all in the name of growing our courage.

My mom was one of those original steel magnolias, very charming and very strong. She ran our household from top to bottom and could spot a crumb on the carpet from two rooms away. In typical fashion, it was Mom who forced *us* to confront what was happening to her! She discovered that she'd paid one of the household bills several times, so she went to my dad and said, "Something is wrong."

With a great sense of urgency, we all—Daddy, my brother and his wife, my sister, and me—gathered together to face what was next and to grieve what was lost. We each had a part in the plan to go forward. I was in production with my talk show at the time, and one of the first things I did was dedicate an hour to telling stories of Alzheimer's.

I asked my mother for permission to mention on the air that she had the disease, and she said, "Not only can you, but you have to. You must talk about it to anyone who will listen for as long as you can until there is a cure." She taped an appearance for us in which she came on and said, "Hi, my name is Jean Gibbons, and I have Alzheimer's. My message is that if you have this disease, you should not be ashamed." (To see this segment, go to **www.leezagibbons.com**.) I always had great respect for my mother and was in tremendous awe of her, but never before had I been so proud of her courage and sense of compassion.

The saddest part for me is that when she was diagnosed, Mom wasn't done yet. She had this amazing life of loving and being loved, which she couldn't remember. She had emotions locked away in her mind, dreams in her heart, and words she was waiting to say. She was the one who always told me, "Take a chance, honey. You only regret the things you don't do." It's so ironic that she exited the planet before she had the chance for another take. It's one of the reasons reinvention means so much to me.

When she was in the early stages of Alzheimer's disease, Mom blessed us all with the tremendous gift of sitting us down and saying, "If I get hostile, if I cry and kick and scream, I want you to know that it is the disease talking, not me. Right now, while I can tell you, I want you to know what my wishes are for my care."

What a remarkable thing it is for us to have known what Mom wanted while she still had her cognitive abilities. If my mother hadn't had the ability to face fear and stare down her new reality, I don't believe we would have been as empowered or brave while helping her in her greatest time of need. She used her disease to teach us about courage. Every time a mother tucks her child into bed during a storm, or sings a song while her child gets a shot at the doctor's office, she is teaching that child about courage. When we don't react to a petty and hurtful comment or when we never fail to respond to social injustice, we give courage a chance to grow stronger.

"Courage Is Fear That Has Said Its Prayers"

All I have to do is think about my lifelong friends Terri and Zaidee, and I get the biggest smile. This is my favorite picture of us. Together we can face anything. They are among my strongest examples of facing fear with grace through all the changes in our lives. These two just stare it down and plow forward.

Terri has that kind of light-hearted energy and positive spirit that makes you just want to be with her. You'd think her life was all rainbows and butterflies. But one of the things I love about Ter—and what I've learned from her example—is the resilience and the courage it has taken for her to re-create her life in the wake of unbearable hurt.

No parent should have to bury a child, but Terri did. She lived not only through the anguish of losing her baby daughter, but also the heartbreak of losing her husband in the prime of life with no warning when an aneurysm hit while he was on the basketball court. She used the pain to spearhead change and get defibrillators courtside throughout the state of South Carolina. She grew her courage from fear and used it to open up enough to fall in love again and heal herself and her family. She dared to risk being hurt once more; and when she married her new husband, Lane, I became stronger and more hopeful that I too could begin again.

That's how we all must think: We're always in training, and it's never a solitary journey. If we face fear and choose to move past it, we're doing so for those around us as much as for ourselves. There's a ripple effect, and our loved ones benefit every time we act with bravery. Z has also made friends with her fears many times.

Zaidee gave me a little framed quote that I keep on the counter in my powder room that puts all this in beautiful perspective: *"Courage doesn't always roar. Sometimes courage is the quiet voice at the end of the day saying, 'I will try again tomorrow.' — Mary Anne Radmacher."* This, along with the quote by Karle Wilson Baker that makes up the title of this section, really helps me through the tough times.

As you've seen, having courage doesn't mean you're not afraid; it just means you're determined to continue in spite of your fear. There is no way to become braver if you don't acknowledge that facing fear is the way you're gonna get there. Put fear in its place: in the footnotes of your story. Or in the acknowledgements, where you can thank your friend called fear for all the life lessons.

What follows is an idea to help you along the way.

The Bravery Box

You've probably noticed by now that I'm a huge fan of baby steps. I don't believe you have to force big changes on yourself in fast and furious ways. As long as you're dedicated to facing what you fear in whatever dose you can stand, you've already made progress.

When thinking about what requires you to be courageous, you might find there's a list of things that frighten you, everything from trying a new food to dealing with the unpredictable. To help with this, try creating something I call the Bravery Box. You can use an old shoebox, a plastic container, or whatever type of box you like.

Write down on separate pieces of paper the things that frighten you. Maybe you're avoiding talking with an estranged family member or friend, are afraid of starting an exercise program, or are averse to setting up an Internet business. All those things (little and big) that hang over you and lurk like skeletons in the closet—write 'em down. Then fold up the papers and place them in your Bravery Box.

The trick is to keep the container in sight. Every day as you go about your business, make sure you can see that box of things that freak you out. You cut those fears down to size and only gave them a little strip of paper to live on. Then you literally closed the lid on your fears.

Sooner or later, I hope you'll open the darn lid and realize that it's not Pandora's Box after all. When this happens, pick a piece of paper (don't peek), and do whatever it says. If you chose "Meeting new people," make it your mission for the day, week, or month to meet someone new. If going that far is too much at first, no worries. Decide to do something, though, that gets you on the road to working on that fear. Maybe it's buying a book about overcoming shyness or perusing the Internet for social groups or hobbyist sites.

Ultimately, what the Bravery Box will do for you—at the very least—is bring your fears to the forefront. Your apprehensions have been transferred from mind to paper, which means you're now consciously admitting to them and thinking about ways to solve them.

Dale Carnegie said it best: *"Inaction breeds doubt and fear. Action breeds confidence and courage. If you want to conquer the negative elements in your life, do not sit at home and think about it. Go out and get busy."*

Somewhere along the way as you begin your personal Take 2, you'll realize that those fears you wrote down in the box belong to the "old" you and they have no place in your new life. As you face each thing on the list, bid it a fearless farewell by taking it out of the box and burning or shredding it. This can be done in secret or you can share it with those who support you. Either way, it gives you a rite of passage; and then you can replace the Bravery Box with a Gratitude, Wish, or Dream Box. Those are fun, too!

Friends gave me a Box of Courage during a time when I had to make a very difficult decision. They put quotes and their own thoughts of encouragement into the box. Every day I opened and read another reason why I could face the moment of truth in my life, another validation that I could conquer the thing that kept me awake at night and caused my heart to race. It was tremendously helpful. In time, I passed on my box of courage to another friend—more proof that as we grow, others do, too.

Further Steps for Facing Fear

Every day is a blank page, a new chance to find the courage to change. If you were afraid yesterday, it doesn't mean you have to be today. Fear doesn't define you; it can be the friend who shows you what you're really made of. But as with making any new friend, sometimes you need to break the ice. Here are some things to keep in mind when warming up to courage.

Have a Courage Symbol

Superman wore his *S,* and Dorothy had the ruby slippers, so why can't we have something, too? It could be an object, a photo, a letter, or a poem to carry with us or turn to when we're looking for a zap of courage.

When I need an extra reminder of the power I hold within myself, I like to think of a single wing. My friend Bobby gave me this symbol one year for Christmas as a reminder to trust. One wing reminds me that I'm blessed with already being halfway there, and I can always grow another wing or be given another wing when it's time to fly.

Other times when I need a boost, I visualize the tall palm trees that line the street on my drive to work. Impossibly tall, leaning in over the road, they bear up under their own weight because of the depth of their roots. They may bend, but they don't break.

Learn the Art of Positive Self-Talk

Before you dismiss this as another plea for positive thinking from one of the converted, think about this: The quickest way to psych yourself out is to listen to the noise in your head, that old self-doubt that creeps in just when you worked up your gumption. I'll be hitting this topic full swing in the next chapter, but it's helpful to keep in mind for the purposes of courage.

Whether you realize it or not, you carry on a dialogue with yourself much of the time. To successfully face down fear, you have to become aware of what you're saying to yourself. This often happens in meditation or prayer, and it's your best defense against fear. Sometimes the messages you tell yourself may not be so good, so you'll have to take charge of them and make sure that what you say makes you stronger.

You get what you focus on—end of story. So focus your thoughts on where you want to go rather than on what you want to avoid.

MY TAKE: LEEZA'S LENS

My Need For Speed

I learned the lesson of focus in a race car in Pasadena. Ever since I did a few laps on a track with Tom Cruise while he was filming the movie *Days of Thunder,* I've known the meaning of "the need for speed." There's something intoxicating about it, and I wanted to get me some. So when I was invited to drive in the Celebrity Grand Prix, I couldn't wait to zip up that sexy orange jumpsuit. I'd taken weeks of driving school to get ready; and before race day, my instructor rode around the track in the car with me to help me prepare.

I was a little nervous, and a lot excited. I'd just had Nathan (my third baby), and speeding along like this was so opposite my usual safety mode—even though I'd been looking forward to the opportunity. Normally I drive like a little old lady, and all I could think about was hitting a wall and crashing. In driving school, I'd been taught to look past the turn toward where I wanted to go and to think ahead, but when I got on the course for real, I could barely think at all. As I drove the track with my instructor, the noise was deafening and I was stressed. The straps over my shoulders felt tight as I looked over at my teacher from underneath my heavy helmet to get signals on how to take the curve. I saw him holding up two, sometimes three fingers, telling me which gear I should be in to negotiate the turn.

It was going well as we approached the final bend. My instructor was holding his hand in front of him doing a gesture I'd never seen before, but I remembered he'd told us in class that even though it seemed counterintuitive, sometimes the best way to go into a curve is to give more gas rather than less. He was doing this unfamiliar motion with so much emphasis that I figured I'd really better step on it.

Well, I hadn't seen it—although apparently *he* had—but there was a yellow flag signaling an accident on the course. I careened around the corner, and before I could react, I broadsided the tow truck that was on the track to remove a disabled car and driver. *Oh no!* flashed through my mind. This was my big fear—hitting the wall. At the moment of impact, I saw the outline of a man go flying through the air. This was the guy who was rigging up the tow. *Oh my God. I've killed someone,* I thought.

When the crash was over, I looked at my instructor and saw blood coming out from under his helmet. Maybe I'd killed him, too! In reality, he'd hit the windshield and had a small cut over his eyebrow. The medics took me to a triage tent where I found out everyone was fine. The man I saw flying from the crash scene was really just leaping to get out of

the way and wasn't hurt at all. I was fine, too, except for my bruised shoulders and chest, along with my bruised ego. I proclaimed that there was *no* way I was racing the next day, but I knew I had to get back out there and face my fears. I "got back on the horse" and wowed the crowd on race day with my next-to-last-place finish.

I learned that it's true: We get what we focus on. Where you look is where you go, on the racetrack and in life. My instructor still has an L-shaped scar across his forehead to remind him that Leeza was there. I still have the lesson to put my energy and attention on what I want rather than letting fear steal my thoughts and put them squarely on what I don't want.

I often refocus my thoughts with affirmations. This is the best way I can think of to make sure your thoughts are taking you where you want to go. Think of it as training your thoughts with a few spins around your mental track. These positive statements are a great way to reroute the grooves in the brain to take on a new belief, or to anchor an existing one. Here are some of the ones I've been saying lately:

The more I give, the more I receive.

Money and opportunity flow to me effortlessly, and I am open to receiving the gifts of infinite abundance.

I am healthy, and my body and mind work perfectly.

I say my affirmations on the treadmill, in the shower, and while driving to work. Repeating them for a few minutes a day is amazingly effective. Don't believe me? Try it! We can choose to be kind to ourselves and be our own greatest champions; or we can be our own worst enemies, slighting ourselves with a sharp tongue and living with razor-sharp regrets.

Fuel for Fear-Free Living

In the TV business, we often use a technique called "rack focus," where we bring a scene or a person from a fuzzy, soft, amorphous shape to crisp, sharp focus. Life has a way of doing that for us as we grow older. We can more easily see that our relationship with ourselves may have been built on lies. Chances are, the pages of promises you've made to yourself in the past could fill a book. Most of them were probably derailed by fear. Well, this is *your* story, and you're the writer and producer and director—so revise those pages, prepare for Take 2, and put your future into focus!

Fearlessness is an "F word" that you definitely want to have in your life, so let me give you a few more warning signs of the bad stuff so you can invite it to exit your life. Fear often masquerades as a regret or excuse. Think of those conversations that begin, "Someday when all this settles down, then I'll . . ." or

"If only I had more time, I'd . . ." Stop it. Change that mind-set. It's just fear getting the upper hand. Try saying "Next time," instead of "If only."

Use oxygen as your fuel and simply breathe in and out, telling yourself there's no situation that is more than you can handle right now. Remind yourself that you *can* do it differently than you have in the past. You've got to own your disappointments and fears before you can let them go, just as you did with the Bravery Box. Ten purposeful breaths while you focus on what you want can bolster your courage and pull the rug out from underneath fear, so you can lock it up, close the door behind it, kick it out—whatever visual image works for you, use it.

If you've never had this kind of courage before, you can acquire it. That was then; this is now. Do people change? As you discovered in Chapter 2, the smart ones do!

Laugh in the Face of Fear

Humor is to be taken very seriously because it's useful in disarming fear. A good dose of "light therapy" always works for me, by which I mean keeping things light. Not letting the enormity of any situation get to you is always the right choice, even in life-or-death dramas.

My dear friend Cheri (a fellow reporter/performer) is great at staying upbeat. When she was scheduled to have a major, life-saving surgery, everyone close to her was on edge about it. Her strategy was to find the humor in it all. On the day of the procedure, she woke up early in her hospital room to do her most diva-like hair and makeup. By the time I arrived at 6 A.M., she was already glammed up, complete with the perfect hair, which was soon to be covered by one of those awful blue surgical nets.

As I rounded the corner of the hall to her room, I caught sight of a priceless image: Cheri in a yoga pose on the bed, chanting softly, wearing the blue net as a beret. (You can see from the picture that she even managed to look pretty in that!) I knew it was all to keep her mind off the procedure she was about to have, but

I think she may have done it more for me than for herself.

We were trying to "out-brave" each other, and in doing so found common ground that neutralized the entire event. Cheri offered to let me wear her *5 Alive News* jacket from back in the day when she was a reporter, as we joked about how I'd be live on the scene, reporting every move the doctor made, each surgical instrument he called for, and any young interns worth mentioning!

When the medical staff came to wheel her off, it was showtime. I started a countdown as she sat straight up in the little hospital bed: "Okay, direct from Cedars-Sinai, you're on in five . . . four . . . three . . . two . . . one." Right on cue, the double doors closed, and I looked around me. Even the bored desk nurse was laughing.

MY TAKE: LEEZA'S LENS

Find Another Way In

Many times when I was a little girl, my mom would sing me to sleep with "Que Sera, Sera" by Doris Day. The lyrics make it clear that things are going to happen the way they're meant to, and we can't forecast the future. My mom focused on that part, but I got stuck on the idea that there's nothing we can do about it.

I don't believe in that message anymore; it can't be good enough for any of us. Whatever we make of our situation, *that's* what will be. But we can't make it better if we can hardly make it through.

You must believe that your essence is strong—that you're a strong woman *and* a "woman of strength." The little poem on the next page is one of those things that found its way to me in an e-mail. There's a much longer poem written by Luke Easter that elaborates on these ideas; but a friend sent this version to me after it had made the virtual rounds of women on the Internet, all of whom had found ways to make it their own.

Be a Woman of Strength

*A strong woman isn't afraid of anything. A woman
of strength shows courage in the face of fear.
A strong woman works out her body to keep her muscles
in shape. A woman of strength works on her relationships
to keep her soul in shape.
A strong woman wears a look of courage on her face. A
woman of strength wears a look of grace.
A strong woman makes mistakes and vows to not let that
happen again. A woman of strength learns from those mistakes
and knows they are among the greatest gifts in life.
A strong woman prays she will be strong enough for the
journey ahead. A woman of strength knows that it is within
the journey that she will become strong.*

You can also find the poem by Luke Easter at **www.leeza gibbons.com**. I'd love to hear your descriptions of what makes you a strong woman *and* a woman of strength.

Please know that I'm not expecting you to reinvent yourself by simply reading this chapter. (I wish I possessed that level of hocus pocus!) But this moment is offering you a new chance to change. You belong to a species built to adapt, and there are examples of this everywhere.

One shining star is entertainment news personality Giuliana Rancic, whom I was asked to introduce as one of the "women of achievement" at a charity event recently. Even before we became friends, I admired her work ethic, her great reputation, and the success she's had as an Italian girl who started out not knowing any English. I cohost

51

America Now with her husband, Bill; and the two of them are great sources of inspiration for my husband, Steven, and me. They've built an entertainment empire starting with Giuliana's job on *E! News* and Bill's success on the first season of Donald Trump's show *The Apprentice*.

Achieving is something this couple knows. In a few short years, they've written books, starred in their own reality show, hosted prime-time events and TV shows, and charmed millions of fans. When we think of people who have success like that, we assume they're able to accomplish and inspire because they have navigated the journey well and are smart and strong. That's true, of course, but I think these two are also successful because they know how to deal when things derail.

Giuliana and Bill have an adorable little boy. His arrival was not only a miracle, but also a testament to Giuliana's ability to face fear and to change. When she found out that she had breast cancer at age 37, she wasn't about to let that destroy her version of happily ever after—she just found another way.

After having challenges conceiving, Giuliana was told that the treatment for her cancer would mean putting her eggs at risk, so she chose to have a double mastectomy and harvest her eggs in the hopes of having one last chance at being a mom. She made a change, let go of what used to be, and faced what her reality had become. Giuliana took her darkest hour and turned it inside out by moving forward and facing her fear.

Her son, Edward Duke, was born to a surrogate, but he's the biological offspring of Bill and Giuliana. Dreams are worth holding on to; it's the path we take to get there that we need to release. Giuliana was flexible on her way to happily ever after; she called for another take, and for that, she's truly a woman of strength *and* achievement.

A strong woman prays that she will be strong enough for the journey. As you know from my Transformation Proclamation, which I shared with you in the Introduction, I've promised to seek out opportunities and turn down the noise of competing voices in my head so that I won't sabotage my success with self-doubt and fear of rejection (my own or anyone else's). I've promised to own my power to effect change in my life and in the world. After all, I have sole custody of my thoughts and myself. I've promised myself that I'll resist the urge to duck and hide when it begins to feel overwhelming.

Eleanor Roosevelt had the right way to look at this. She said, "You gain strength, courage, and confidence by every experience in which you really stop to look fear in the face. You are able to say to yourself, 'I have lived through this horror. I can take the next thing that comes along.'"

Do you want to do the same? Good, because life doesn't stop for anyone, and change is the inevitable sure thing. Growth, however, is the part of change where many people opt out. No matter what, and no matter when, I hope you choose to stay in the game and grow. You just have to believe you're worth it, so let's spend more time looking at that.

❈❈❈

INVESTIGATE, NAVIGATE, NEGOTIATE

You know how a lot of shampoos come with directions on the bottle instructing, "Lather, rinse, repeat"? Well, think about this part of your life story as being the part where you "wash" yourself of old hurts, stripping away that dull layer of doubt and inertia. The plan now is to: *Investigate, navigate, negotiate.*

Here's the way I see it: If you're on a search for the truth, you'll find it. If your goal is to be enlightened, you already are. Once you walk in the light of discovery, you can never go back to the darkness of indecision and apathy. I believe what's most significant about calling for Take 2 is committing to it—that step changes everything.

By now the energy in your life is probably in flux and your brain has been signaled to be on alert for new instructions, so think about this: *Investigate* who you really are (and create who you want to become) by being brutally honest with yourself. Once you're in the zone, you'll yearn to learn it all, but there's no hurry. Focusing on a finish line is contrary to the effort. Instead, just *navigate* the current. Be aware of where the wind is coming from, what storms are building, and adjust your sails. If you still manage to get off course, that's cool. In fact, that's the point, but you just adapt and *negotiate* with whatever's new on your horizon.

Investigate, navigate, negotiate. Repeat as necessary.

Chapter 4

ASK YOURSELF: ARE YOU WORTH IT?

*"We cannot think of being acceptable to others until
we have first proven acceptable to ourselves."*

— MALCOLM X

As you've seen already, my mother provided me with a reliable compass for life. Whenever I feel lost or unsure, I can usually find answers (or at least inspiration or a laugh) in Mom's kitchen-table wisdom. She knew from the get-go that I was competitive and what a huge advantage that can be. She also knew it was a potential trap and a revolving door of disappointment. Sometimes I feel like I'm playing hide-and-seek with self-identity.

Mom always told me, "Think of yourself as a thoroughbred, honey. Thoroughbreds don't look at the other horses; they just run their own race." That tried-and-true wisdom has been pulled out of my back pocket a lot. Comparing yourself to others breeds vanity or bitterness. I've tried to remember that as I run my race, but I'm not sure Mom had all the facts about what a competition it would be.

Sometimes you hit the ground running, feeling confident about reaching the finish line. Other times—more often—you may feel as though you're sinking in quicksand as you watch your fellow racers find their cadence and progress farther along the road than you do. I'm a big fan of having people around you who are inspirational and who can set a productive pace, but to compare your successes to anyone else's will just make you feel empty. The number one piece of advice most business leaders and life coaches give is to simply be yourself. That means if you uniquely play to your abilities, express your strengths, and have confidence and faith in that process, then you won't waste time measuring your position and growth against someone else's.

At the 2012 London Olympic games, gold medalist Rebecca Soni broke her own world record in the 200-meter breaststroke, doing it in a way that was hers and hers alone. The breaststroke presents the greatest technical challenge of all the strokes because of the resistance created by the way the arms and legs push through the water. No one can figure out how Rebecca does it so fast. Her stroke isn't fluid and certainly isn't the standard approach, but she owns it. What I learned by watching her was that she was comfortable and confident in her own rhythms, and she relied on that to get the gold. Rebecca wasn't focused on the swimmers in the other lanes; she was concentrating on her own goal. She also had a coach who believed in her and her method.

If you happen to find yourself dealing with people who don't or can't support your vision, don't waste time trying to get them on your side. Let go of the resistance and team up with those who can see your originality and your approach to the race.

There's an English proverb that says, "When an envious man hears another praised, he feels himself injured." Oh, you can use others and their accomplishments to inspire you, guide you, and set the pace, but you have to run your own race. Like Mom said, that thoroughbred has blinders on to ensure that he stays focused on what's in front of *him* and isn't distracted by the other horses. *When you get sidetracked or sucked in by the feeling that you're not keeping up, not learning enough, or not evolving quickly enough, I want you to visualize yourself in a set of blinders to keep you facing forward in your race rather than seeing where you are on someone else's track.* It's the only way to work on self-worth.

Self-Esteem Sabotage

If you don't believe you're worth it, you might as well let go of that branch and let the quicksand swallow you whole. Even if you have to fake it (and for a long time, I did), just feed yourself the words and images to support your vision of a confident woman worthy of her own respect.

I have to tell you, this can be really challenging. Many women are tempted to skip this step and go straight to self-sabotage. It's my contention that despite the fact that they know deep down where they'd like to be, they're stuck because they don't think they deserve better things. Their self-esteem might have started out intact, but the wear and tear of life's realities has wreaked havoc on their beliefs about what they're capable of, how strong they can be, and how beautiful they are—inside and out.

Do you ever look at pictures of yourself from high school or college? Perhaps you've turned the pages of the photo album for your wedding or baby shower and grimaced. Maybe you thought, *Gosh, I was so young—look at how clueless I was. If I only knew then what I know now. . . .* Who isn't guilty of falling into the biggest trap of all, comparing herself today to her old self? *Look at how happy I was. I was working then. I was adventurous . . . and so thin. I'm just a shell of my former self now.*

Whatever the words, it all points to struggling to build or keep self-esteem and being incapable of seeing that change is just one choice away. This is the part of your story where you get to make it up. Look for every opportunity to affirm where you want to be with this self-esteem stuff and say it out loud:

"I'm a really confident person because I believe in myself."

"I'm loved and lovable. I attract success to me."

"I'm taking yoga classes because I'm worth it."

"I won't settle for less because I deserve to be happy."

If you have a tendency to tear yourself down, repeat these kinds of supportive statements throughout the day and then go about the business of making them come true. Check out more at **www.leezagibbons.com.**

It can be helpful to think about where your self-worth went. Did you give it away piece by piece? Maybe there's a past regret or mistake that you just can't forgive yourself for, so each "failure" has chipped away at your self-esteem. For example, my friend Cameron is brilliant, beautiful, funny, and loving, but she refuses to read the headline for her own story that says so! She's become accustomed to tearing herself down, and it has gone on for so long now that she believes it. Cameron was afraid to interview for a job, so she fell back on her familiar put-downs: *Why would they want to hire me anyway? There are so many others who have more experience and are younger. Of course I didn't go for a walk today like I'd planned to because I'm just not a motivated person; I'd fail at this just like I fail at everything else.*

Cameron is a single mom, and even though she desperately wants to get married, she refuses to date, saying, "I need to lose some weight first. Besides, who wants to go out with someone like me with a kid and not much else to offer?" Listening to her became so tedious for those of us who love her that we just eventually stopped trying to talk her out of her self-deprecating despair.

The reasons and ways to destroy self-esteem are infinite and very personal. But what we all have in common is that at one time or another, we've secretly questioned or wondered something along the lines of *Now what? Nobody's going to want me, hire me, or love me. My chances are all behind me. It's all downhill from here.*

Get over yourself! You know that saying, "If you don't take Paris with you, you won't find it there"? It's so true. Things are typically what we expect them to be—the world is as we see it. On my kitchen windowsill, I have this inspiring Wayne Dyer quote displayed: *"When you change the way you look at things, the things you look at change."* It's one of my favorites, and it reminds me that I get to choose what to believe about myself and how to receive the input I get from the rest of the world.

Body Beautiful—Yes, <u>Yours!</u>

One of the many things I love about my husband is that he's a great communicator and very in touch with his emotions. Pillow talk for us can go on for hours! Before going to bed recently, Steven and I were talking about the beginning of our love affair, and he shared with me something that he's said before in different ways. He said part of what attracted him to me was that I was so sexually confident and so comfortable and secure with my body. He told me that it was like I was announcing to the world, "This is me. This is my body after three kids, and I'm celebrating it."

I had to smile because that's not how I was initially feeling at all! But I decided to act "as if," telling myself that I was sensual, sexy, and secure. That would be *my* opinion of myself, and I just had to let Steven form his own opinion. He did—it worked!

But that's the deal, isn't it? People take their cues from us. If we think we're valuable, they'll treat us that way. I try not to compete with younger, firmer women with child-free bodies where stretch marks have yet to appear. I had that time of my life. This is a different time for me, and this is the body I walk around in. I made a deliberate choice to want what I have and to praise it. As Oprah Winfrey says, "The more you praise and celebrate your life, the more there is in life to celebrate."

Let's look at what older women can teach us about being comfortable with where you are now. Some of these things I learned from male friends who told me what they found attractive in a woman; some were passed on from the goddesses who are ahead of me in age.

Most older women have learned to look people in the eye, be engaged in conversation, ask questions, and listen. Strength, optimism, and trying your best are attractive; trying to be the best at everything is not. Sharing your journey is something that bonds you to other people. Complaining, whining, or being victimized by your journey is something no one wants to hear.

And, ladies, let's just retire the question, "Do I look fat in this?" He probably doesn't care, he probably doesn't think you do, and you probably don't.

If *you* are concerned about whether you look fat, then make the decision for yourself and consider changing the outfit, for heaven's sake. But to be constantly concerned about the size and shape of your body and making excuses for it isn't sexy. When you get ready for Take 2, you can begin to call a truce on this one.

This middle-age thing kind of sneaks up on us, though. I never thought about what it would feel like to be at the halfway point in my life. I didn't know I'd swallow a handful of pills each day to fuel my body and feed my brain. I couldn't have predicted I'd rub on creams to balance my hormones and give me the energy I used to take for granted. I didn't grasp that hot flashes would ever really happen to me, except for the kind that hit when the flashbulbs of the paparazzi go off at the Emmy Awards or something.

I thought that by the time women evolved to this place, we wouldn't feel pressured to diet, get a new nose, and transform ourselves to be more marketable to this consumer society where we eat up sound bites like morsels of real wisdom and dread the ravages of time like the plague. We fight back hard, don't we? As well we should, in my opinion. But as my friend Suzanne Somers taught me, there is no face-lift, liposuction, breast implant, or injection that will save us from the fate of all living things. We grow older. What's the operative word? *G-r-o-w!*

Our looks simply change. They don't fade, and we don't lose them—they just change over time. The edges soften as our emotional edges relax, and we don't need those looks because we're more secure and understand what true beauty actually is. I also think we change so that we're reminded it's our time to move off the stage and let the women coming behind us dance in that spotlight while we find our *own* music. It's always playing somewhere else, if only we would let go and listen.

You see, we're all moving toward the next stage—marriage, mommyhood, middle age, menopause, magnificence! Well, at least that's been *my* track, so far. Wherever you are on the path, it's inevitable that you'll have to move forward. I think it's a dance of holding on and letting go. Each stage, each age has gifts and surprises, and each one has its own choreography. But at some point you have to take off your corsage and leave the dance . . . or at least you must walk over to another stage. Once you're there you can learn the steps to *that* music, but the tune will be different.

Eventually you'll find your groove, and it will be like the easy cadence of a waltz—one-two-three, one-two-three—with you gliding through it. But when you're learning the new routine, you may trip up; you might step on toes. Think about the posture of a dancer in the waltz: head up, shoulders back, ready to receive direction and new steps. Let's be open like that, ready to receive whatever's next.

I've said that life is a dance of holding on and letting go. So hold tight to the lessons and the love, but release the failures, the regrets, and the unique expression of yourself that belonged to *that* particular time. Open the door and step through to what's next. Bring your overnight bag to the new destination and fill it with the one thing that will keep you happy, fulfilled, joyful, and successful: your self-confidence.

The Confidence Cycle

Why are you who you are? Don't worry, this isn't going to be an existential exploration—but it *is* probably the most fundamental question you can look at if you want to change and grow. Whatever you believe about yourself, why do you think you believe it? Is this who you want to be and choose to define yourself, or have outside sources lent their influence? Let's say it's the latter; and you have a core belief that comes from your parents, spouse, boss, teachers, children, and friends. You're lazy, naïve, gullible, a poor judge of character, and a spendthrift. You can't take a joke. You're temperamental, quick to judge, and terrible at math—you know the list. And you believe it! Well, guess what? Beliefs aren't static, and you can change them whenever you want.

Give up the blame game. Your self-esteem—or lack of it—doesn't come from any outside source telling you that you're worthless. But it doesn't come from accolades either! It grows from you earning your own respect by facing something new, doing the right thing, and *taking a chance.* It springs from challenging yourself to do difficult things. Sometimes the toughest thing of all is announcing to the world who you really are or would like to be and then sticking to your guns.

I know the elusive and clichéd search for self-esteem seems like the ultimate chicken-and-egg scenario, but I'd rather think of it as a confidence cycle. You start with vapor, really—only the slightest belief that you might be worthy. Then you take a baby step toward a goal, make a small change in facing fear, and suddenly you have real evidence that you're worth it. You realize that you're in charge of making it happen. You complete the cycle. It's like condensation coming from the earth, gathering up in a cloud until it erupts with rain. You can't give yourself the credit that becomes self-esteem unless you believe you deserve it, and you can't create that feeling unless you first have some self-esteem. Oh, why can't anything be simple?

But you have to start somewhere, right? Here's where you get your confidence cycle working for you. Let's just begin by conjuring up some of that old magic that you felt at least once in your life when you accomplished something, big or small—maybe it was a promotion or visiting a friend in the hospital. Please don't forget those daily moments that go unrealized, because they're by far the most significant in your life and the lives of others. Give yourself credit for doing something right, something good, and you have the basic stuff to build on. Now I ask, *What are you creating in your life today? What are you doing that adds meaning? Have you ever really learned to take custody of your decisions and abilities?*

We're taught to do the laundry, balance a checkbook, and make a living, but who teaches us to do the following things:

- Honor our feelings
- Create boundaries and protect our hearts
- Live authentically regardless of the handcuffs the outside world wants to put on us
- Say no effectively
- Say yes with trust and faith
- Take the limits off living and back it up with a daring vision

Those are some of the skills your parents and outside critics may have missed—the important things. These accomplishments make you proud of yourself; and chances are, they happen through quiet victories known only to you. We can all encourage each other to reach higher, but you alone have to believe you deserve it first.

All this talk of change and transformation and starting over means a lot to me. It's my truth, and I've seen it work when it's applied with faith and expectation. But if you don't feel you're worth it, you're doomed at the starting gate. You must, above all things, hold yourself in high regard.

We have enough naysayers out there trying to lower our expectations of ourselves and each other. Don't get sucked in. The signals we get from the world tell us that now we have less faith in people, in the kindness of strangers, and in the understanding of the important roles we play individually in the world. In this extreme-media culture of 24/7 news, reality television, and continuous entertainment, we've come to hail celebrity and notoriety above all else; and we move so fast that there's no time to observe ourselves and our own contributions to society. Well, this is where we get to hold up the mirror and see it differently.

Author and philosopher Erich Heller wrote a lot about reality. His best-known statement is: "Be careful how you interpret the world; it *is* like that." I use that quote all the time because it reaffirms my belief that we get to make it up. This is an inside job. There's no way to measure it, Google it, or get overnight ratings on our self-worth. We're a look-at-me nation now more than ever, so it's easy to dismiss our daily accomplishments as insignificant. If it wasn't reported on Yahoo! or streamed on YouTube, then it's almost as if it isn't real.

You get to redefine what's real for *you* and let the rest bounce off your shield of self-worth. *Even if your peers, husband, kids, or co-workers think life isn't fair; nothing ever works out; and the world is just an ugly, dog-eat-dog place, you can put on another pair of glasses and see through another lens. I personally think rose is an underrated color.*

The Upside of Being Unreasonable

My friend and inspirational master Tony Robbins always encourages us to have "an unreasonable expectation." I love that! It gives us permission to go way beyond what we think we can do, and it takes away the logic part. In that unreasonable zone is where you'll find visionaries, leaders, and change makers of all kinds.

When there's so much cynicism about the state of the world, it's easy to lose hope. *What's the point?* we might think. But let's look at people who saw something better and made it happen. Did Nelson Mandela ever lower his expectations or lose hope?

When the Wright brothers came up with their flying machine, do you think anyone found that to be a reasonable thing to attempt? I mean, Wilbur Wright didn't even have a pilot's license! Did it make sense for Rosa Parks to get on that bus and say no to the status quo? It was unreasonable, and it changed the world. Steve Jobs never would have created Apple if he had a need for others to think it was a reasonable thing to shoot for. These people don't have anything on you or me—they aren't better or different. They just had the guts to go for it based on a belief that they could make it happen regardless of the logic or reason.

We have to condition ourselves for this, though. When we've been told to be reasonable and realistic all of our lives, we need to give ourselves much more latitude to dream without squashing the ideas for being too "out there." Dreams always come a size too large. Every great idea and invention started as someone's vision. Your thoughts become things, and your mental energy expands to create the realities of your ideas. That's why it's so important that you do the mental preparation with something like the Transformation Proclamation I shared in the Introduction. Your thoughts will move the energy in your life to create your new reality.

Be very specific as you lay out your plan for your second take. What *exactly* do you want? Now you need to get to the *why:* What's the *reason* behind what you want? Want to be rich? Great. Why— what for? Want to lose weight? What's the reason? Getting to the heart of what truly motivates you helps you live on purpose; and when there's purpose, there's lasting action. It's an exercise in unleashing the power of your intentions. And don't get bogged down in the *how* of it all—that's not your part of the picture. Instead, focus on *What is it?* and *Why do I want it?* and watch what happens.

Create Your Dream Factory

I'm really big on dreams. I think they're the primal screams for happiness; but, as they say, a dream is not a plan, and hope is not a strategy. When you talk about something, it's a dream. When you schedule it, that's a plan! We always seem to be pushing toward something, but how many of us can define what that something is? Lily Tomlin said, "I always wanted to be somebody, but now I realize I should have been more specific." Love that! So, let's be specific: *I want a better relationship with no resentment, more money for vacations, a house in Rome, to run a 5K, a career like Meryl Streep* . . . fill up your dream plan with lots of reasons why.

Every day we learn more about the power of the mind to manifest reality. By now, legions of people subscribe to the notion that we're the co-creators of our existence along with a universal force. (Some call it God, some say it's love or source energy.) Well, the universe only knows yes; it's the ultimate affirmative energy. So if you believe, *I'm a fat slob and a failure,* or *I don't want to end up like my sister,* the universe will answer yes and keep delivering that to you. If all you can think of is ending up like your deadbeat sibling, since the universe gives you what you focus on, then bingo—you get more of the things that are like your sister, or what you fear most. Any drama magnets out there?

I think this all points toward conditioning ourselves to expect more and back it up with action. As my pal Tony says, "Expectancy is the atmosphere for miracles." The goal is to work toward changing your psychology so that your best self automatically kicks in. Begin to expect that things will go your way; believe that your dreams are on their way to you. That training allows for the energy to get going and flowing the way you want it.

When you believe that you'll be successful, watch it happen. Have faith that the world is filled with people who are mostly good, and you'll draw them to you. Expect that you'll make money or make a difference—whatever it is, you are the architect of your life. Brick by brick, pillar by pillar, *you* create the situations in your world, or at least your reaction to them. You're never a victim unless you choose to be. Remember: When you change the way you look at things, the things you look at really do change. (Thank you, Wayne!) I think you are part of something bigger than your own personal journey. I guess what I'm saying is you really can change the world by changing the way you view yourself, beginning with developing and nurturing self-esteem and the belief that you're worth investing in to get what you deserve out of life.

What's Your Worth?

I've met with presidents and royalty. I've parachuted, zip-lined, and gone parasailing and hang gliding on several continents. I've interviewed the biggest movie stars and the most pitiful prostitutes and drug addicts, and you know what? Until I got to know myself, none of that was meaningful. I used to keep journals and write about what was happening in my life. It was a diary of typical stuff: my hopes, fears, dreams, and desires. I pulled out one of these small leather books this week, and I was surprised to see that even at age 25, when I was traveling the world, making good money, and living a full life, I wasn't valuing it. In many cases, I wasn't even feeling it because I was so feverishly looking for myself.

One of the entries read: *I really have to do more and accomplish more. I feel I'm behind.* There's that green-eyed monster, comparing myself to others. Another was: *I don't fit in. What if I go through decades without ever making my mark?* That's my panic, failing to see the steps I was taking. I suppose much of that may be the usual quest for meaning and egocentric arrogance that accompanies a person's 20s, but now that it's in my rearview mirror, I have the perspective that allows me to see that I was "spooling" like a computer that's stuck and can't figure out what it's supposed to do next. I was failing to find meaning in my efforts and daily accomplishments because I didn't think I was enough unless I had a big job with a big title, making lots of money and changing the world.

You may have already figured it out, but I'd like to share a few more things that I learned when I chose to run my own race and not get stuck in quicksand. It's not as difficult as you think to rediscover the importance of championing and loving yourself. Yes, a lot of how you view yourself does come from the messages and opinions that have been ingrained in you over the years, so begin by sifting through all you've been fed about how you should behave, how much you should weigh, what you should wear, where you should shop, and on and on. Maybe some of it is useful. Whatever you don't agree with, throw out. Decide today what you're worth, and take some time to chart your course. Be specific, like Lily said. Make sure you have people around you who will be the wind in your sails.

Dear Past,
    Thank you for the lessons and wisdom.
    Thank you for being my teacher and for
       giving me a classroom for change.

Dear Future,
    I'm ready.
    Let's do this thing.
    I'm going for an advanced degree.

Bask in Your Backstory

Believe it or not, charting your new course doesn't mean disregarding past adventures. In writing and storytelling, there's something called "backstory"—a literary device that provides a history or background to promote fuller understanding. Diving into your backstory can help you recover your self-esteem because it provides the context for where you are now and why you feel the pull to change. Don't turn away from your history, and don't judge your place within it. Who knows what gems you might uncover once you blow the dust off? Look for guidance to chart your future course and assistance in owning your actions—past and future. This is a similar process to some of what you learned in Chapter 3, but the primary goal here is to focus on becoming your own support system for the change that's on the horizon. When reviewing your backstory and pulling aspects of it to help build your second take, you might find some of the following prompts helpful:

— **Are you proud of your behavior?** Your self-esteem is affected by how you behave. If you've ever had a not-so-shining moment, join the club. Maybe you reacted to an adversary in a way that you feel isn't the best representation of who you truly are, or went along with a poor decision for the sake of "going with the group." Harping on the things you did or said that you aren't proud of breeds resentment of yourself and lowers your self-confidence. So if you stayed with the wrong guy for too long or cheated on that test back in high school, it doesn't give you permission to define yourself as unlovable or disingenuous for the rest of your life. Beliefs can be changed, starting with how you view your actions. Don't make your regrets all for naught. Instead, use them as character-building tools, acting as compasses for the better decisions and behaviors you'll exhibit today and in the future. It's like what Maya Angelou is often quoted as saying: "When you know better, you do better." The past doesn't equal the present. Make peace with this.

It might help to perform a ritual to move on. One day, write down the torments from your past, big or small. Cry; scream; or be sad, depressed, or worried. Experience whatever you need for the moment.

Next, take the list, make a scroll out of it, and put it in an envelope or small box. Find a spot in your yard (or use a large pot if you don't have a lawn) and bury this blast from your past. Then in the same spot, plant something that will grow in spite of all the bad stuff that's hidden at its roots. Knowing that you buried your burden and planted new hope that grows stronger every day will make you smile.

— What are the major milestones—negative or positive— you've already reached? It's amazing how many women have amnesia when it comes to how much they've really been through and survived. Try this exercise, which I call the Tell-All Timeline: List each of the major periods of your life and write in one or two (or more!) big milestones you faced. Maybe it was grappling with the death of a pet when you were a little girl, or something heavier such as the loss of a loved one. Head into the teen years and give yourself high marks just for surviving high school intact! Be proud that you made it through your first broken heart. What happened in your 20s that you're proud of or that tested your faith and strength? Move on through the years.

What you'll see, as I do when I study my own Tell-All Timeline, is that your courage only grows and grows. With each test aced and behind you, you're ready for the challenges ahead. Writing all of the ups and downs from your backstory is a powerful tool, as there's nothing more concrete than seeing your courage and self-worth displayed right there in black and white.

— When was the last time you paid tribute to a victory? Create an event around it, make others part of your celebrations, and keep on striving and finding joy in the journey. The small steps you make stack up and must be recognized in order for them to grow into the leaps that you'll soon be ready to take. Patting yourself on the back reminds you of every job well done and increases self-esteem. To that end, I actually had a small "Happy Divorce" dinner with some close friends when my marriage ended. I was proud of my courage to finally take action and face my fear of failing.

— When was the last time you told someone your story? Reveal your life. Tell your history to your kids, a friend, or a mentee in bits and pieces through conversations, pictures, and music. They'll learn to appreciate you; and better yet, you'll begin to see yourself through their eyes.

MY TAKE: LEEZA'S LENS

My Dancing Diaries

Sometimes you don't have the time to work on yourself in the manner discussed in this chapter. Sometimes you just have to show up and say, "Screw it!" Don't be a spectator in your own life. Every day in every way, be present, connected, and deeply entrenched in the present moment. Overthinking can be a trap sometimes, so often the best approach to take on new challenges is to just step into the ring. That's what I did when I accepted the invitation to appear on *Dancing with the Stars*.

A fan since its first season, I'm shamelessly devoted to the show. In season four (against my better judgment), I became one of the spray-tanned, glittered-out contestants, convinced I could mambo with the best of 'em. A glimpse through my *Dancing* diaries reveals that this was a moment of truth for me. It was less about judges' scores and talent, and more about life lessons and finally coming to terms with many of my issues. What could those be? Well, when I said yes to the show (in a moment

Backstage with my kids after my foxtrot

of temporary insanity), I called my therapist and told him I'd have to suspend our visits for a while.

"I'm not going to have time," I explained. "Besides, this is the perfect platform for me to deal with my control issues, fear of intimacy, and that *You're not enough* voice in my head." Truer words were never spoken.

There were so many lessons I learned during my ballroom adventure, but here are my top three:

1. Be coachable. Let's start with the control business. You know, we Type As are delusional enough to think we can always handle, take over, or manage most anything better than anyone else. We sweat, hyperventilate, and get bossier when we feel threatened or out of control. When I met my dancing partner, Tony Dovolani, I was in a tail-spin of torture. Ultimately, I learned to let go of control and be coachable. (Although if you ask Tony, we could have used this lesson a bit earlier!)

The most successful people are the ones who are the most teachable. When you're willing to learn, you aren't wasting time and energy defending what you already know or being embarrassed by what you don't. Having virtually no dance experience, I had to be open to Tony, who'd already been a professional ballroom dancer for many years. It wasn't

easy—on many of our rehearsal days I felt like a second grader who was being scolded because she hadn't memorized her math facts. Letting go of defensive-ness and opening up is key in life, and it was essential with this dance drama. We had no time to develop a safe, mu-tually respectful relationship—we only had four days to learn a routine! I've taken that lesson with me: In life, those who are open to others' input, guid-ance, and advice usually go further with less anxiety.

2. Ask for help. I was one of those self-sufficient, inde-pendent women who (formerly) found it uncomfortable to ask for assistance. My *Dancing* diaries reveal that I was able to drop this hang-up in no time!

We're not alone in life's adventures, yet we invariably try to handle things ourselves. Not me, not this time. First, I got my kids on board, and they were my biggest fans. Then I put out an APB and gathered up a team of Ballroom Buddies, with members ranging from my life coach and nutritional guru to my Pilates instructor and goddess circle of girlfriends. To ready myself for this terrifying experience, I started on day one with a cleanse. Determined to reap the benefits of more mental clarity and injury prevention, I packed my little lunch box with beet juice and various other disgusting items. In just a few days, I started getting migraine headaches and muscle spasms, so I nixed the cleanse, but not my team of supporters.

Regardless of the outcome (I was eliminated in week four after a pitiful paso doble), I learned how meaningful it is to share a common goal, how great it felt to have a team of supporters, and how alive I felt sharing this experience.

3. Right now, you are enough. We all question ourselves every now and then. We gaze into the mirror in stunned disbelief at the image that's staring back. We look at our children's behavior and wonder what kind of parent raised kids like that. We compare our careers with others and wonder why we're not more successful and making more money. Dancing gave me lots of examples of why this doesn't work.

Amid a sea of sexy, young, talented celebrities (who could actually dance!), it was a reach to remind myself that I was enough. I turned 50 on the show, and at that time I was the oldest contestant ever on *Dancing with the Stars*. On the first day of the production, all of the celebrities got together to do the title shoot. This is the opening of the show where all the dance couples are introduced. I felt like a transfer student at a new school who didn't know where her desk was.

The professional dancers had such command over the space and set the tone for the glam factory. If I hadn't already been stressed to the max about my decision to do the show, standing next to Paulina Porizkova (supermodel) and Shandi Finnessey (beauty queen) would have been enough to put me over the edge. They were cool, confident, and gorgeous—not to mention stick thin! I began to hyperventilate at the thought of having my legs peer out from underneath a shimmery costume, exposing to the world my broken capillaries, cellulite, and pastiness.

When Lisa, my makeup artist, began to apply paint, I was just sure I looked like a drag queen. I slumped in the chair and fixed my eyes on the floor since I didn't think screaming was the right call. Putting on the costume didn't help. It was purple and

gold and resembled something worn by a majorette reject. I allowed it all to overwhelm my self-confidence until my head pounded and I was dizzy and felt like throwing up. (Hmm, maybe it wasn't the cleanse.)

The professional dancers tried to reassure me, but I'd already convinced myself that I wasn't enough for this show. After that, the universe did everything it could to prove me right. I couldn't even find a natural smile for the stills, not to mention manage a simple turn to camera with Tony. The purple eye shadow that Lisa so skillfully applied couldn't camouflage my insecurities. Who wears purple eye shadow with pink highlighter? Not me. I felt like an imposter, and nothing that came out of my mouth that day sounded like me.

A hot bath that night helped me bounce back a bit, but the train had left the station and I was already on board. By focusing on what I didn't want, I got more of it. I thought constantly about how nervous I was, how difficult it was to learn the steps, and how out of place I felt. When I hit the dance floor, those were the voices in my head. The crowd of internal critics was running amok, and I couldn't quiet them.

It wasn't until I got eliminated that I could see all this. It had been a risk, and I'd taken it. I'd tried my best, learned something new, and moved out of my comfort zone; and I wore a hot leather mini with a cape and totally owned it! I was more than enough; I was proud.

These days I watch the show safely clad in my T-shirt and pajama bottoms, with a sense of solidarity with those wide-eyed stars who freeze like I did when the big voice announces their names. But I know now that on *Dancing with the Stars,* as in life, my mom's simple advice applies: Show up, do your best, and let go of the rest. If only I'd kept that in mind when the spotlight was on me and the judges' paddles were raised with low scores. But hey, it happens—to all of us.

Find the Funny

We've been taught that it's never gracious to laugh at people, but what if that person is you? What if you took your latest fumble, mishap, regret, or misfortune and simply found what's funny in it? Sometimes we have to laugh just to keep from crying, as the proverb goes, so I say take humor seriously and apply it to build your self-worth.

You're probably asking yourself, *How the heck does laughing at myself build self-confidence? Wouldn't it actually do the reverse?* Those are good questions, to which I answer no. Instead, it allows you to realize that the things that didn't work out weren't final or fatal. And when you laugh, you're more likely to perceive the consequences of risk as less serious and take failure less personally; and *that* will keep you open to change instead of fearing failure.

Here's a case where the joke was on me, so I laughed along. After one of my first Academy Award red-carpet appearances, I was skewered by the fashion media for wearing a "hat" with my dress. Now you can call it a hat, but I have to agree with the critics who said it looked more like a UFO or a satellite antenna! The truth is that it really was horrible, and I don't know what I was thinking. I got a D minus from one reviewer who said he would have given me an F, but I just looked so darned happy! The next day I

THE PRINCIPLE OF ENOUGH

Yours is the only opinion about you that truly counts. What you think about yourself is enough. Don't worry about the cackling of others, especially the judgmental ones who don't even know you. Instead, focus on being loved by your family, respected by your peers, and at peace with yourself.

I did an interview once with a mother who killed her young daughter while drunk behind the wheel of her car. As I talked with her in front of a live audience, I couldn't imagine the torment for this mom. But she told me that she wanted to tell her story to help others, so I helped her give voice to her pain. In the days after the show aired, I got e-mails and phone calls from people who thought I was too hard on her and those who felt I didn't press hard enough. Working in the media has taught me to follow my own moral compass and know that I'm judged not by the ratings, fan mail, hate mail, Facebook "likes," or comments on social media, but by the sense of fairness that I offer each person who crosses my path.

had to do live interviews in Australia, and I started off each one by saying, "And if your viewers are lucky, they might have a chance to win the headpiece I wore at the Oscars!"

The more you try, the more you grow and gain self-confidence. When you have a sense of humor, you take over a room— it's as simple as that. Own it, take charge, and people will gravitate toward you. This reminds me of a great quote by Jarod Kintz: "Laughter is the sound of the soul dancing. My soul probably looks like Fred Astaire."

That's the idea! The more in command you are, the more you feel worthy and confident in your ability to do the job or rise to the occasion. So commit to finding humor wherever you can, and laugh with abandon. Especially when the joke's on you!

What was I thinking?

People who can laugh at themselves and find humor in lost causes, broken hearts, detours, and derailings give hope to others and make them feel good. And people want to keep company with those who make them feel at ease and free to fumble in their own way. Want to disarm your foes, open strangers' hearts, ease every burden, and light up more rooms than the Clapper? Have a well-developed sense of humor. And that doesn't only mean being the one making people laugh; you must learn to be the brunt of the joke as well.

If you need more reasons to make this change, consider that people who laugh often have stronger immune systems and lower blood pressure. Laughter stimulates both sides of the brain, making it more alert and open to learning, so look at your life and find the funny.

Who Do You Think You Are?

How we see ourselves is exactly who we'll become. At the beginning of this chapter, we looked at how others define us and how those beliefs sometimes take over our own. Have you ever had anyone ask you, "Who do *you* think you are?" It's a great question, isn't it?

Maybe it's not until we get challenged that we're really forced to look at who we are and who we want to become. I have my first-grade teacher to thank for challenging me at an early age. I was a good kid, but a bit of a smarty-pants in school. One day the principal proclaimed during morning announcements over the loudspeaker that we were celebrating Horace Mann Day. From my front-row seat I blurted out, "Who is that? He must not be very important if I've never heard of him!"

My teacher walked over and said, "Leeza Kim Gibbons, just who do you think you are? Do you think you know everything?" I can still see the smirk on my face beneath my badly cut bangs disappearing as I turned red with embarrassment. She did me such a huge favor that day when she dared me to think about who I was. (And I found out who Horace Mann was.)

I think this is a fundamental question that we should all ask ourselves every once in a while. Go through the list in your head right now: Who *are* you?

I'm an optimist; I'm forgiving; I'm a believer in dreams. I'm a loving mother, a dedicated daughter, and a passionate wife. I'm a career woman and a philanthropist. I'm someone who can keep a secret. I have compassion, and I care.

Those are some of my answers. How would you respond? Hopefully your list will be a powerful validation of who you really are. It will no doubt wind up different or better than the list of things imposed upon you in the past by outsiders. Describing yourself as a survivor is stronger than saying, *I'm chronically ill.* Saying, *I'm a thriver* beats saying, *I've had a lot of challenges.* Believing you're a champion for change is better than saying, *I'm a complainer.*

When you can reframe your experiences and turn negatives into positives, and when you can uncover the truths and dismiss the lies, you'll become accountable to your backstory.

Can you see the worth in all the events of the past? When you discover that these acts are reinvention in motion, you'll have proven what I have been saying to be true: Beliefs are not static and *can* be changed.

Now that you've made the decision to put yourself first in life, made some needed adjustments, mustered up some courage, and rediscovered your self-worth, what in the world are you gonna do with all this power? I sense a hint of the unknown in the air . . . and it's incredible, isn't it? Join me on the track to authenticity, where you're running your own race!

Chapter 5

BUST THE BALANCE MYTH

*"Life is like riding a bicycle—in order to keep
your balance, you must keep moving."*

— ATTRIBUTED TO ALBERT EINSTEIN

I realize I may come off as a person who's really got her you-know-what together. To a certain extent maybe I do, and that surely didn't happen overnight. But who am I kidding? There are a lot of days when I think, *How the heck am I gonna pull this one off?* In fact, many times when I sit down to write, I have to giggle as I channel my grade-school teacher and ask myself, *Who do I think I am, dishing out advice?* But I've arrived at the place in my life where I can see what my gifts are and what I have to offer; and I've stopped worrying about whether anyone finds value in them or not. I'm serving it up and sharing it, letting go of the outcome. When I write about the omnipresent time trap, though,

I sometimes feel disingenuous, because this is a lesson that's on automatic replay for me—it just keeps coming back! But they say we teach what we need to learn, so here I am.

If only I could take my own advice. When I committed to writing this book, I knew I had to figure out how to make all the pieces fit; but like most of you, I'm spinning at a dizzying rate. How would I make it work with all the other stuff in my life? I know I have a boatload of blessings, but sometimes I feel like I need to jump ship! At the time of this writing, my list includes sitting on the board that oversees the California Institute for Regenerative Medicine (CIRM), California's stem cell research agency; spearheading my nonprofits, Leeza's Place and Leeza's Care Connection; hosting the shows *My Generation* and *America Now;* being an ambassador for AARP; and developing a new scrapbook line and a new jewelry collection. I *love* my life, but it's large! Forgive me for the apparent chest pounding—but I'm proud of the things I'm involved in, and I want to give them all my best. If you notice, however, this list doesn't include the highest-priority items: spending time with my family and friends, exploring my spirituality, and that all-important "me time" I spoke about with such conviction in previous chapters. Now who's got their s - - t together?!

Do I panic? Sure, sometimes. Does stress creep into my life and wreak havoc on my sleep patterns, hormones, moods, and body? You bet. And I have no doubt that you have as much (or more!) on *your* plate. Let's just run down a theoretical list. Aside from the big stuff like managing your family and career, or any random day you have to settle a fight with the kids while online banking; work on expanding your mind while working out to slim your thighs; be a vulnerable lover at home and a tough butt-kicker at the office; offer encouragement to your friends; delegate tasks to your employees; pluck your eyebrows, shave your legs, and wax your bikini line; and strive for the success of Heidi Klum, the sexiness of Beyoncé, and the strength of the women on the WWE. All in a day's work, right? Phew! Did you recognize your life in this list?

While you're embarking on your path to take back your life, the tricky part is that *you have to find the time.* Reinvention and re-creation takes focus, energy, and nurturing; but if you're out there playing the role of Jane-of-all-trades, how do you get back to your core essence? If and when you do figure it out, will you be dragged off in a straitjacket as a result? Some people say the answer to this conundrum is to "find balance" in your life. I mean, come on . . . how many magazine articles, books, and blogs try to tackle this one? You may be relieved to know that I think all that balance business is bogus.

This Just In

The propaganda that has been spreading like wildfire through the self-help world for years is this concept of balance. Oh, it's a great idea. When it's explained and taught by spirituality circles, pop psychologists, and the editors who create the headlines for beauty magazines, it sure sounds terrific: "12 Ways to Create a More Balanced Life," "How to Find Balance in a Chaotic World," "5 Tips for Better Work-Life Balance," yada yada.

If you search for "balance in life" on Google, a whopping 2.5 *million* results pop up! That's a lot of talk about an issue that causes so much guilt and turmoil in our lives. Maybe it's because an entire generation of women who have fought for their right to "have it all," along with generations of women who have come after, are now up the river without a paddle, barely keeping it together as they navigate the responsibilities of their lives—and losing themselves in the process. Have you ever thought, *I need to create more balance in my life* when you felt overwhelmed, underproductive, overexposed, tired, fat, or ugly? I sure have.

Trained as a journalist, my job as a reporter has been to present the facts. Now, as a columnist, I've been given the wonderful opportunity to veer a bit from an unbiased viewpoint to share the perspectives I've gained through my own experiences. So as a reporter, columnist, and a fierce supporter of the well-being and quality of life of all women, here's some breaking news from the Land of Leeza:

BALANCE IS BOGUS

Yep, that's right, the 2.5 million results on Google look great and may provide some temporary relief, but it's a trap. Balance is a myth—it doesn't exist. No one has it, or at least no one can sustain it. It's my opinion that redefining what the term *balance* represents is a critical step in actually creating more of the time, space, and energy required to focus on you and your transformation journey. Give it up and let it go. Don't make balance your goal.

MY TAKE: LEEZA'S LENS

It's about Navigation

As you probably already figured out, I came of age during the height of what was then called the women's movement. (Sounds kind of quaint now, doesn't it?) My wonderful, forward-thinking parents encouraged me to do it all and to be all that I could be—a tremendous gift for which I have always been grateful. At the time, I could see no restrictions on my dreams, no barriers to my ambitions. I was determined to be one of those have-it-all types: a woman who could juggle a career, marriage, car pools, and breast-feeding without breaking a sweat. I was going to combine the best qualities of Marlo Thomas from *That Girl* (one of my early inspirations) and Mary Tyler Moore, along with a little Joan of Arc. And later I also wanted the thighs of a 20-year-old, the craft skills of Martha Stewart, the power of Oprah, and the Mother of the Year award. I wanted to volunteer to feed the hungry, make my husband dizzy with sexual delights, and never chip a nail or run my stockings.

It's no wonder we feel so stressed and inadequate. (Or maybe it's just me. Am I projecting here?) The time tyrants compete for space in our heads with the voice of reason, which is easily suppressed. For me it used to happen daily—that nagging feeling that I should be doing something more productive. Forget that I might have just made breakfast, managed to remember to throw in a load of laundry before I drove my son to school, conducted a staff meeting, taped several interviews, and done my Christmas shopping on the Internet while waiting to take off on a transcontinental flight. I'd still manage to feel uneasy about taking a moment to just let it all stop—or maybe it's just that the lull in the action felt so foreign.

This, I find, is getting much better with age. I've stopped thinking about wasting time, spending time, or saving time. Now I think about how I *invest* my time, and it's paying off in some pretty big dividends, most notably in my sanity and serenity. These days I know it's not about balance; it's more about *navigation*—finding the right mix of emotional, intellectual, spiritual, and physical elements to make me a complete woman. I take satisfaction in knowing that if I just do my best in this moment, it will put me in the best position to take care of the next one.

Some days it's all you can do to focus on one of those dozens of demands vying for your attention. And I think that as long as you're focusing on *something,* there's not a problem. I still write a script in my head about what I hope will happen in a day, but now I've learned to never expect it to come out exactly that way. This is all tied to another favorite "F word": *flexibility.*

Why Is Balance a Myth?

Balance is an outdated model by which we measure success, but we are strangely obsessed with it. It's a pretty empty goal, besides the fact that it's just not possible. It seems as though a balanced life is supposed to tell the world, "Look at me—I have it all." And we've been programmed to believe that's a desirable thing. I think that's a lie. Maybe it's been different for you, but have you ever realized that you were the last thing on your mind? You're probably the last item on the list (if you make it onto the list at all); the first to be blamed, but the last to take credit. I had to hit the wall as a martyr before I was ready to give up my membership in the society of perpetual people pleasers.

This kind of talk usually prompts my kids to roll their eyes and advise me to resist the urge to hand out my snappy, bumper-sticker sound bites as quick fixes to life's most perplexing problems. I've decided to do with their advice what they tend to do with mine: Ignore it!

I don't want to simply create a campaign slogan for a culture that values multitaskers and has created a generation of self-identified superwomen. I'm talking about reframing "me time" and seeing it for what it is: an essential action to keep women on the front lines of their lives without unraveling. It was hard for me to manage my job in TV and radio, handle my three kids, be a good wife, run my charity business, and help care for my mom. My survival tactic was pretty simple: When I was on the high wire, I didn't look down. I learned, however, that ignoring my constant state of overwhelm didn't work for me, and it won't for you, either.

Balance seems to mean that we divide our time equally among our work, children, spouse, family members, and health maintenance. That's gotta be a joke, right? If you were to draw a pie chart of your life, would the dividing lines be equally spaced, or would some portions be wider than others? I would guess the latter. That's not balance—that's priority setting. I like what the late Stephen Covey had to say on this subject: "The key is not to prioritize what's on your schedule, but to schedule your priorities."

What I know now is that having it all is about finding the *right mix* of emotional, intellectual, spiritual, and physical elements that make us complete women and productive employees or entrepreneurs. It's that sliding scale of disproportionate (unbalanced) amounts of each that make it work.

For instance, when I became a mom, I knew that my children would redirect my professional choices. My challenge has always been how to honor my commitment to my kids and my desire to put them first while pursuing a career I love. The thing is, the message we all wanted to believe was wrong—we *cannot* have it all. I realize now that I don't even *want* it all! Everyone who's a mom can testify that you can't really love your children equally. They each need different things at different times, and it will inevitably be off-kilter instead of in the equal  portions that the term *balance* implies. Caregiving—whether parenting, grandparenting, or assisting someone aging or with an illness—requires that you give what the person needs when he or she needs it, not when you have time so that your day "balances" out.

So there are points in my life that are rich in mommy time, and my work suffers. There have been many shows or appearances I've had to do with sleep deprivation and without preparation. That makes me uncomfortable. I'm a professional—some may even say a perfectionist—and I have angst over things not being as good as they can be. But I chose to be a mother, and I'd rather let down an audience or a production than disappoint my children. That's not balance. It's making choices on a daily basis about what counts and what doesn't in that moment; it's about accepting that something's gotta give, or else I'm going to make myself crazy and hurt others. I love the way Bette Midler looks at it. She says, "I always try to balance the light and the heavy—a few tears of human spirit in with the sequins and the fringes." I've interviewed

Mary Ann Halpin Photography

Bette several times, and she always makes sense to me. Who's to say what's light and heavy for you? It's a very personal thing.

So if balance is a myth, how do we change our mind-set to find the right mix; navigate our lives more productively; and most important, make the time for ourselves necessary to create a powerful jump start for our second take? Kick it old school, as my kids would say.

The Leeza Gibbons Retro Approach to Having It All

Does this sound like an infomercial, or what? Sometimes the price you pay for trying to have it all is experiencing as much guilt and exhaustion as exhilaration. In her landmark book *Gift from the Sea*, Anne Morrow Lindbergh spoke for millions of us when she put words to the conflict that rages in the hearts of many women:

> Woman instinctively wants to give, yet resents giving herself in small pieces. . . . How can one point to this constant tangle of chores, errands, and fragments of human relationships as a creation? . . . The space is scribbled on; the time has been filled. There are so few empty pages in my engagement pad, or empty hours in the day, or empty rooms in my life in which to stand alone and find myself.

That was in 1955. If you're lucky enough to find that empty room in your life, what do you see there? Sometimes when I'm standing in that emotional place, I envision my life as a movie projected on the wall, and I see how often *flexibility* and *forgiveness* have played a role, two "F words" that have characterized my journey, whether I knew it or not. (I've since added *fearless* and *fabulous*—proof of my evolution!) I see the time when I was invited to the White House to receive an honor, and it occurred on the same day as my daughter's school play in which she was a dancing dalmatian. I

opted out of the solo-in-the-spotlight award where I'd be singled out for some great accomplishment in favor of being anonymous in a sea of parents applauding what was in fact my greatest accomplishment: my daughter.

With time to reflect, I see all the big moments in my life—like getting my star on the Hollywood Walk of Fame—along with smaller, more intimate moments, like being backstage with a little boy named Pat, who gave me a star he'd made of tinfoil and told me I was the "nicest, funniest TV lady" he'd ever met, even though I was the only one he'd ever met. I see myself reading *The Cat in the Hat* for the 48th time and walking a teething infant up and down a dark hallway at 3 A.M. There's the time the tooth fairy forgot to come, and Lexi put a note saying "You owe me," under her pillow the next night. I see myself dashing around like a maniac looking for my lost car keys while breast milk seeped all over my new silk blouse and my interview with Michael Jackson was given to someone else because I couldn't get it together.

Life is mostly lived in this vast gray area, rather than clearly differentiated blocks of black and white. I've learned to stop trying to achieve that mythical balance or to have it all and instead concentrate on *enjoying the things that matter most*, which is the heart of the Leeza Gibbons Retro Approach.

I'm simply talking about being clear with yourself about what your values are and then pledging allegiance to them. It doesn't mean giving up your career and becoming June Cleaver, hitting the boardroom when you'd rather be in the baby's room, or giving up your husband or kids to join a radical ashram. It just means striking a realistic mix, on a sliding scale, between the people you love and the work you love (paid or unpaid) without the expectation that these things can ever come out "balanced" in equal portions.

These are lessons I offer you and that I try to remember and practice daily:

1. Own Your Life

It's the ultimate work of art, and it's all yours. Put yourself in charge of your own happiness, and you'll be in the best possible hands. Success is living life on your terms, and only you know what you want. When you decide to get real about running your own show, it might be difficult to let go of the understudy who was doing a pretty good job. I don't know about you, but in the past, I subconsciously created a veneer, a persona of sorts, to lull me into thinking I was doing all right. It was painful for me to admit that I was teetering, ignoring my dreams, or silencing my feelings, so I just pretended that my life was cool and I was totally together.

If you've shrouded yourself from what's really going on in your heart, it may be painful to give that up because the false image might look better than the reality. Let it go anyway. You may have to grieve for the version of yourself that you thought would emerge as you grew older, stronger, and wiser but for whatever reason didn't. This is the time for you to learn what you really need and how to go after it—things like finding a job that feels more authentic, getting more time for yourself, editing people out of your life who no longer fit, or simply having a good cry. It may not always be a pretty picture with a neatly tied bow on top. But it will all be *living*, and not from the wings but from center stage.

When I arrived at that point, I found that I didn't need applause, approval, or my name in lights. All I needed was the quiet satisfaction of knowing that my life is my own creation.

2. Love Your Work

Whether it's in the paid workforce or as a stay-at-home Chief Everything Officer, this is your unique print on the world. I do believe the adage, "Work is its own reward." Humans are hardwired to be productive, but I think work (and I'm including any effort here, from volunteering to parenting) is an extension of who you are and not a separate chamber apart from the other dimensions. When you love what you do, you love yourself.

I'll never forget the moment when I was expecting my first child, Lexi, and I'd been sent on assignment to England by *ET* to interview Paul McCartney at his studio in Sussex. I'd always loved the Beatles, but Paul especially, so it was already a magical moment—but then it got even better. In a spontaneous moment, he started singing "She Loves You," serenading my swollen belly. As he leaned over and cupped his hands so that my unborn baby could hear those words, I knew that the two most important things, my personal life and my work, had come together; and it was sheer bliss. The photo of that moment remains one of my favorites.

It was the first time I was aware that I'd made choices, even before Lexi was born, to share my work with my children. For right or wrong, good or bad, it's what I've always done. I try not to complain or give them an expectation that work is just a time suck to be tolerated until it's over. Think about the whining we adults can do! Who wants to grow up when what they see of the working world is an obligation to just get it done, have a drink, take a bath, and try to forget about it while dreading the next day?

Even though there have been plenty of times when I've felt overextended and exhausted, I've always been grateful for what I do, and I try hard to show that to my kids. It's a privilege to work, to offer something of value. Whether it's a shiny clean floor, the formula for a new medication, a TV show, or a spreadsheet, autographing your work with excellence is a sure sign that you value your own effort. When you do that, it keeps work from being drudgery and helps your path make sense. As Theodore Roosevelt put it, "Far and away the best prize that life offers is the chance to work hard at work worth doing."

Whether you're making a beautiful flower arrangement or manufacturing a part for microscopes, knowing that you're contributing to something outside of yourself helps create pride, and *that* is a beautiful quality

One year during a particularly sweltering summer, there was construction on the campus of the University of South Carolina, and it looked like a miserable task to be part of that crew. I walked by while the guys were taking a break, and just to be nice and pass the time I said, "It's a hot day for laying brick, isn't it?" One of the men looked up at me, pulled his bandana out of his back pocket to wipe his face, and said, "No, ma'am. I'm not putting up a brick wall—I'm building the future. I know someday my kids will walk by this building, and they'll be really proud that I helped create a place where the brightest minds will be changing the world." I walked away with a lot of respect and perspective.

Think about parking-lot attendants, cashiers, or office administrators who are visibly happy on the job. Their positive energy is like a fragrance that hangs in the air and spreads to anyone who interacts with or even sees them. One of my sheroes, Barbara Walters, once said that "To feel valued, to know, even if only once in a while, that you can do a job well is an absolutely marvelous thing." Agreed. Love your work; it is part of you.

3. Treasure Your Friends

Your friends are your best investment in you. Make time to laugh, play, and pour your heart out to those people who know you best and love you anyway. Cultivate these relationships with every ounce of your being, and you'll know immeasurable joy.

Few things are as comforting as the knowledge that there's someone out there who "gets" you, and if you're lucky, you'll have several of those someones. Maybe a few will know instinctively how to be your friend, but it's more likely to be learned over shared experiences. Some inspire you to reach higher, and some listen with such active participation that you believe they really do feel your pain. You'll call others for a rule-breaking romp, and some will call you out on your stuff when you've managed to fool everyone else. The point is they're all holding up a mirror so you can see yourself more clearly.

Friends reflect back to us the parts of ourselves that we need to dust off more often, the parts that need to be kicked to the curb, and the parts that need to just come out and play. My friend Tricia lives in Seattle, and although we rarely speak to or see each other, she motivates me in little ways that count. She reminds me of my optimism and calls me her "yellow" friend because to her, I'm sunny. When I forget that about myself, I love to see an e-mail or text from her.

My sister, Cammy, is my best friend. Along with my sister-in-law, Anne Marie— and Zaidee and Terri, of course—Cammy knows me well enough to intuit when to back off and when to stand up. When I was going through my divorce, she let me cry, feel rejected, and be depressed, right up to the part where I talked about how much I needed to put the relationship back together

Cammy and Anne Marie

and make it work. Cam drew the line at lunacy. She let me sit with feeling inadequate, insecure, and a host of other hurts before she held the mirror up so I could see that, while I may experience or feel those things, they are not who I am.

It's scary to let others see who we really are when we become so skilled at hiding even from ourselves, but part of treasuring your friends means taking a risk and understanding the value of mutual disclosure. I learned this a bit late. Now I talk a lot about the need to stop achieving and start receiving. I can't always be the "fix it" friend who finds the answers, the resources, or the way out. Sometimes I'm the one who needs fixing, and I have learned the beauty of letting my friends take care of me until I can get back into the pilot seat. Sometimes we have to be the gardener who tends to the soil, and sometimes we're the flower who seeks the sun and blossoms. Good relationships will allow you to be *both*.

4. Pick Some Pacesetters

There are several people I look up to, whose sheer effort makes me want to be better. My list is made up of women I use as inspiration to set the pace for me. Yours should reflect the individuals who have what you want, the ones who handle things the way you'd like to and have attained the goals you wish to accomplish. These are like mentors whose way of being in the world helps refine your own direction.

Olivia Newton-John is at the top of my list and has been for years. Aside from her girl-next-door beauty and impeccable reputation, Olivia set the pace for me by starting over and staying strong. I can't blame her personally, but she also inspired me to chop off my hair to look just like hers in the '80s when her *Physical*

album came out. I rushed out and bought headbands just like the one she wore on the cover. I was working in Dallas at the time, and the fashion section of the newspaper nailed me for hanging on to this trend long after it had passed. Our show was taped and then went into reruns, so Olivia and the rest of the world had moved on while I was still sporting the look. (I've since learned the lesson about trend versus style.)

I couldn't believe it when I moved to L.A. and got an assignment to meet this iconic beauty at her home in Malibu. Now we're friends, and she remains one of the most generous souls I've ever known. I look to Olivia for grace; her fearlessness facing her breast cancer is legendary. She sets the pace for me with her measured ambition and her inherent competitive nature. I'm inspired by her commitment to personal growth; she always seeks ways to become smarter, stronger, and more spiritual.

Finally, Olivia shows by example how passion and purpose move mountains. When Olivia gathered up an international team of walkers to take on the Great Wall of China, I couldn't wait to be one of them. The idea was to take steps along this historic divide in honor of all those battling cancer whose own steps might be limited.

I embarked on this adventure the day after I signed final divorce papers, following years of trying to make my marriage

With my Aussie friend Rachel Gordon on the Great Wall of China

work. On the walk, Olivia talked to me about having faith and knowing I was worthy of love. I'd been betrayed and felt foolish and naïve, but I saw Olivia embrace her new love and life without any trace of anger or resentment. She gave me hope that I could have that, too.

The days I spent as part of her mission opened me in new ways as we raised money and awareness for Olivia's dream of a cancer-and-wellness center in Australia. It took her almost ten years to make that dream real; by the time it opened, I'd married Steven, and he and I traveled to Melbourne to support Olivia and celebrate this enormous victory. She was characteristically modest, but I really understood when she said this was the best thing she'd ever done. Just like a pace car at the Indy 500, Olivia is the first one on the track setting the cadence and mastering the curves ahead of most everyone.

MY TAKE: LEEZA'S LENS

Women Who Helped Me Find My Way

In my days of jumping rope and tea parties, I watched a lot of TV and got a lot of mixed messages from the women on the small screen. It's no wonder that much of my generation grew up searching for an identity. We had Donna Reed and Harriet Nelson representing one view of womanhood, followed closely by Peggy Lipton from *The Mod Squad* and Goldie Hawn from *Rowan & Martin's Laugh-In* showing us something else. In between, we had women fulfilling men's fantasies like on *I Dream of Jeannie* or women hiding their real power like on *Bewitched.* From Agent 99 on *Get Smart* to Lisa on *Green Acres,* I watched them all; and I'm sure parts of each made their way into the woman I've become.

I loved *Shindig!* and *Hullabaloo* and began to hatch a dream that I'd be a girl singer. One summer, my friend and I went to the dime store and bought matching magenta polyester jumpsuits, grabbed our hairbrushes to use as microphones, and choreographed a song-and-dance routine that would have made Diana Ross jealous! Secretly, I thought that one day my poor, pitchy vocals would improve and I'd fill out the costume and step into my place onstage. Flash forward 25 years: I was interviewing Diana Ross, and it was all I could do not to break out singing, "Stop! In the Name of Love."

Ultimately, it was Mary Tyler Moore and Marlo Thomas (bless them) who emerged with more relatable expressions of being women with careers and ambitions, but they were still a bit helpless at times and hapless with men. Where were the images of women who had careers, husbands, children, and friends *and* were content with their choices? Okay, I admit it—that *would* be dreadfully boring to watch!

My point with all this is that you have to figure things out for yourself and ultimately merge the messages you get along the way into your own unique expression. I've sure had my attempts to get it right and even lied to myself along the way. It all comes back to knowing who you are and understanding your own story before you can add another person to the plot.

Trying to match the image of what I thought was a successful woman from my upbringing or from TV kept me from knowing who I was and prevented me from finding my own story. But now in my second take, relationships don't fail, they end. What counts is the effort and what we walk away with. If we're lucky and smart, we learn the lesson before we move on. If we're not, we keep getting more lessons. I know I did.

I was caught in a spiral of trying to force things to be the way I thought they should be, and I left no room for what actually was. I was so concerned about trying to find a definition that fit for me in work and in love that I failed to realize I could write one for myself. What a revelation! I'd spent years trying to find the middle of the seesaw with my career and personal life, but I'd never considered that I could come up with my own story and let go of my attachment to a definition that no longer fit. More specifically, I didn't have to feel like a failure for no longer investing in a marriage that had left both sides struggling and gasping for air. And when I finally did take responsibility for the next take, it included the basic truth that I deserved to be honored and loved both for who I was and who I was not. The new version of myself is a woman who will never apologize for trying.

My story became one of valuing my attempts, learning the lessons, and accepting the past as the perfect teacher it is. I fell in love with my reinvention, and I found a man who fell in love with me. I've never been emotionally broken, but I was a little lost; never empty, but a bit hollow in places. Once I knew my own story, I wasn't afraid to open up the book so that Steven could read from the pages and form his own conclusions. Wow, *that* was a big difference. I didn't try to manipulate, influence, or control his opinion of me. What he thought of my body, my age, my parenting—whatever—that was his work. My part was to let him see it. I was (and am) a woman in progress, ever evolving on my journey, always growing even when it seems I'm off the path or out of step with what I *thought* was going to come next. In my story, what happens next has often been more meaningful, better, and more fulfilling than what I envisioned. I promise it will be that way for you, too.

"Don't Fix It, Cuz It Ain't Broken."

Don't you wish there could be a global summit to deal with how brutal we women can be regarding what life choices we've made? I mean, ladies, wouldn't you like to celebrate options and not judge them? One of the most polarizing talk shows I ever hosted was about working moms versus stay-at-home moms. By the end of it, you would have thought the stay-at-home moms were committing crimes against humanity and that the working women were the devil incarnate. Neither side needed approval from the other because each felt validated by her own choices—and yes, that's the point! There was no "disability" associated with either choice. Not a single person there felt broken or wounded. Yet many of them stood waving fingers at each other, preaching and admonishing. At the end of it all, each held more tightly to her labels. The real victory would have been to find more tolerance for each side and more celebration for all of us, an all-around high five for the progress we've made.

Sometimes, though, when we feel backed into a corner, we get defensive, like someone is trying to break our spirit. I've learned that things don't break, people don't let you down, and opportunities don't fall to pieces in order to make you bitter and give up. Things break so you can put them back together again stronger, on the way to becoming who you're supposed to be. Or maybe the thing that appears damaged is really perfect.

There are lessons about this everywhere, and for me, lots of them are found in the kitchen! Cooking always teaches me something. There's nothing natural about it for me, and I'm intrigued by what unlikely ingredients really do go together. My mom would sometimes go by recipes, but most of the time she added her own interpretation to a dish to make it uniquely hers. I've decided to be that way with most things now. Sometimes there's a recipe or a formula to follow, but many times there's greater satisfaction in finding our own way to mix it up—adding or omitting the things we know we need for the final product to be just right for us.

While I'm not much of a cook myself, I do know that when trying to blend family life with work, there will always be a few lumps in the batter. My solution has been to learn to like it that way and to stop apologizing for not getting it right. That's tedious for everybody. Maybe we don't have to fix it cuz it ain't broken. Arguably, *no one* gets it right all the time, but we all get a chance to have another chance. That's become more than enough for me.

I've changed my expectations and become kinder to myself. I used to have a cartoon on my desk that showed the thoughts of women waiting for the bus: *Think positively, stop worrying, be myself, take a risk, be open with people, don't slouch, be more aggressive, start my diet . . . mmm. I know there's something else I'm supposed to do today. My metric for a successful day—and, in fact, a successful life—is now: Did I try my best? Did I grow? Can I let go?*

As my friend Holly told me, "Let go or be dragged!"
All right then. Movin' on!

Creating a Life as Sweet as Pie

As I mentioned previously, life doesn't tend to be perfectly proportioned into equal slices of pie. If yours is, then that's great, but for me, some portions have been heaping servings of bedtime rituals and car pools and homework. Other times, things like exercise and meditation were barely a crumb of the crust. The mix is never the same for me, but the one constant is that I get to serve up the pie of my life in any way I need to on a daily basis, just never in equal slices. The realization that this was okay was freeing to me, as it gave me permission to give all of my attention and love to the slice on my plate at the time.

In one of the many letters he wrote to his son in the 1740s, the Earl of Chesterfield offered the following advice: "There is time enough for everything, in the course of the day, if you do but one thing at once; but there is not time enough in the year, if you will do two things at a time."

This is so true. Our brains aren't even wired to do more than one thing at a time, at least not well. It's the myth of multitasking, and neuroscientists have been trying to get this through our thick skulls for years now. The poor Earl of Chesterfield knew this almost three centuries ago! But we women will never admit that we can't close a business deal while stuffing a Thanksgiving turkey and simultaneously reading over our child's college-entry essay.

Don't just take my word for it—even Harvard researchers agree about this myth. Peter Bregman, writing for the *Harvard Business Review,* says that not only is multitasking not useful, but it actually lowers productivity—and not just by a little either, but by a whopping 40 percent! If this doesn't encourage you to focus, listen to this: *Too much multitasking can ding your IQ and limit your ability to focus on the big things in the future. So, as it relates to balance, we are back to one thing at a time.*

My question is this: How big are *your* slices of the pie? Where are your long-term goals and short-term dreams? Do you have ambitions for better health, a deeper relationship, or a change of course? Because if you can tell me that you have each slice of your pie equally portioned on your plate, then great—you've achieved "balance." But those of us who have been dishing out so much for so long need to find the right serving sizes so we can make room for what we need to fill our lives. How do we do this? How do we navigate the responsibilities and commitments we've made while still being able to point back to ourselves in the end? Without doing so, we'll never be able to get perspective and call for a second take; we'll just keep dishing out until the last morsel is consumed, most likely by someone other than ourselves!

As a Southern girl from the land of okra and sweet iced tea, don't you think I'd also be an expert on pie? Well, below are some recipes I've created throughout my life that I hope can also help you bake a life as sweet as pie. They've worked for me but have taken a lot of practice. Use them exactly as I have or make them your own—mix it up as you feel necessary.

1. Accept

The fact is there's no way you can have it all, all the time. Can we just move on past this, please? Instead, learn to make happiness and sanity your priorities. Put them above everything else. Once you free yourself from the false expectation that in 24 hours you should do 24,000 things, the energy and focus you need to help you make changes in your life will come naturally.

I'm bored to tears with conversations about my long to-do list. It got so ridiculous that at one point I started subcategories: *pending, needing action, delegate, urgent,* and so on. Insane. The list stressed me out, and I never got to the point of turning it into a "Ta-da!" list the way Oprah talks about. So I've accepted it.

Now I see the onslaught of action items as normal. It's a big life, and it's gonna get filled up. In fact, I have my own definition for the constant clutter: SNAFU, which for me stands for Situation Normal All *Filled* Up (instead of the original meaning: Situation

Normal All Fucked Up). Of course, most often, the standard definition applies, too!

I know a lot of people depend on me, and I'm sure the same is true for you. As women, one of our greatest joys is being able to nurture and care for others. But what would happen if you put caring for yourself in a permanent place at the top of your list? I promise you, everyone will benefit. We all instinctively know this, but the better you care for yourself, the better it gets for everyone who depends on you. Loving yourself first is the ultimate selfless act.

2. Create Your Retro Approach

What this boils down to is simplicity, which I think translates to sanity. And you know, it's not so simple to achieve simplicity! The trick is not to resist. We're all in this river of life. Maybe you're truly going with the flow, or maybe you're swimming upstream. Maybe you're in the raft paddling along, or you're the one with water wings trying to stay afloat. Maybe you're on the banks, not ready to jump in, or maybe you're offering an oar to someone else who's gone overboard. Be aware of where you are on the river and know that your position is going to change. Be okay with all of the options, but try to be present.

Enjoying the simple stuff in life seems wonderfully old-fashioned to me, which is why I joke that's it's "retro." But downshifting to enjoy lunch with a friend while not thinking of the ten million other things you have to do is pretty simple. So is relishing your nephew's debut as a snowflake in the nursery-school holiday sing-along without feeling anxious about canceling that conference call. This is one of my emerging skills. In my life, instead of piling on the work projects and trying to do everything I'm asked (a habit I acquired when I was young and hungry), I'm now on an active campaign to simplify.

Create your sanctuary. Honor your story. Ask yourself, What's expendable? What do I need to let go of? And then delete it from your life. When in doubt, cut it out! No apologies, no explanations, no looking back.

Can you make a list right now of what's nonessential in your life? How about just one thing? Hey, that's one piece of the pie that's no longer spoken for! Once you get that slice of time back, you get to decide whether you want or need to reassign it, but at least it's *yours*. That's all it takes.

3. When You Can't Spare It, Share It

There will be times that your commitments and responsibilities will interfere with the people you love in your life. That's when it helps to divide and conquer or align with an ally. If you can't spare the moment, then share it! For instance, I've always tried to use my work to impart my values to those who look up to me. But whoever needs your attention—whether they're children, aging parents, other family members, or friends—they all simply want you to have time and energy to spend on them, and they want you not to be burdened by your life.

I get caught in this trap sometimes. When it came time for bedtime stories or acting as a caregiver for my mother or a support system for my dad, I was sometimes so exhausted that it could pollute my special time with the ones I love most. I often pushed through and then felt resentful when I was so depleted. Why didn't I get that they could understand pressure and demands? Why didn't I share the situation and admit to being temporarily burned out? Why couldn't I ask for help and open up to receive it?

I always wanted my children to see the joy I get from my work and the fulfillment it gives me to also be there for them. It's important for them to see how I can be of service by what I've chosen to do and to be a good mom by modeling limits and sacrifice.

When my youngest son was in elementary school and sat down to do his homework, I would sit beside him and do my research and reading as well. I hope he saw that it takes discipline and that learning is a lifelong pursuit. He also often saw Mom get frustrated and walk away for a moment rather than lose it, but he learned that when you value something, when you really want it, there's a price to pay. We learned to share our homework time, and I got to feel good about being with him in a meaningful way rather than guilty about stressing over my work alone.

So if you're already immersed in your mission to make a change and think the time you need is being sucked away by work or anything else, find a way that you might be able to incorporate your family or friends. Can you share your intent to make a transformation with your son or daughter? Could you show a friend your action plan, or at least let her in on the big dreams you have for yourself? This way, when it comes time to have to offer them just a sliver of the pie instead of the large piece they've been accustomed to receiving, they'll be supportive and happy for you. And who knows, maybe you'll inspire them to find the strength and time to call for their own Take 2.

4. The Drug Called Multitasking

Multitasking really is like a drug for me, and it feeds on itself. The more I do it, the more it becomes a rhythm for my life. As I mentioned before, the truth is that I (like most women) think I'm pretty good at it. But it feels like a one-night stand or taking a job you're not proud of. Once you've made it through, you don't feel good, and chances are you can barely remember it all.

I know I talk about this a lot, but we have to get real here, ladies. Multitasking means misery. I know, I know, this seems counter to all we think and have believed. I can only tell you what has become true for me. I'll always want to do a lot of things, and I want to do them faster than most, but I'm trying to adopt a one-thing-at-a-time philosophy. Original, huh? Well, it is to me! Training my brain to focus on a single task is a constant reminder of how much opportunity for growth I have. Besides, now that I've learned that multitasking leads to less productivity and lower IQ, I'm really motivated to reform!

I've never been a stay-at-home mom. I totally support and applaud those women who have made that noble choice, but I decided to be a mother and have a career. Many women have no choice; they *have* to work to provide for their families. I've been lucky to have flexibility with my profession. So far it's worked for our family, but I've come dangerously close to the limit. Oh, I can get it all done—the problem is what kind of shape I'm in when I get to the end of a particular marathon. If there's no time to enjoy the journey and share with those along the path, then what's the point? The saying is true: What you do is how you make a living, but what you give is how you make a life. You can't give on a meaningful level to anybody if you're always busy in the eye of the storm.

5. Learn Physics

Never the science buff myself, it took a while for this principle to sink it; but once it did, it made a world of difference. *You can't be in two places at once.* I can't promise to be there for my husband and the kids and then jet off to a health summit. I have to stand and deliver. There are almost always choices to be made and consequences to be lived with. I might not be able to say yes to as many projects as I used to, but I have said a resounding yes to my personal happiness. I've finally realized that I'm worth it. When you're making time for yourself and finding the mix that helps you create the woman you strive to be, remember this law. It will make all the difference in honoring your commitment to yourself.

6. Create a Sanity Sanctuary

What happens on the days when you just don't know who gets which piece of the pie or how on earth you'll find time for your endeavors? Go with your gut. I know that sounds like a cop-out, but as women, don't we know how powerful our instincts are? They truly never let us down.

I learned this the hard way. Like many women, I was raised to be a good girl, to not rock the boat, and to be grateful for what I had. As a result, there were frequently times in my life when I ignored my gut instincts (big mistake) and allowed others to define me. I became whatever they needed in order to make them happy. So when you're figuring out your own mix for the day, go with your gut, and the solution will present itself every time.

The one thing you should never be uncertain about is that you deserve what I call a "sanity sanctuary"—a place to go or something you do that reminds you of who you are. This is different for each of us: 15 minutes on a yoga mat, a phone call to a friend, or maybe an ice-cream treat. Find the touchstones throughout the day that center you.

If we don't have a firm grip on who we are, the others in our lives are often shaky, too. What kind of a lesson is it for our daughters in particular to demonstrate that Mom is a martyr, or Mom is so busy that she doesn't care enough about herself? In this case, I mean caring about the soul, not the external self. We find time for the external stuff—polish our nails, color our roots, and all the rest. It's much more important to take care of our heart, our soul center; that's fundamental. (I'll talk more about this in Chapter 7.)

7. Give Yourself Permission

Believe me, I know! A woman's work is never done. You tell yourself you're doing what you have to do, and I'll bet you are. The bills are paid, the dishes are done, your husband is fed, the kids are in bed, and your parents are taken care of; but truthfully, how are you when you get to that point? And how do they feel about that exhausted, burdened woman who's dangerously close to depletion? They'd probably rather have a wife, daughter, or mom with more energy and a lighter outlook. No one cares that you're getting it all done. That kinda hurts sometimes, but I think it's true. Checking things off that big to-do list really only matters to those of us who are so desperately trying to make it happen. The men in our lives don't want us to be perfect, and neither do our kids.

So after having three kids and a husband whose ideas of peace, serenity, and order never seem to match mine, my advice would be to ease up on your expectations and give yourself permission to fall short of the goal. There are no awards. No judges will be dropping by to make sure you're measuring up. Be kinder to yourself than you think you can be. Take off some of the edge by doing things well, but at your pace, and always find time for you. Usually this is when I ask myself: *Am I trying my best?* If the answer is yes, let go of the rest.

"If Mamma ain't happy, ain't nobody happy" was written in needlepoint over my mother's kitchen sink. I've finally realized that is so right.

MY TAKE: LEEZA'S LENS

Lessons from My Children

If you have kids, as you begin to reclaim your life and start living by your own rules, I'll bet you find that the previous rules of parenting don't seem to fit. What other people think of your approach to being a mom may seem a little less relevant, too. I've finally been able to get over myself as a parent. I give myself high marks for effort and realize I don't have to win any awards to feel validated. For example, I'm not as competitive as younger parents for things I know aren't meaningful, like the newest gadget or the trendiest party, and I'm more introspective than ever before.

Like most parents, my kids are so much a part of me that I can't even think of re-creating my life without examining their role in it. Goodness knows I've tried to be the best mother I could at every stage of their lives, and I'm still trying. Having two adult kids (Lexi is 23, and Troy is 21) and a ninth grader (Nathan) means that the rhythms of motherhood are different for

From our annual pajama holiday photo shoot '07. I hope they don't kill me for this!

me from when I was packing lunches, making playdates, and assisting with science projects. Now I'm helping them establish credit and figure out how to achieve the right mix of dreaming and doing.

Mostly I love the teenage years and admire the unique individuals my kids have become. But I still see them frozen in time as those trusting little souls who'd rather stay home and build forts and have grilled-cheese sandwiches and tomato soup with me than do anything else in the world. I've found it's true what my own mother always said to me: "When they're little, they step on your toes, but when they're bigger, they step on your heart." I raised my kids to grow up, be independent, and live on their own one day—and damn it, they've had the audacity to do just that! I always thought I'd have more time with them around the kitchen table and in the passenger seat of the car to impart all the wisdom I was sure they needed.

The alarm buzzer went off before I could get under the wire with another life lesson or dispense another pearl of wisdom. I see now that there's no finish line with parenting. My heart still skips a beat when I pick up the phone and hear my dad on the other end saying, "Leaps [his nickname for me], it's Pops." I realize he still sees me as his little girl, and our relationship has grown richer over time. It can be that way for any of us.

There's no age of emancipation when it comes to the emotional process of parenting; and just like with other aspects of your life, you get to hit the reset button. I'm not talking about having another chance to experience the first day of school, summer camp, or the prom, but the real opportunity to see it all through different eyes.

The mind is like a screen, and we're either cleansing it or polluting it with our thoughts, which create our experience. We have to mind and monitor our thoughts, because that's how we create our own reality and how we bring about change. So think about getting another shot at being a good mom. This isn't to say you weren't a good mother before or that you aren't one now; but chances are, no matter what ages they may be, you're parenting different children with each new experience. Sometimes parents and kids grow and forget to tell each other. It's never too late to redesign the whole relationship.

I took my middle kid to lunch the other day. It was one of those rare moments when our schedules were in sync, so I suggested that we go to a little sidewalk café that I like in West

Hollywood. I immediately started thinking that it might not have been a great choice for my pizza-loving, burger-eating son; but as we walked in, he said he was glad to know about the place since he thought his girlfriend would like it. We sat outside, and when he walked in to get our order, I watched him brush his long hair back from his eyes and remembered every screaming match, door slam, and frustrated moment of disconnected tension. As a teen, Troy was the one labeled troubled and lost. In retrospect, I see now that he was no more of those things than any other adolescent; even so, he struggled, and we responded the best we could.

Troy is the sweetest kid on earth, and we each know how much we're loved by the other, but his newly claimed adult status meant that I could look for another way to connect with him. On this day, I wanted him to know that if we chose to, we could wipe the slate clean and redefine our relationship to one another.

I told him, "Honey, the first couple of decades in your life have unfolded in a certain way based on who we were at the time, and how we both reacted to the changes that came with your growing up. We can change it, you know."

He was confident and didn't hesitate as he said, "Mom, I guess I felt like you haven't really taken time to know me and to understand what I'm about now."

I continued nibbling at my salad but looked him square in the eye. "Well, darling, I thought I tried to." As I stumbled, he picked the conversation back up with, "I really appreciate that you've been reaching out, but I'm not you. Maybe I'm not who you thought I would be, but I like who I am."

"Troy," I said lovingly, "I like who you are, too. How come you've never talked to me about those feelings?"

Then my son said something I never expected: "It's been hard growing up in the shadow of a giant, Mom. Everything you do seems to work out, and people support you, and everybody knows you're strong. You care about different things from me, like making a difference and changing the world and all. I just want to be who I am and chill."

I give him a tremendous amount of credit for stating the obvious and for serving it up along with the extra salad dressing. That was a defining moment in our relationship for me. The truth is I'd heard sentiments like that before, but always in a heated war of words when I'd sometimes hunker down in my foxhole of righteousness and be unable to receive them. I no longer needed to be right, and I got a chance to start over with my son.

I've found that as you commit to coming clean with yourself during your second take, you're more willing to let your kids see you as you really are. This is a time when you can get past the notion that you have to be a perfect parent. As I said before, your kids don't need you to be perfect, and they don't want it, either! It puts way too much pressure on them. Apparently, I got the memo too late.

Years ago, when my daughter was 16, we were driving together somewhere in a comfortable pocket of silence. Seizing the moment, I asked her what her experience was like getting to this point in her life, having me as her mom. I was expecting her to gush with gratitude about all the experiences and opportunities she'd had, to talk about how secure she felt, the respect she had for me, and the pleasure she got from knowing about my career and sharing in my success.

Unfortunately, way too much time went by before she uttered a single word.

She finally said, "Um, Mom, we should probably find a good time to talk about this later."

If there was a mother's cross to hang on, I was there. Lexi told me that basically, being Leeza Gibbons's daughter was not a cakewalk, and that even though I never put any pressure on her, it was obvious that people expected a lot from her.

I was thinking, *Oh my gosh. I didn't realize that my celebrity status had been such a mixed bag for her.* I was never aware that my daughter was that conscious of who I was in the public eye. Maybe I was a little naïve, but it never occurred to me that this was factoring into her experience of herself. I was too busy being her mom. I'd seen everything through my eyes and never detected a single sign that she saw it differently. We have to dare to care enough to ask and be prepared for what we hear.

So when you're focused on who you want to be and how you want your second take to go, if you're a parent, think about what that means. Bring your kids into the process, and you'll probably get to learn a few things that might surprise you. You can call for a redo on your role as a mom, just as you can in all the other areas of your life. I feel more peaceful about my parenting now because I finally realized it's not about getting it right. It's just about *trying every day.* Live and learn, Take 2.

8. Wear Your Emotional Sunglasses

I was having lunch with my friend Tricia the other day. We were catching up over a steak quesadilla and blended margaritas, and predictably we started talking about our kids. Neither of us has little ones anymore, and we have been surprised that it's so much more challenging that we had anticipated as the kids grow older. She said, "I'm parenting harder now than I ever have." I completely agreed that when you have little kids you have little problems, but big kids bring big problems. We also realized that while we'd always continue to try to be great moms, actually being great women *for ourselves* was the platform not only for our personal success, but also for our families.

I arrived at the halfway point ahead of Tricia, and we were talking about her induction into the wisdom years. She told me that a couple of years back, she'd been thinking about what qualities she wanted to develop for her arrival at this milestone of being 50. She'd asked the universe to deliver her to her fifth decade without any clinginess. Not without vulnerabilities, but without neediness.

Tricia told me in the months that followed she'd continued to focus on that, so she wasn't surprised when many of her relationships that had been built on codependency began to erupt, disintegrate, or break at the seams. She was "shedding" and in a sense being reborn, but she said it was hurtful because some of her friends hadn't been able to accept her as a whole and complete woman who wasn't dependent on them.

As we walked to the parking garage to get our cars, I realized that Tricia has been on a journey for truth and her own enlightenment for many years, but now she was ready to pay the price of admission. Birth is painful; it's not an easy fit coming out of that canal, and Tricia saw that it's not a smooth transition when you step into your truth either. The light can be so bright that it hurts a bit. I advised her to wear her emotional sunglasses.

The thing is . . . you're searching, right? You're looking for a way to change, for a way to be more fulfilled, and for the tools you need to sit down and get going on your second take. Nobody knows you better than you know yourself, so the best way for me to help is to show you where some of the land mines are on the journey. As I mentioned earlier, I want you to let go of the notions of having it all and balance. They're traps.

John Adams has been quoted as saying there are only two kinds of people: those who are committed and those who require the commitment of others. I want you to be one of the former, so commit yourself to doing the work and learning what you need to know. I want you to raise your voice in your own best interest and sing it from the mountaintops. Be like a bird that doesn't sing because it has an answer; it sings just because it has a song! And as they say, the forest would be mighty quiet if only the birds that sang best chimed in. You don't have to wait till you've become the highest version of yourself to celebrate. Be happy about the process—sing it loud and proud!

I think you can tell I'm a big fan of what it means to be female. To make the point, let me share you with the words of Alexis de Tocqueville, the French statesman writer who came to America in 1831 to study our democracy and left impressed with one of our country's other great natural resources.

"If I were asked," de Tocqueville wrote, "to what the singular prosperity and growing strength of that people [Americans] ought mainly to be attributed, I should reply—to the superiority of their women."

To which I reply, "Amen."

Chapter 6

FIND YOUR STORY, MAKE IT COUNT

"There are no extra pieces in the universe. Everyone is here because he or she has a place to fill, and every piece must fit itself into the big jigsaw puzzle."

— DEEPAK CHOPRA

It was one of those perfect L.A. days, sunny and 72 degrees. All the requisite beautiful people were on display in their places at the Ivy restaurant on Robertson. I was having a catch-up lunch with my girlfriend and former producing partner Debra. She's a hard charger with a soft heart—you know, one of those professional women who got a little tough going up against the boys, but not so tough that she lost her femininity. We hadn't seen each other in a long time, but that didn't matter. We jumped right into such easy banter that I looked up from my grilled veggie salad and realized that two hours had gone by.

We were in dissection mode, exploring feelings, decisions, paths taken, and doors wide shut. In my view, this is one of the most meaningful ways to find your center, picking apart all that you want and don't want now. Examine it all. Lay it out as neatly as you would an outfit for a special occasion. Stand back and invite someone to share your process, or at least be a sounding board as you give it a whirl.

For Debra, it was a time of transition with a potential end result of transformation. Like some opportunities, this one had arrived as a sort of dead end thrust upon her. She was no longer entertaining big job offers with bigger salaries and unrestricted power. Instead, she was hustling for chances that she'd turned her nose up at before. Ageism? Maybe. A changing economy? Definitely. But I think there's also something different that happens to us (blessedly) at various junctures along our journeys. It's what I call "shedding."

Shedding is the process of transitioning from one stage to the next, usually prompted by something external, but inevitable nonetheless. It's coming to terms with who we are now and who we need to become to keep growing. "I tried to volunteer at my daughter's school while I waited for the big job to happen," Debra said, "but it's just not enough." She quickly began to explain that she thought it was wonderful to volunteer, and she was grateful to have a chance to be involved in her daughter's life, but she didn't feel like it was for her. To which I replied, "So? It doesn't have to be."

This was familiar territory for me. What fits, what doesn't? I love to take inventory! Debra was judging herself for not being where she used to be and feeling disappointed that she wasn't thought of in the same way by the business world. Her knee-jerk response? "I'm just gonna get out of the game."

It's probably our first line of defense: *If the coach doesn't pick me in round one, I just won't play at all.* It wasn't really the work Debra was missing; it was the validation, the respect, and the thrill of being part of something. I've been there. When I left my job at *Extra* to start my nonprofit, I worried and wondered what it would mean to not be on television every night and not get the big check that goes with it. At our lunch, Debra and I talked a lot about what we "need" to feel. Is it egotistical, are we addicted, can we never be okay without a high-octane career? Are we really valuable without a salary to demonstrate our worth?

I told my friend to be comfortable with this uncomfortable feeling and to know it's serving her best interest. When it bubbles up inside, making her feel awkward in her own skin, it's like standing on the precipice to a new self.

As Debra prepares for her second take, she's found herself at what storytellers call a turning point. All main characters must come up against a conflict, or else a tale isn't worth telling. If you've ever felt like Debra—not living authentically, somewhat lost or going through the motions, concerned, and confused about all that has led up this point in your life and what comes next—then you're simply experiencing what every hero who's worth her salt goes through. It's a chance for metamorphosis. You're about to go up against the conflict that will test your virtue and reveal the strong, courageous woman you've always been.

Conflict is the critical element every story needs. If Scarlett O'Hara didn't have a war to contend with and her own personality flaws to overcome, *Gone with the Wind* would have been boring. Nobody wants to read hundreds and hundreds of pages about a beautiful, rich Southern girl with all the men at her beck and call, the prettiest dresses, and Daddy's land to inherit, and have that be the end of the story. We need conflict for the story to continue and be interesting enough to make us keep turning all those pages.

I realize this sounds like a daunting task, but believe it or not, most of the work has been done—at least in terms of what we've already discussed in this book. The hard stuff has all been laid down: finding your courage, setting priorities, building self-confidence, and creating the space to focus on your dreams and goals or to reinvent your life to your liking.

By the time you're calling for Take 2, it's really about taking all of this inner work you've been doing and turning it outward. Once the foundation has been put down, it's time to build your dream house. Set your goals and make them happen.

MY TAKE: LEEZA'S LENS

Lead with Your Strength

There's a saying that nobody cares how much you know until they know how much you care. I think that's especially true in business, so in all situations, dare to care. Let it be known that you have passion and that you invest emotionally. Smart women use what we've got in business and that means our intuition, the ability to collaborate, nurturing energy, and softer strength. Believe me, I've worked with a lot of ball-busting women, so I know that approach can work, too. But I've seen more examples of women being happy with their power if they decide to express it in a way that's more organic to who they are. I'm not saying play small, and don't be in anyone's shadow. I'm just saying use what's natural to you in business—and that usually means that you care. Never be afraid to show that. If you find you're involved in projects with people and things that don't matter to you, you're going to need to find a way to engage because the reality is that you'll be more successful if you really care.

This was brought home to me while covering a story I didn't want to do. When I was a new reporter in Dallas, one of the first assignments I was given was to cover the Mary Kay convention. In the early 1980s, it was a national seminar given by the cosmetics queen. I was downright huffy about it. "Come on," I moaned to my assignment editor, "those are the hyper ladies with the pink Cadillacs."

Well, I walked into a convention hall filled with smart women all focused on getting smarter—strong women dedicated to getting stronger. Mary Kay Ash herself was holding court, and I was mesmerized. She'd found a way to unlock something for those women that they'd never dared to show before. She'd unleashed their ambition, their desire to accomplish goals and win victories for themselves, and their determination to break out of their domestic boxes. If a pink Cadillac was the lure for that, I said okay, bring it on. What I saw was a woman setting the tone and the example that if she could build her empire by leading with her feminine strengths, so could we all.

Mary Kay once said that "An average person with average talents and ambition and average education can outstrip the most brilliant genius in our society, if that person has clear, focused goals." She also liked to insist that "Attitude determines altitude." She built her multimillion-dollar business on a "you can do it" platform where P&L didn't stand for Profit and Loss; it meant People and Love. She wanted to live in such a way that when she died, others would say, "She cared." When Mary Kay passed in 2001, her legacy as a passionate woman who redefined caring had long been secured.

I interviewed her only once in her offices in Dallas where she had all pink lightbulbs put in (better light for a softer complexion). What I experienced that day has never left me: We all do better when we lead with our strengths and use what's organic to us. It's never a mistake to show how much we care.

The Upside to the Downside

As she prepares for Take 2, my friend Debra is at a turning point. She can choose to face the conflict and slay the dragon; or she can abandon the challenge before her, making the second take less interesting than the first. If Rocky Balboa had bowed down to Apollo Creed, we would have left the movie theater. There's no story if you walk away from your challenges.

Let me break this down simply: We're born, we do a bunch of stuff, and then we exit. The trick is to make the most of the middle part. And the good news is that on your life's ride, you get more than one shot at standing up on the surfboard. There are lots of currents to knock you off balance, but they're actually pushing you to reinvent the life you want.

Conflict is just a rougher word for *change;* and we already know that without change, we die. So let whatever it is—your own insecurities, an unsupportive spouse, money issues, a terrible boss—thrust you to the crest of the wave where you can ride it fiercely, maybe for the first time in your life.

At the point of the transition is where you'll find the most opportunity. That's what I meant when I told Debra that the awkwardness she feels means she's closer to self-discovery than she thinks.

You were meant to have a life of richness and abundance. We all were. So I always say supersize your dream. Without vision, the rest becomes a meaningless rehearsal that never makes it to Broadway. I'm not saying that you need to buy a Harley and strike out in some state of rebellious defiance, but maybe just take some baby dream steps—write a page, buy some paint, call for a loan, whatever it is. This is the action part of the plan, and if you're anything like me, you're not afraid to get your hands a little dirty.

We're desperately working, pushing toward something, but how many of us can define what that something is? Many of us simply don't know where we're going, so we can never realize how close we are to success or when to change course. I've met and interviewed people who run the gamut from wildly successful entrepreneurs and entertainers to teenage welfare mothers and battered wives. Certainly not all, but many of them talk about the daily barrage that wears them down to the point where they get a little lost or numb. Hope is forgotten, and dreams seem like a luxury not easily afforded.

The question is how the heck does that happen? How do we regress from the blank slate of our infancy to a place that's so unfulfilling? Needless to say, I don't have all the answers. I just know that in the story of my life, the many transitions and conflicts have proven to me that my journey only gets better as a result of my reactions to the things I never saw coming and my actions toward creating my own life starring *me*. My second take works in a way that the first one didn't.

Note to Self . . .

I remember being a young girl, sitting cross-legged on my bed in Irmo, South Carolina, writing stories about my future in a spiral notebook. They were extraordinary adventures of challenge and triumph. I had no doubt that the chapters in my notebook would one day become real.

From early on, I had a sense that everything was possible and that life was a wonderful gift to be opened over and over again every day. My dreams got bigger as I grew taller, and my parents took each new declaration about my future with the seriousness I intended. Even at a young age, I admired the talking heads on the news; I was certain that the anchors and reporters had the greatest gigs on earth (something I still believe).

I didn't have much use for playing with dolls at that time, but boy, could I weave some dreams with my Barbies. Mine were news reporters and anchors and they had names: Nancy Dickerson and Barbara Walters, two of the coolest pioneering newswomen of the time. I used to imagine that when they weren't interviewing politicians or covering breaking news or world events, they ran businesses on the side and had an entire charitable division for giving back.

I was dead serious when I played and was very annoyed when my little sister, Cammy, always wanted to butt

With Cammy, Christmas 1967

in. "I wanna play! What can I be?" she pestered. Usually I'd get exasperated and give in by telling her, "All right, all right. You can be my assistant!" (Even then, I was exploring my life lesson of dealing with control issues.)

In high school, Walter Cronkite was my ideal of credibility and humanity; I worshipped him. By the time I got to college, though, my focus zoomed in on my favorite female newswoman who was creating a lot of controversy. Barbara Walters generated big headlines in 1976 by accepting a five-year contract with ABC for a million dollars a year, becoming the first female network anchor and making more money than the men—Walter Cronkite included. I announced to my friends that I wanted to be like her and that someday I'd make a million dollars, too. They laughed at me.

As always, I ran to my mom, who started making a chocolate cake so we could talk things over (that always seemed to make things better). By the time we were ready to put our masterpiece in the oven, she said, "That's okay, honey, don't listen to your friends. They don't have vision. You'll show them."

Note to self #1: Have a vision.

✦

After I became established in the business, I wrote Barbara a fan letter. I'd been sitting alone at my kitchen table in Hollywood watching one of her specials, and I got that wonderful feeling that comes when your hero doesn't disappoint. I'd been so invested in her and always watched her reports as if she were somehow blazing the trail for me. Her excellence and her victories became mine. I tried not to gush in my note to her, keeping it semiprofessional. She replied with a warm handwritten note and has never failed to offer encouragement and support.

Oprah has done the same. I was at the Academy Awards one year when I found myself outside one of the after parties with Ms. O. At that time, I was executive producer and host of my own show, *Leeza.* The format for afternoon talk shows had become exploitative and tawdry, so I was proud of myself and my staff for being responsible and respectful. Oprah approached me and said, "Keep doing what you're doing. You and I are doing it the way it should be done."

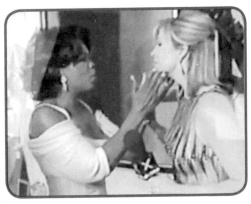

It was generous of Oprah to put me in her company, and I heard her wisdom echo in my ear many times before I went onstage to tackle a show. A few other times she sent me notes of congratulations.

From those two outrageously successful women, I learned that generosity of spirit is key. I took a cue from their second takes, and I rarely miss an opportunity to make a call, write a note, or take the effort to support and encourage those whose path I share or who are coming up next.

Note to self #2: Be gracious during your quest for success and especially when you're basking in it.

✦┈✦

As I mentioned earlier, when I was a child there were very few role models who had what I wanted, except Marlo Thomas as *That Girl*. I dreamed of a life just like hers in New York in her cute little brownstone apartment with her exciting job, that great flip of her hair, lots of independence, and a fun boyfriend. I wanted all of it. Well, maybe I wanted all of it except for the boyfriend, Donald— he was a bit of a dweeb.

Well, just a few years out of college, there I was in New York City, living in a brownstone very much like *That Girl's*, with a job on television that took me all over the world doing exciting things! Maybe there's more to the practice of visualization than some like to believe.

It was then that I found one of my first mentors, a female ex-ecutive named Bobbee Carson, who was responsible for hiring me (along with my dear friend Andrea Ambandos). She was young, smart, well respected, and married—as close as you could get to having it all. I watched Bobbee be strong in business through inherently knowing her value and living by her convictions. She knew how to make unpopular decisions and still retain her sense of worth. In a room with the top brass or in front of a live audience, Bobbee never allowed a person or situation to back her off her position. She used to remind me that I'd been good enough to get the job, so I needed to trust that and be myself, turning off the voices that were trying to persuade me otherwise.

In the early days while I was trying to find my groove on the air, she'd say, "You know who you are; don't be afraid to own your ideas. Autograph your work with your performance."

Note to self #3: Stand your ground.

I learned early on that my gift was to communicate. As I mentioned earlier, one of the first storytellers I tried to emulate was newsman Walter Cronkite. Of course I knew that I'd never hold the same place as this most beloved of journalists, but I wanted to be trusted the way he was. I wanted people to believe me when I delivered a message. He had such warmth and was so comfortable and secure with himself. He could tell you about the most monumental event, yet his humanity still emerged during the report. From the Kennedy assassination to the moon landing, Cronkite put it all in perspective live on the air as events unfolded, and somehow made us all feel better just knowing he was on the case.

It was pretty much the same deal with Dick Clark. I adored him—the host of hosts, the kind of guy you'd invite into your home and spend time with because he made it all so comfortable. I loved the way Dick interviewed his guests: always careful not to humiliate anyone, respectful, quick-witted, and versatile. I wanted to be that way.

When I moved to Hollywood, I learned of Dick's keen business sense. He took control of his career and recognized that he was the most valuable commodity he had. I was a frequent presenter at the awards shows produced by Dick, and I marveled at his ability to master that environment.

Courtesy of Getty Images

There he was writing copy, supervising talent, managing the audience, timing the segments, and calming nerves—the ultimate executive producer in his perfect setting.

Note to self #4: Be good at being yourself.

When I was working at *ET,* I was offered a chance to cohost the Miss USA and Miss Universe pageants with Dick. During these opportunities, I watched him closely and often asked for advice. "Respect the audience," he told me. "Understand all aspects of the business." But mostly he said, "Be grateful every day. You never know how long it's gonna last." For Dick, the answer seemed to be as long as he wanted it to. Even after having a stroke, he fought his way back on the air, and I got misty-eyed every New Year's Eve to see him in Times Square, signaling a new year with a new version of himself.

I loved Dick. He and his wife, Kari, were committed to taking on whatever came next. I guess life was like a live event for Dick. The countdown begins, you get a cue, and you go on. He played it that way until the end. When I got my star on the fabled Hollywood Walk of Fame, Dick came and spoke at the ceremony. For someone who'd grown up idolizing this man, wanting nothing more than to work in his industry, it was a moment that secured my faith in dreams

With Dick and my buddy, former *ET* cohost, John Tesh

123

coming true. Along with so many others, I cried when he died; we lost so much with his passing. While the world seems a little less vibrant without Dick Clark in it, his programs, projects, and friendships are lasting testaments to a life well lived.

In 1994 while I was working at Paramount, I created my own production company, Leeza Gibbons Enterprises; and I began to get serious about developing the kinds of programs that reflected the things I cared about and believed in. When it came to creating programming success, one of the giants in the industry is Arnold Shapiro. I knew of Arnold—everyone did. He's the Oscar- and Emmy-winning producer who made an indelible mark with his documentary *Scared Straight*. They don't come any finer. I approached Arnold about partnering with me on some projects, and I remember being in his office for the first time.

Hundreds of awards lined the walls and shelves, but there was no attitude. Arnold acted as if he had all the time in the world for me. Bingo—there it is. Find successful people, and often they're generous and have the ability to focus on the individual or situation in front of them at the time. I made a note of that, and then I siphoned off a bit of Arnold's creativity.

We were trying to convince the networks to do a documentary about child abductions, which would teach parents the lures pedophiles use. Although now that seems like standard fare, at the time it was provocative and edgy, and we were experiencing many obstacles in our pitch meetings. Arnold taught me to be creative and find another way in, to believe in my projects, and to be patient. He always said, "Don't feel defeated when you're told no. Wait a while and those people will be gone. You'll go back in there and try again!" Ah, the voice of experience.

Note to self #5: Take your time. Let success marinate.

✦◦✦

From Arnold Shapiro I learned that, as a good producer, you have to know everything that's going on but trust those you hire to deliver. I watched it work on his sets. He brought me on to host a wonderful series of documentaries called *Teen Files,* and whenever I arrived on location, Arnold made sure all the members of my team were treated with respect and appreciation for their talents. He never insisted that people stay in their departments. A good idea always wins, whether it comes from the craft-services guy or the hairstylist. I run my business that way today. I ask all kinds of people for opinions, and I listen to what they say. I'm amazed at where answers and ideas come from, and I often think of this great mentor and the influence he's had on my life and my business. Thank you, Arnold.

Arnold and me taking ourselves very seriously!

Note to self #6: Be coachable and open to learning from others.

As an aside, I have to laugh about *Teen Files,* because at the time we produced the series, I never envisioned that my own children would be forced to watch it in school one day! I can't imagine many things worse than the day my son sat down next to his classmates and heard the voiceover: "Now, *The Truth about Sex,* hosted by Leeza Gibbons."

"Nathan, isn't that your *mom?*" a voice called out as Nate sank deeper into his seat.

Kids, I'm really sorry.

Full Steam Ahead

One thing I know for sure is that the only way to get ahead is to get started. The good news is that any change depends mostly on the mental prep work, and you've done that. Now it's time to get down to business and look at setting the goals to make your dreams come true.

When you give voice to a dream, you're in essence changing the rules of the game. You begin to take control of your life and steer it in the direction you decide. This is big stuff, and if it marks a departure from your everyday routine, you're likely to get some "pushback" from family and friends. It's like awakening a sleeping giant, and that means others have got to deal with you on your new terms. We teach people how to treat us anyway, and we get to decide where the boundaries are, so don't be timid.

Show up for this new spin-off version of yourself with confidence and commitment. Having done this before, I have to tell you that there will be some who will accuse you of being grandiose or a Pollyanna. Just say thank you and move on. From where I stand now, I see that the drawback of *not* showing up to create the rest of your life is far greater than being made fun of by others for your ideas of what comes next.

For me, hitting the reset button meant simply admitting to myself what I wanted *now* and then going out and getting it. That's what always worked for me when I was younger; but after a certain age, I found myself not trusting it and unconsciously putting limits on what my life should look like. I'd think, *Maybe I shouldn't be so ambitious anymore. Should I start slowing down . . . start wearing sensible shoes?* Heaven forbid!

So whenever I came across a bridge that seemed a little shaky or a conflict that I perceived as outright catastrophic, I decided to look to some of the women in my field who'd already been where I wanted to go. They're among the women I admire most: Katie Couric, Diane Sawyer, and Maria Shriver. They didn't run from change; they rewrote the script.

I talked earlier about my admiration for Maria, and my feelings about Katie and Diane are similar.

Katie Couric took over the anchor chair at *CBS Evening News,* knowing that she'd be a target of criticism. But in the end, it was worth the risk because she knew she had a chance to make history and show her daughters by example how to step up and accept challenge and opportunity. She's much more than her perky, girl-next-door public image, but she was never embarrassed by that image and doesn't try to deny it. It's her stock-in-trade, her calling card; and she's a smart cookie who knows how to allow that window to open so many opportunities, including her new talk show, *Katie.*

Diane Sawyer has never tried to be in the boys' club. She's used her brains *and* her beauty to create a place of her own in the newsroom. Always a lady, never a pushover, Diane has the respect of her colleagues because she put in the time and sweat equity to deserve it. She adapted, grew, and changed at every step from beauty queen and weather girl to becoming the first female correspondent on *60 Minutes* and now the anchor on ABC's *World News.* She's timeless and beautiful, and because she's so comfortable in her own skin, we're all comfortable watching her.

Look at the people you admire, and drill down to see what their lives stand for. At the base, I'll bet you find a lot of reinvention and change and never a failure to take action.

If you want to transform your life, you have to "name it and claim it." Let go of the wishing and hoping, and get down to the doing. So what does it mean to be *you* right now? And how do you identify, set, and achieve the reinvention you've committed to?

Make It Up

You've probably heard of vision boards. They're used to create the future by envisioning what it could be. Before you can arrive at your destination, you have to know where you're going, and the board is like a visual blueprint or map. Think of it as your outline for Take 2. Don't worry—you don't have to be artsy or know anything about crafting. It can be created digitally (we'll link you up at **www .leezagibbons.com**), or you can go old school. Yours can be as basic or as elaborate as you like, but you have to get the dreams out of your head and onto a board, piece of paper, or digital page. This isn't a step to skip.

Some people like to cut out pictures, words, phrases, or mantras from books, magazines, or newspapers and paste them on a board or wall. A few years ago, I did a board with pictures and the words *dream home.* Now I live in just such a place, complete with a mag-nolia tree outside as I envisioned! I wrote *true love,* and now I have it. *My body is strong and well* and *financial abundance* were on my board, too. As I added each word or picture to the board, I allowed it to permeate through my cells. I expected it to happen. I could feel what it would be like to drive up my driveway into a safe haven with the love of my life. That's the key component—you have to *feel* it into being.

My childhood and young-adult notebook acted as a vision board in and of itself because I took my internal thoughts and wishes and brought them into the physical world when I put pen to paper. Or consider these words from Norman Vincent Peale: "Change your mental habits to belief instead of disbelief. Learn to expect, not to doubt. In so doing, you bring everything into the realm of possibility."

Dreams are our very own, hatched from the purest places. Write down your goals, think about them every day, and envision them coming true. Smile knowingly as you imagine what it feels like to make it all hap-pen. You've had that sensation before, right? Think about when you ace a test, learn something new, or get into those jeans and look hot. It only gets better.

Many people have used vision boards as ways to manifest what they want, such as cars, clothes, money, and cute boyfriends. All of those things are terrific, but try to dig deeper and visualize the person you want to be, getting in touch with the woman behind the curtain. You know some of my heroes already. I wanted to be respected and trusted like Walter Cronkite and Dick Clark. I wanted to be as fearless as Barbara Walters and Diane Sawyer, as well as wildly successful like Oprah. I wanted to create change in the world the way Maria Shriver does and to be as entrepreneurial as Suzanne Somers. I wanted the grace of Olivia Newton-John. As I've described, these people became my pacesetters.

I believe that when you prioritize your virtues so that they're higher on the totem pole than material wealth, you'll receive both tenfold. Who has what *you* want? Use them as a guide, a source of inspiration, and evidence that it can happen. Make a list of your own pacesetters.

Shorthand for the Long-Term

Do you ever see other people doing things you want to do or who look and feel the way you want to? I do, and I've used those images to inspire my own reinvention. As I described, I've gleaned lessons from watching those who were living the life I wanted—from Maria Shriver to Barbara Walters to Dick Clark. I never let what they said or demonstrated go unnoticed. I looked for their wisdom and trusted in it, making mental notes to myself along the way. That's the idea behind the ten tips that follow. They're guideposts, continually helping me embrace conflict, stay focused on my goals, and remember why I've embarked on Take 2 in the first place. They're a bit of shorthand for setting and attaining long-term goals so that getting started on your second take is easier.

1. Don't Be Afraid to Look Behind the Curtain

At our recent lunch, my friend Debra and I had a heart-to-heart and took inventory of her life as she dissected her choices and thought about how to proceed. Taking inventory requires courage. It's like peeking behind the curtain to recapture the *rest* of your identity—the part you haven't been showing the world—and to help you evaluate what you really want and the best methods to going about getting it.

When we explore ourselves, we'll always find that the essence of who we are began in childhood, when we were much more authentic. Usually when we're in this pure place of youth, we hold a vision for ourselves, as I did when I wrote in my childhood notebook. Peeking behind the curtain and remembering that dream is an important step in setting new goals or awakening the ones lying dormant in our subconscious.

We need to have vision, and I believe that my act of writing down my dreams and discussing them so vividly with my mother and friends, or anyone else who would listen, had a little something to do with them coming to fruition. Taking inventory will set your own plan into action as you sharpen your vision of yourself. The next step is to determine what resources you need to keep your vision in focus.

2. Determine What Resources You Need

Going after your primary goals for reinvention will likely mean you need to rely on some sort of physical, spiritual, financial, and emotional resources. The solution is something I discussed earlier—YES: Your Empowerment System. Find the YES in your life, and you'll be on the yellow-brick road.

When I did the local news, I worked with a woman who was one of the anchors. She was Ms. Queen Bee, and she knew it. Composed and confident, she strutted through the newsroom with perfect posture and perfect anchor hair. Like everyone else, I always admired her from afar, but one day I had the nerve to talk to her as we reapplied lip gloss in the ladies room. I asked her such a generic, broad, pathetic question that I was embarrassed almost before it came out. I dipped my lip brush into impossibly pink gloss and asked, "How do you do it?"

To my astonishment, she replied with a very thoughtful answer: "You have to know who you can count on for support and always know who's got your back. Plus, you'd better learn to be your own best friend, or it can be brutal out there."

Those words never left me.

Part of the YES approach to life means activating people or programs to tighten your grip on change. You have to know where to go for strength when you feel weak and where to find a shot of adrenaline or a kick in the ass. I've identified these people in my life and informed them of their role. "You're my circle of certainty," I told them. "If I get lost, when I waffle on my goals, when I can't seem to tell the mountain to get out of my way, I need you to keep me committed."

When I take care of myself physically and emotionally, I also provide the basics for all my dreaming and scheming. There are no shortcuts. My target is 150 minutes of walking or biking a week, along with not overindulging or skipping meals. The time to relax, meditate, soak in a bubble bath, and laugh—these are nonnegotiables. Strong muscles, a sound brain, and a serene spirit are all necessary for my grand adventure, and this is my way of feeding them so they can nourish me.

Spiritually, there has to be a connection to source energy for life to make sense. When you develop this relationship, everything else seems to fall into place. I think the *pursuit* of truth and wisdom is more important than actually finding it. In my opinion, the glory goes to the seekers.

3. Test-Drive Your Dreams

This is one of my favorite mental notes because it's one of the most effective when it comes to getting out of traps that sabotage us. How many times have we set a goal only to find when we finally achieve it that it doesn't make us as happy as we thought it would? Are we thankless fools? No. Are we confused, undeserving, or incapable of being happy? No. I think that so many times we've simply outgrown our goals and dreams but don't know it. By the time we buy the red Ferrari that was the apple of our eye for so long, we realize it's really the silver BMW that feels more like us. Or we discover it's not a car we need in order to feel valuable or successful; maybe we're looking to go on a volunteer vacation instead.

Ever get the guy to finally ask you out, only to decide he's not really your type? Have you nailed the job but think maybe you should go back to school or switch careers? Our bodies, minds, and souls are ever changing and growing, so why wouldn't our goals do the same? From time to time, it's important to test-drive your dreams, to make sure that the energy and resources you're about to expend to make them happen are actually worth it. You don't have time to waste, so you must assess what you want. *Does this fit with who I am today? What does it mean to be happy? Has the definition of success changed for me? What do I need now in a relationship?*

Don't be afraid to test your heart, your head, and your soul often to make sure your dreams still fit. Sometimes you'll outgrow them, add on to them, adjust them, or change them; and that's cool. The idea is to never abandon them, because without vision, your true self is lost and your life will never make sense.

4. Kill Your Darlings

Writers sometimes get attached to their words. For instance, I might write a sentence or come up with an idea that I think is the most eloquent, pithy, or ingenious thing since Facebook; that expression then becomes my "darling" (or if you're a Southern gal like me, "darlin'"). But then, in walks an editor, director, or network executive who has a better idea or thinks your metaphor isn't so original. It becomes difficult to drop your initial idea that you love so much. In the writing community, there's a saying for this: "Kill your darlings." And it hurts.

The same idea applies to the previous tip of test-driving your dreams. Often you become attached to a goal that seemed great when you first set it, and many times you let that goal contribute to the definition you have of yourself. For instance, I once knew a teacher who for her entire career really wanted to be a screenwriter. It was something she'd pursued as an on-and-off hobby since she was in her early 20s. When she finally reached her late 40s, she had to admit to herself that she'd never written a full script. Ever. She asked herself, *If I love something so much, why don't I participate in it?* She then test-drove her dream during a school break, deciding to get out her laptop and her story outline and finish what she'd started almost two decades earlier. What she discovered was that the arduous process of writing no longer excited her. In fact, it fatigued her. It was time for her to abandon her screenwriting dream.

But who was she now if she wasn't a striving screenwriter with creative ideas and a desire to be influential in cinema culture? In essence she had to "kill her darling" and in the process uncover the hard fact that she didn't really know who she was or what she wanted to do. She'd held on to the screenwriting dream in order to salvage a part of herself, even if it was a false part. Teaching was never her passion, and that hadn't changed. Once she'd killed her darling, she freed up a lot of emotional, mental, and creative space that allowed her to test-drive new dreams and discover what would fuel her moving forward.

It takes courage to abandon old ideas of yourself, but peeking behind the curtain every once in a while will help you waste less time and maximize your next take.

MY TAKE: LEEZA'S LENS

Don't Edit Your Chance at Love

It sucks that when you finally make friends with the woman in the mirror, the reflection has the audacity to change.

At the very essence of being female is creating life. Whether we choose to do so or not, our bodies are designed for this purpose, and so a vital part of a woman's self-image is her fertility. The loss of that aspect of our identity, that sense of fertility, is scary. It gives us a sense that we're running out of time. We may feel as though we're literally and figuratively drying up. So imagine how frightening it was for me to start dating someone in his 30s when all of his peers were cranking out kids and filling up car seats like there was no tomorrow!

All right, let's go there: "My Cougar Chronicles: How Dating (and Marrying) a Younger Man Saved My Life." When we met, Steven was 38 and I was 51. A mutual friend introduced us, saying we had a lot in common and should meet. Okay, fine. I was *so* not looking for love—or even for a dinner companion. My life was chugging along after a divorce that had taken forever and threatened to take my soul with it. I wasn't broken, so I sure wasn't looking for anyone to fix me,

dine me, wine me, or otherwise try to reach the walled-off sections of my heart that I'd so skillfully protected. I'd made peace with the notion that maybe I'd just take one of my gay friends to red-carpet events and let my goddess circle of girlfriends take the place of boyfriends or—God forbid—a husband.

So when Steven asked me out to dinner, I showed up wearing my highest pair of boots, BlackBerry in hand and purse thrown over my shoulder, for what I was sure would be a go-nowhere couple of hours. He was nice enough, cute, and smart. I went straight into interview mode (my comfort zone) and proceeded to dominate the night with a million questions about politics, his growing up in Beverly Hills, you name it—anything so I wouldn't have to be engaged in a topic I wasn't ready for. I waited and waited for the "ask"—the reason for the dinner, the agenda Steven surely must have. When it never came, I sprang up from the table, declared that I had an emergency at home with one of the kids, and fled from valet parking with a peck on the cheek and some head-scratching questions.

What was that about? I mean, this man was 13 years younger than I was. Surely his interest in me wasn't romantic. He was on the school board, so maybe he saw me as a political ally or a potential donor. I didn't let the thoughts linger; sure enough, months went by and I didn't hear from him.

The next thing I knew, I was having lunch with Steven after my assistant had too quickly said yes to the appointment. "He wants to meet with you about some ideas for work," she said. Okay, what the heck—90 minutes out of my life, and he might have something interesting.

That was the beginning. Under the protective bubble of work, I could exhale and really get to know this dynamo who was spending several days a week with me sharing energy and ideas on my career and my charity. Flash forward to a fund-raiser for Rodney and Holly Robinson Peete's HollyRod

Foundation to support families dealing with autism and Parkinson's disease. It was a swanky affair held at the top of the Hollywood Hills.

I didn't see what was coming, but I did something I'd never done before—I let go. I wasn't trying to protect or defend a point of view, and I wasn't trying to present myself as anyone other than me. I was experiencing that thing called *mindfulness,* where I was fully present. As much as that allowed me to get to know Steven, it revealed myself to me, too. As we listened to a live band entertain the crowd, we were so wrapped up in each other that the rest of the world was just intruding on our private party. Steven put his arm around my waist, and that was where my "happy beginning" started.

My sister gave me a little dish that says, "Sometimes, right in the middle of an ordinary life, love gives you a fairy tale." It happened to me. Steven isn't my usual type. He's not in my age demographic, and there are dozens of other things that wouldn't make him the obvious choice. Primarily, he has a soft confidence and isn't a larger-than-life personality sucking the oxygen out of the room—in other words, a total break from my typcial pattern. Maybe it was because I was so sure we weren't going to be involved with each other that we were each able to let our guard down and stretch out a little.

I *knew* he was a great guy. In fact, in the beginning I insisted on hooking him up with wonderful women in child-bearing years who'd be good with him. After all, I assumed he'd want to start a family. This was a big lesson Steven taught me: I was borrowing tomorrow's trouble that might never come. He said, "I know how to take care of myself in our relationship. I'd rather focus on what I have versus what I don't have." Gradually, I learned to focus on *my* work in the relationship and not try to impose my thoughts about how *he* should feel about me—my weight, my age, or any of the rest of it.

We married on the rooftop of the same hotel where we had our first date, back when I would have never imagined falling in love again, much less with him. It all came down to Steven giving me permission to be *me* and celebrating what that meant. I'd never been comfortable enough before to recognize that what I had to offer was worthy and desirable without me having to morph into a smaller version of myself where the light is always dimmed and I'm always walking on eggshells. I've discovered that it's far better to count my blessings and not my stretch marks. No regrets, no excuses, no looking back . . . spoken like a true reformed cougar.

Here's the upshot: Keep your heart open without regard for your previous ideas of what will make you happy. Don't edit your chance at love by bringing a list of challenges and problems to a new situation. Never give up on your fairy tale, and don't predesign your prince.

photo by Christian Scott

5. Forget What Other People Think

No matter the goal—new or old, test-driven or otherwise—you'll never implement it if you make a habit out of caring what other people think. Remember what Bobbee, one of my first bosses, told me: "You know who you are." You have to silence the noise and partner with yourself when the going gets tough and it's time to take action. I had to remind myself of this crucial mental note recently, after I married my husband, Steven, in 2011.

Steven is 13 years younger than I am; and as soon as we started dating, I became the target of every cougar joke imaginable. From Twitter and Facebook to calls from distant relatives, everyone was talking about our relationship. At first I was a little self-conscious, but it didn't take me long to realize that none of it mattered. I knew that missing out on such a rich, deeply satisfying relationship was simply not an option. So I took a deep breath and made friends with the woman behind the curtain. The rewards are many, but at the heart of it all is the fact that I've never felt more like me than I do right now.

6. Discover What You Think of Others

On the flip side of that mental note not to worry about others' opinions of you, I believe that you should take a close look at what you think of the people who share your life. Value yourself and your time enough to realize that it's a great privilege when you allow others to really see you and share your days, dreams, and desires. Make certain the ones you let in are worth it. It takes a lifetime to develop a reputation but only a moment to destroy it. Be careful of the company you keep because you become the people you share time with. If you work for a jaded boss or have a lazy business partner, chances are you might become a bit jaded and lazy yourself. If you have lunches with Negative Nellies who seem to never have a good day, it will be much harder for your optimism to fight its way to the top of your thoughts.

Disingenuous, ungracious, arrogant, ignorant, or unmotivated people aren't the ones you need to be around right now—or ever—especially as you embark on your transformation journey. Finding supportive people who have made great changes in their own lives or have a pure desire to see you grow and be happy should be a priority.

My star on the Hollywood Walk of Fame (1997)! Talk about surreal. . . . My little Nathan was brand-new. My sweet mom was already showing signs of Alzheimer's disease, but we thought she was just drinking too much. My sister, Cammy, covered for her.

With Mom and Dad "on Golden Pond" (2002). That's what they call their little lake cottage. I remember holding on tight to Mom, who had recently been diagnosed with Alzheimer's and was emerging as a proud advocate.

A kiss for luck (1988). One of my favorite pictures of Mom, during one of our many hellos and good-byes. We traveled everywhere together and loved exploring new places.

All smiles in South Carolina (2012). Here I am with my sister, Cammy; my sister-in-law, Anne Marie; and my brother, Carl. No one makes me laugh more than they do. Typically when we get together, we break into song followed by balancing spoons on our noses—don't ask!

My 50th birthday in Hollywood (2007). What a goddess moment it was. I was still in the competition on *Dancing with the Stars*, but that night, my favorite dance was when all of my kids—Troy, Lexi, and Nathan—joined me on the dance floor to celebrate our blessings. (I don't know how Lexi got that tiara away from me!)

photo by Christian Scott

Wedding bliss in Beverly Hills (2011). Look at these smiles—we were soooo happy. Lexi and Troy got ordained as ministers so they could perform our marriage ceremony, while Nate handled the rings. Pretty cool, huh? There were *no* other guests other than the kids, Steven, and me. We picked flowers from our yard, and Lexi sang, "Bless the Broken Road."

A matrimonial hug (2011). Steven and I consider our union to be evidence that miracles really do happen. He is the best plot twist of my second act!

photo by Christian Scott

Cowboys Stadium in Dallas (2010). My Cowboys-obsessed Steven could hardly keep it together when I surprised him with tickets to join Roger and Mary Ann Staubach in their suite for the game. They are now used to our over-the-top excitement! I used to live in Dallas, and I still love it there.

Times Square (2008). I was shooting for my makeup line, Sheer Cover, but clearly I was not in a New York state of mind! The city is a mixed bag for me, since my show *Two on the Town* was canceled when I worked at WCBS, and I had to sell my cool brownstone on West 57th . . . but then again, that's how I ended up in L.A. working for *Entertainment Tonight*!

Just Shoot Me! (2002). Remember that TV show? This was my cover shot for the fictitious *Blush* magazine. I remember Dean, Keith, and Julie (my friends and fabulous glam squad) getting me ready, and I kept thinking I was so fat! I have given up that kind of obsessing, thank God.

Steven's 40th birthday (2010)! I surprised him, and we had the best time. No one was happier than I was to have him *finally* hit the big 4-0! (He was 38 when we started dating.) Or as my son Nathan put it at the time, "You're finally eligible to date my mom!"

At home in Hollywood, with Maria (1995). This woman is my lifeline. Technically, she is my housekeeper, but in reality, she is my surrogate mother and my "soulkeeper." Maria and I have been through it all together and come out smiling and stronger on the other side. There is no one I respect more. I love this lady.

Near Shimla, India (2008). I took my daughter on a graduation trip to India, and brought my sister along, too! Thanks to our dear friend who set everything up for us, we had the most amazing journey, including this rafting adventure near the Himalayas. I had some of the best meals of my life on that trip!

...ngo with Tony (2007).
...ere I am on Season 4 of
...*ing with the Stars*—this
...efore it became like an
...ne-sports competition!
...ear it was like therapy,
...ot camp, and worship-
... all in one! I still have
... not-so-secret dream to
...om dance with Steven.
... promised me for our
...ersary. . . . I think he'll
...ood in a red sequined

Mother's Day (2006). Every year I tell the kids that what I want for Mother's Day and Christmas is for them to just brush their hair and take a picture with me! Second choice is for them to write me something by hand, so usually the photo wins out. They may look all angelic in this shot, but trust me, it was preceded by lots of resistance! On Christmas, I make them all dress in the same pajamas . . . just imagine the eye rolling that goes with *that!* I treasure these photos (and secretly, I think they love them, too).

Production behind the scenes, West Hollywood (2010). On this day, I think we were shooting something for HSN. The first time I remember reporting for the camera was in sixth grade. I was doing a mock report of the Pilgrims landing at Plymouth Rock in my "Cronker Walkite" persona (Walter Cronkite was my hero!). I've been at

7. Learn the Confidence Game

If you still find yourself concerned about what another person might think, do, or say once you've made the big changes you're planning, it's time to learn how to play the confidence game, aka the tried-and-true "Fake it till you make it." This always bears repeating: If you don't think you've got it, act *as if* you do, and those critics won't know the difference. Their reaction to your fake sense of worth will change, and therefore your reactions will be more positive. After a while, you'll find this reverse psychology actually creates an authentic sense of self-confidence and accomplishment.

Remember that your brain doesn't know the difference between what's real and what's not. That's why you get to tell it what you want to be true and watch it happen.

8. Declare Your Value

In your jobs, your relationships, and the world, you deserve to be paid well for your time and talent, and you deserve to be treated well. This begins with others seeing the way you treat yourself, another reason the previous tips are so important. I do believe we teach people how to treat us by setting the example ourselves.

Are you worth the effort of putting up boundaries around your optimistic heart when people are negative? Do you deserve to get enough rest to be at your best? Are you going to let people take advantage of your good nature and run all over you? You have to know what you're worth, and you have to know that you deserve dignity, respect, and cooperation. Anybody who says or thinks otherwise can be kicked to the curb!

9. Be Aware of the Power of Words

I saw a video on YouTube that showed a blind man on the street with a cardboard sign next to him that said, "I'm Blind. Please Help." He had a tin cup into which people had thrown a few pennies. A woman who was passing by changed the words on the sign; and afterward, everyone who walked by felt compelled to leave money. The man was stunned by the effect a few words had created, and he asked what she'd done to his sign. She told him that she "wrote the same, but different." She'd changed it to read: "It's a beautiful day, but I can't see it."

Although the video is an ad for an online content company rather than a documentary, their message still rings true: "Change your words. Change your world." People who own their power are aware of this and take it seriously. Furthermore, scientists have long noted the power of words to affect your emotions and actions.

At my foundation, we created an awareness-building fund-raiser for our work supporting family caregivers. My belief was that we had an opportunity not only to educate people about what we were doing, but also to encourage change agents of all kinds to come forward and to recruit new volunteers. We called it "Dare2Care."

I wanted to involve some of the thought leaders in philanthropy, and I was really excited about what Jessica Biel was doing at the time with her Make the Difference Network. I decided to reach out to her because I knew she'd understand what I was trying to do. I'd almost given up, though, when I got a message that showed me the power of words. Jessica left me a voice mail telling me that she was so supportive and appreciated what I was doing and wanted to help me. She was

encouraging and positive. It came at a time when I really needed those words. For her, it may have been just another message; but for me it was a reminder that I should keep going, reinvest my energy, stay focused, and believe. Whenever you have a chance to be that person for someone, do it. When Jessica showed up to support our effort, I thanked her for that initial voice mail that kept me in the game. Remember what Khalil Gibran once wrote: "All our words are but crumbs that fall down from the feast of the mind."

10. Downshift and Trust the Process

Learning is a lifetime process. According to Mark Twain, "Training is everything. The peach was once a bitter almond; cauliflower is nothing but cabbage with a college education." My college education, both in and out of the classroom, was like boot camp for real life. And what I learned in real life is that things don't happen overnight. Sometimes the coach doesn't choose you for first string, but that doesn't mean you quit.

Why are we in such a rush to know everything anyway? Why is it we need to see instant results and not let things percolate? Transformation is an organic, inherent process, and it's within that progression that we learn the most. But sometimes we just don't see the value in that. Instead, we measure ourselves only by the end result. Let's say you're well versed in painting with oils—perhaps you even teach a class to others who share your passion. If you aren't picked to exhibit your art on the walls of some gallery, then you've failed, right? Of course not! The fact that you're artistic and help others develop their talent would be thrown aside in that quest for accolades.

If you can slow down, you'll find that the frantic rushing, deadlines, and need to achieve take you further and further from what you may really want: to find meaning. When you downshift, meaning comes as a by-product. You stop feeling as if you're failing because you've let go of that arbitrary schedule for success.

Just for once, change your relationship with time and allow your inner truth to reassure you that things are unfolding exactly as they should. Nobody succeeds on the first try, so redefine success and do what Arnold Shapiro advised: Believe in your projects (that's *you*) and be patient. View the time that it's taking to achieve your transformation as its own lesson, and in the meantime become coachable. Accept the help you need instead of acting like the female version of John Wayne and going it alone.

You'll learn an invaluable amount from others if you engage in the process of transformation instead of closing your eyes and holding your breath through it all, hoping you survive to bask in some glory. Remember: There is no glory, there is no story, if you don't embrace the challenge.

Embrace the change

Chapter 7

LET YOUR SPIRIT *SOAR*

*"The tears of faithfulness to your beliefs cleanse
your spirit to envision the road ahead. Everything
is possible for the person who believes."*

— ADLIN SINCLAIR

Why are you on this journey? What do you really want? How
do you make your second take count? Here's what I believe: You
must pay attention to when your soul is singing in harmony with
your actions. What does that groove feel like, and what occurred
so that you fell right into it? When life syncs up and purpose meets
passion and compassion in action, that's what I call your *soulprint*.

If you're like me, you want to believe that your life matters and
that your story will be a lasting one, filled with a renewed energy
that transforms your work, relationships, and soul. In order to
truly experience deep change, however, you've got to have faith.

Without it, there's no need to bother facilitating any action. If fear is faith in reverse, that means you mustn't be afraid of change.

I've talked a lot about change, and your interest in it is probably part of why you picked up this book. Doing so has caused the energy to shift in your life. Change has its own momentum, and while you can feel its strength, it's also intangible. If you don't believe anything that you can't see, touch, or measure, then no matter how hard you try, you won't be your own agent of change. Chances are you'll miss the best part of your story—the part that says you're a spiritually evolving person who questions and challenges, but who also has the daring faith to keep climbing without having to see the top of the staircase.

On my dresser I have a pair of wings. My husband doesn't really care for them, and I guess they do look a bit strange. They're just a pair of gold wings on a pedestal, but I love looking at this piece. Beside it is a little framed quotation: *"Though fragile they may seem, your wings are stronger than they appear, so fly."* It reminds me that we already have everything we need. It's our choice whether or not to dust off the wings and take flight, trusting that they're strong enough. Make the leap with faith that you'll find somewhere safe to land or that your wings will support you until you do.

You've come to this book to make bold changes in your life, so you must have faith deep down that the change will happen and that you're the person who can do it—you just don't know when. It's desire and expectation that pushes dreams forward, but we aren't always in charge of the timetable. Sometimes we wait decades for our evolution. When it seems that our progress is unexpectedly halted, that all doors are slamming in our faces, it's rarely true. It's just hard to accept that maybe the growth comes from mastering the lessons that are here right now before we get to move on.

My friend Dean Banowetz is now well known in the beauty business as "the Hollywood Hair Guy." No doubt he dresses the tresses for your favorite stars these days, but he came to Hollywood

as a young man from Iowa, number 13 of 15 kids. This is a guy who knows about being patient and waiting your turn. When his turn for success came, it led him to becoming the force and the face behind the InStyler hairstyling tool. His strategy was simply to keep at it. He tells me, "When one door closes, lock it, redecorate, and build a bigger door." When you can see yourself locking that door with a giant deadbolt without any reservation, resentment, or defiance, you're ready to launch into what's next.

I think that if we're lucky, we pass the quest for personal evolution to the next generation. We empower those who come after us to see that a search for meaning *is* living a meaningful life, and that no story is complete without purpose. To create a difference for others, even those we might never know, we put our energy out there and keep the faith that as we reach for our own growth and connect with meaning, we give the universe the greatest gift we can offer.

Let me break that down a little bit. I think we're here to try as hard as we can, contribute whenever we can, grow as much as we can, and offer kindness and compassion to ourselves and others. Regardless of what you think the meaning of life is, it's hard to be against those things, isn't it? Think about it . . . if we had more people focusing on that, it truly would be epic.

Faith is the voice that will be whispering for you to keep trying when you feel like giving up. Trust its delicate urging, because it won't be as loud as the waves of defeat shouting for you to move on or give in. And while I encourage you to trust in the new energy you're creating, also remember that time, courage, patience, and commitment are necessary ingredients in the elixir for lasting change. But you don't have to go it alone—in fact, you can't, because change is a team effort. Yeah, yeah, I know that they say you come in alone and you go out alone; but it's the stuff in between that moves all of that energy around, makes use of it, and benefits from it.

You've probably heard the expression that life is like the dash that connects the birth and death dates on a headstone—your story is what comes in between, just like that dash. The way we're connected to each other is also all about what's in the middle. How we work together, relate to each other, and support our efforts is where the rewards (both internal and external) exist.

Any contribution is a thing of value. We're just trying to make ours matter more. And as we carve out our path, calling for another take in the name of re-creation, we must remember that it's not what's on our résumé or in our obituary that lasts. Instead, we need to consider what emotional collateral we spend while we're here. What we have to offer is what we give away.

What does that mean—our money? Yes. Our time? Absolutely. Our talent? That goes without saying. But what about our intention? What about the support we give with a simple smile or a positive glance? What about the way we fuel a project by doing our very best, the phone call to a friend in need, or the faith to keep pushing after we've been told no four or five times? Those are the things that have energy. I think those are the things that last, and calling for Take 2 means that you can incorporate these gifts into your life even more.

Buddha said, "Just as a candle cannot burn without fire, men cannot live without a spiritual life." *The way we get to live forever is through memories stored in the hearts and souls of those whose lives we touch. That's our forever fairy dust. It's our comfort, our emotional nourishment at the end of the day and the end of a life.* It seems to me that we should spend our time in a conscious state of creating these meaningful moments that live on, and that includes in our journey toward change. This means transformation in the highest form.

What I'm talking about is crafting a spiritual life, with connectedness to others and a deep understanding of the self. Making this choice has helped me keep faith and hope constant in my quest for happiness and meaning. Creating a spiritual life that is mine alone has been the source of the very energy that affects me and those with whom I share my life, and that will live on after my job on Earth is complete. It has led me to a life of intention, which I believe means doing good work that lasts.

What Is a Spiritual Life?

I'm not talking about religion or doctrine. You don't have to believe in God or even a higher power (although many do). Crafting a spiritual life means discovering an inner path that enables you to find out who you really are, to define the essence of your being. You simply live by deep values that are highly personal and define how you treat yourself and others. You determine what your intentions are for how *you choose* to live.

None of this is mysterious or difficult, and there are many ways to incorporate spiritual elements or practices into your life. It can be done in a car, at your desk, in the grocery store, at bedtime, or anywhere you like. Some people meditate or pray; others engage in a contemplation exercise in which they develop an inner life for themselves beyond what they experience in the hurried world. When you hear the terms *finding your center* or *mind-body connection*, know that they're just another way to talk about spirituality and the ways you incorporate it into your day.

If you've never thought of yourself as spiritual, now is the time to rethink that. The very fact that you're reading this book tells me that you are! Tapping your natural connection to the rest of the world comes with ease once you get started. A rewarding and enriching process, incorporating spiritual elements into your life will bring serenity, focus, intention—and, most important, constant faith in yourself and the change you're trying to make. Once you create the connection between your mind and soul, you won't want to stop. It will be as if an old friend is opening up her arms to wrap you in an embrace of warmth and security.

Why is crafting a spiritual life even necessary when gearing up to produce transformative and positive energy? I find that it's because spiritual experiences help us connect with others more deeply. We're more aware of our place in the world and that we aren't meant to be isolated. My friend Troy (my son's namesake) always said to me, "We are all on loan to each other from God." It always made sense to me. You never know whose life you're touching or where your influences may come from; but spiritual people are open to being moved, and that's enough.

When we're able to reach out to others with a true understanding of universal connectedness, we become happier and more loving, patient, tolerant, forgiving, accountable, and harmonious than ever before. And do you know what all those qualities equate to? *A strong energy encasing an inner stability comprised of faith in oneself that makes lasting change inevitable.* I realize that sounds a bit verbose, but it's actually simple, isn't it? Change is our natural state of being, and once we have faith enough to stop resisting it, we drop the fear and pick up the certainty that it exists to serve our highest purpose.

Helping your spirit soar can take some digging. Like most things that are worthwhile, you need to invest in the idea of a deeper connection with your intentions and those around you. I find that the least intimidating place to start when crafting a spiritual life is with a contemplation exercise. I've asked the question, *Who are you really?* earlier in this book. Here's the opportunity to truly dig into this topic and come up with a deeper answer. I think the easiest way to do it is through creating a mission statement.

The Mission Statement

In business, the mission statement reminds a company of its overall purpose, like a beacon to guide you home if you get lost. It's the same with a personal mission statement. You're in the Better Business, so I think it's essential that you have a foundation to make growth happen. Research shows that companies who write a mission statement get greater returns on their investments and double their return on equity. If you're going through all the effort to invest in yourself and create a second take, you definitely want big returns!

How is a mission statement different from dreaming big or setting goals? Easy: It deals with the macro (big picture) view of yourself, while dreams and goals represent the micro (detailed) view. For instance, when entrepreneurs begin a company, often their very first step is to create a mission statement to convey the overall purpose (macro view) of the company. While there may be many short- or long-term goals that will change or be abandoned, the mission statement is intended to remain constant as a guiding light to the core values of the company's founders.

As you already know, goals can change. They're fluid and flexible, but your mission statement really underscores who you know yourself to be or where you're headed. It's your *intention* for how you want to live, and it represents your inner life. This is the perfect time in your story to write it since it will help you continue with focus, precision, unflappability, and faith.

Don't know where to begin? Think about how you'd like to feel each morning when you wake up or what you seek in life. What attributes do you want to possess and how would you like to react to challenges? Who or what do you want to attract in your life? What's your soulprint? These questions will help you formulate sentences in your mind, which you can then write as intentions.

To help you get started, I'll share my personal mission statement. When I feel as if I'm veering off into unknown territories or entering doorways that don't feel welcoming, this statement reminds me of the inner life I've committed myself to.

Leeza's Mission

To feel joy and spread it with grace and ease.

To seek ways to empower and enlighten through my gifts and talents.

To live authentically as a supportive woman, wife, mother, sister, daughter, and friend within my family of origin and my family of choice.

To seek learning and growth through spiritual and physical exploration of my body, my mind, and my planet.

To live with flexibility and forgiveness for myself and others.

To move forward: ever changing, opening, softening— allowing wisdom to enter my mind and my heart.

MY TAKE: LEEZA'S LENS

When in Doubt . . . Just Connect

Basically I'm a recovering drama queen, and thankfully one of the things that has happened as I've matured is I've realized that the busiest person doesn't always win. My worship of those who return all their calls and respond to all their texts and e-mails in one day has ended. The new model for me is a woman who announces to the world who she is *now*, navigating the days and prioritizing hour by hour. I've let go of "script writing" and expecting certain things to happen, and of feeling like a failure when they don't.

I try to move confidently in the direction of my dreams, knowing that while I can't do or have everything, I'm the only person who has command of my life. I take responsibility for my choices.

At some point in your evolution as a woman, I think you realize you're not the center of the universe, and you're not the sum total of your achievements. Crafting a spiritual life and an emotionally nourishing existence are much better goals that don't have to be difficult. In fact, that's the irony about incorporating more spiritual elements into your life— usually it's the simplest things that matter most.

I often realize this in little moments that might seem inconsequential. Here's an example I know will resonate with you: Not too long ago, my sister called me feeling kind of down. At the time, she was being pulled for time and energy by both her young son and our aging dad. She was tired. I was in the middle of something else when she called and I was a little agitated by the ringing phone. I love nothing more than talking with my sister, but I was having a hard time freeing up my attention to

be present. The sound of her voice snapped me right into awareness, though, and an hour and a half later, I knew I'd made the right choice in turning off the computer and listening to her. I'm her big sister. She knows I understand her like no one else, and she has an uncanny wisdom about what matters to me. A week later, a year later, and especially in that instant, the project I was working on is nothing. The words we shared over the phone transcended the moment. I said, "I'm proud of you; you're trying so hard. Stay strong. I'm always here." She didn't want or need advice. She needed to be heard. Don't we all? She was searching for meaning, and for one moment, maybe I helped her find some.

One way or another, that's what we all do: We search for meaning. I think we can always find it in looking at what we love, whom we love, and how we spend our time. Connection—to others and ourselves—is key. That's crafting a spiritual life. I said before that what we give away freely is the most powerful gift we have to offer. Yet when we make that gift intentionally, the energy comes back to us in good ways, and the adage "You get what you give" rings true.

I'm not in the very least suggesting that we do anything with the expectation of getting something in return; this is simply a fact of universal energy. Giving my time to my sister made me feel good, connected me more fully to her and her needs; and I was reminded of countless times when she has done the same for me. Through this bond, I made a change in myself, in my sister, and in the moment. When I decided to turn off my computer, our relationship shifted, grew, and transformed. I was aware of the present and the power I had within it. It's in simple moments like this that connection works in making lasting change.

Circle of Sisters

One of the easiest ways to connect is to have a circle of sisters. Before I turned 50, I became part of a group of women known as the goddess circle, who had arrived at that milestone before I did. They'd been both wizened and wounded and known love and loss. Although their life stories weren't always the kind with a nice Hollywood ending, they'd chosen to let their spirits dance together in celebration of all the moments that had delivered them to the present. These women have mentored me in beginning my second take, and I love sharing with them—except they have regular dates that they call "cleavage lunch," and I feel I don't have much by way of cleavage to offer! But I always remember the words of the ultimate goddess, my mom, when she said to me as a young girl, "Honey, what God's forgotten, we'll fill with cotton!" She always had an answer!

Friends are the best investment you can make in yourself. When you make time to laugh, play, and pour your heart out to those who know you best and love you anyway, you've formed a spiritual path to your inner self. Cultivate these bonds with every ounce of your being, and you'll know immeasurable joy. I'm lucky that my biological family provided me with strong connections, but you can find your sisterhood anywhere.

One of the very definitions of *spiritual* is an interrelation with others. Forming a circle of sisters that I can count on, trust, and be myself with, for better or worse, is something I only learned with age. I wish I'd known when I was younger that the women in my life would become such a sacred sanctuary. I would have spent less time comparing the size of our hips or breasts; less time wondering what the girl in the next desk in eighth grade knew that I didn't, why her hair was smooth and long just like her legs. I wish I'd been able to peer down that long hall toward my 20s and see that the girls in my sorority were like spokes on a wheel of women who inspired me to reach higher and dream bigger. The girls I looked up to who seemed so wise and secure were really stuck between the tumultuous time of being a teen and the traction of reaching womanhood—just like I was.

When I reached the workforce, maybe if I'd had the magic mirror I would have seen that the women who were my peers in the newsroom weren't competing with me—they'd fought *for* me. If I'd known then what I know now, I might have noticed that the women in my Mommy and Me class had breast-milk stains on their shirts, too, and maybe even stretch marks along with scary feelings about the brave new world of motherhood. I wish I'd allowed myself the solace of the women who would become my goddess gurus—my circle of sisterhood.

The depth of words unspoken when one of your girlfriends shows up and just starts doing what's needed without being asked is also something I learned as I matured. When I was younger I didn't know that hurts parceled out among women diffuse quickly, and forgiveness follows without thought or angst.

When I reached my 40s, I wanted to be a part of a group of women whose loyalty and love would form a safe cocoon where I could hide. I wanted to have a circle of sisters who would push me to take a chance while I knew they were waiting in the wings in case I forgot my steps. To see that in action, I had only to go back to my mom and her sister, along with their best friend from girlhood. Jean, Wayne, and Ginger—I called them the Golden Girls. I saw how they trusted each other to protect the tenderest parts of their hearts. They had no walls, no barriers, and no defenses—and there it was, the thing I hadn't done.

I'd never allowed another person to see past my persona. I hadn't been able to stop achieving and start receiving. I had that feminine fortress around me all along, but I never downshifted from the artificially revved-up pace of my life to notice that they were there, waiting for a crack in the facade. When I threw back the blinds and opened the window wide, they were right where they'd been since grade school.

Zaidee and Terri, my longest-standing girlfriends, are still the other points in the triangle of strength that reminds me I'm never alone. They've always represented safety and the kind of friendship that stays strong through all the changes in life. Our sisterhood goes back to junior high. In fact, I'm the one who dubbed Zaidee with that name, which is now on her business cards and all official documents! There's not a person alive, except her brother, who calls her by her given name, Claudia. I was a cheerleader, Z was in the band, and Terri was a majorette. I guess to the casual observer, we might seem to have very little in common. But spend an hour with us all together and you see that our hearts beat in harmony.

I left our South Carolina home as soon after graduation as I could. While the Palmetto State always holds my heart, my spirit took me to the West Coast, where I've stayed, building my ca-reer and loving my family. Terri is back in South Carolina, and Zaidee is just up a ways in Virginia. We're not the kind of friends who are in constant communication. In fact, there have been spans of time over the years without any real close contact. But we found in each other a harbor that allows us to be exactly who we are. There's no reason to put on any kind of show or pretend, because we know the closets where all the skeletons are kept and what the hot buttons are, so we don't open or push. There's just no need.

In recent years, our annual pilgrimage to the beaches of our girlhood has given us a touchstone and a tradition our kids have grown up with. The white sand and warm water of the South Carolina coast has become the background for three girls who became women in the safety of friendship's hug.

†⊷†

Every day I walk by a framed picture with the words *Soul Sisters* underneath. It's me with my two sisters: one by blood (Cammy), and the other through marriage (Anne Marie). Just looking at that shot gives me a spiritual hug. We call ourselves the Queen, the Empress, and the Contessa! (The titles were Cammy's idea.) We have different lives, different strengths, and even different politics, but we have the same soul. We see each other's beauty, and we fight for each other's sanity when the threads that hold our existence together threaten to fray. Terri, Zaidee, Cammy, and Anne Marie are always among the first words spoken when I offer up my gratitude list, which I always say aloud (more on that later).

It wasn't an accident that I once again gravitated toward some strong feminine energy when I found myself on the Great Wall of China. As I mentioned earlier, I was there to take part in an international walk to support what would become Olivia Newton-John's Cancer and Wellness Centre. The walkers came from all over the world. I didn't know any of the women other than Olivia, but the minute I met Rachel and Chantelle, I knew we'd be friends and conspirators in our mission to make life matter more.

With Olivia as our super chick in charge, we grew closer with each secret we shared. My Aussie friends and I have since spent

time in each other's countries; and even though we each represent different generations, we all fill a need for togetherness that only women with open hearts and trusting natures can. I smile as I look around my kitchen while I write this now. On my windowsill is a framed picture of Zaidee, Terri, and me on our  annual beach trip. Next to it is a photo of Cammy and Anne Marie with me in the middle—that's the *Soul Sisters* frame. On the refrigerator is a shot on the Great Wall of China—my gathering of girls, all smiles fueled by a sense of adventure that is our common bond. And I'm reminded of this great quote by Anaïs Nin: "Each friend represents a world in us, a world possibly not born until they arrive, and it is only by this meeting that a new world is born."

Throughout your own journey toward re-creation, you'll need a haven where you never have to explain yourself or apologize for how you feel, where you won't be judged, and where you'll be supported spiritually and emotionally as you develop a deeper connection to who you are now and where you're headed. I've experienced firsthand how going it alone doesn't work. You wind up suffocating in isolation, devoid of the strength it takes to carve out time to reach out to those who have been waiting for you to rejoin them.

Connectedness is the direct road to lasting change, so craft your spiritual life by entering a circle of sisters—whether it's by rekindling an old trio, nurturing an existing friendship, or reaching out to new women who represent who you are today. Make this endeavor a part of your mission statement if you'd like, and have the faith and courage to put yourself out there and be a part of something bigger—an awareness that will bring the lasting change of your heart's desire.

Be Awake

There's nothing more unattractive than someone who's sleepwalking through life. When you think of the people you admire, the ones you like to be around, I'm certain they're fully present. Everyone is drawn to those who "live on purpose," so as you call for Take 2, know that being awake is crucial from the start. In my mission statement, I have several intentions to *feel* and to *seek*. This means I try as much as I can to be mindful of my actions and the power within the moment.

In your quest for change and crafting a spiritual life, awakening and being aware of the wonders around you will be a determining factor in how successful you are. It's where that faith I've been talking about really comes in handy. Regardless of what or whom you believe in, I think trusting that the universal power always knows what it's doing is difficult. I struggle with this one. It's part of a letting-go process that, if accomplished, helps clear away all of the junk, the ego, and the thoughts that keep us from experiencing life and awakening to its gifts and our innate power to use them in ways we used to only dream of.

How do you live mindfully? Well, in his book *The Power of Now*, Eckhart Tolle says the trick is to be able to detach from your thoughts and observe the thinker in the present. (That would be you!) Sometimes when I do this, I can see how uptight and . . . well . . . ridiculous I'm being. I've learned to look at myself, inhale, and make observations like this one: *Poor thing. There she goes being all defensive. She feels threatened, so she's talking way too fast.* When I can get out of my own way and observe the thinker (me), I'm able to laugh at my behavior and change it.

Being mindful means being attentive and aware of the moment you're in right now. That way you're more powerful and in control of the moment. When you live in the present, you have clarity that helps you keep focused and committed to your intentions.

How do you know if you're awake? If you allow yourself to feel whatever it is that shows up and know that you'll get through it, then you are. I think it has to do with a feeling of "knowingness" —the realization that no matter what, you're okay. They can fire you, call you fat, steal your computer, or lie to your face, but you can handle it. Your car can be totaled, your husband can leave you, someone might post negative things about you on Facebook, and you still know you'll be all right. Oh, you'll be furious, frustrated, devastated, hurt, or worried; but somewhere deep inside, you know you'll deal with it and see it through.

I was having dinner with my friend Ali the other night, and we talked about this quality of awakening. She said that she couldn't really explain it, but she knew that she always had an anchor of knowingness inside her, an understanding that she was unique and that honoring and expressing it would be essential to her integrity. I related to that right away because I feel similarly. When we listen to our consciousness—that inner voice—rather than try to suppress it, life flows more easily. So when we feel different, unsettled, or out of step, it could be that all we need to do is go deep into our core and find that knowingness; and it will help us understand things are unfolding as they should.

Maybe it's your path to move away from your roots. Perhaps others don't understand your choice of husband or job or your relationship with your in-laws. You may do things that others find baffling, but you find impossible to avoid or ignore. Listen to your heart and follow its rhythms, and they'll lead you straight to your core essence.

Meditation

Many people seeking spiritual enrichment find that meditation offers an accessible way to reach deeper into themselves while eliminating stress. The technique has been around for thousands of years, originally as a way to explore the sacred and mystical forces of the universe. Those who practice it say there's no question it's an important part of the spiritual journey.

While there's no way to measure success on that scale, there's a lot of evidence that meditating is a great deterrent to stress. I'll talk about stress management in Chapter 8, but few techniques work as well as meditation. It can also give a boost to your self-esteem, helping you feel optimistic and confident. Even the Mayo Clinic touts its benefits for physical and emotional well-being. There are lots of forms, but mindful meditation—where you focus on your breath and allow your overactive thoughts to float away—is one of the most popular. The idea is to not attach to your thoughts so that when they come back, you can just acknowledge and release them without judging.

I think we move so fast and have such an avalanche of thoughts every nanosecond that it's hard for answers to find their way through, even when we seek them. You really have to still your mind and be open to shift your energy enough to be available for new ideas and patterns to emerge. I like to meditate when I walk; it's a release that always puts me in a better mood.

Try it—no one has to know. You don't even have to have your eyes closed, as you can tell from the fact that I do it while walking. There are countless books and audio recordings that can help you begin your own practice if you feel more comfortable following a guide.

What's on Your Mind, What's in Your Heart?

There's something about writing down your thoughts that simultaneously releases them and allows you to own them. If you can stop yourself from the urge to edit, editorialize, or deny your true feelings, it's surprising what you can discover about yourself.

When you're hurting, take a moment to write down what's on your mind and what's in your heart. Let's say your child has not acted in a way you think she should. What's behind your anger? Through expressing your heart in writing, you may make some discoveries: *I feel guilty that I didn't teach her better,* or *I resent the way she chooses to act when I spent so much time teaching her better.* Maybe your husband mentions the roast you just served is salty. Why does that upset you? Checking in with yourself may determine that it's really not about the beef: *I feel undervalued. I'm not good enough. I don't feel loved and appreciated.*

You may (as I did) discover a pattern of reactions to comments that push your emotional buttons and cause you to freeze up and shut down or flare up and get angry. When that happens, you're being led by your vulnerabilities, which leaves your friends and family in the dark, wondering, *What ticked her off?* Once you start journaling, you'll be much more aware, and you can paint a more realistic picture for your brain to use to process a response.

You can also use your journaling to picture yourself as the person you've always wanted to be. I like to just start off writing, *I am . . .* and let it flow from there: *I am generous and thoughtful, always sensitive to the feelings of others as I look for ways to offer support and understanding.*

The Art of Gracious Living

Be thankful. As often as you can, put your attention on all the good that's evident in your life. Be aware of the flow of abundance, and you'll bring in rivers of emotional, spiritual, and financial wealth.

My friends and family members are daily reminders of my blessings; and like most of you, I try to send notes, texts, e-mails, and cards to show them how much they mean to me. Notes in a lunch box, in a suit pocket, or spelled out in chocolate chips on a cookie always get a smile. But I love anything handwritten, and when I write a note longhand, it forces me to slow down and think about it more.

I also think it's a great idea to create a generational gratitude list. Think of a person from each decade of your life who had a powerful influence on you. Close your eyes and silently thank them, then write them a letter and drop it in the mail (yes, "snail mail"). We live in a cyber world where life is a series of e-mails, voice mails, instant messages, texts, and tweets. It all zips by us without much thought. I encourage you to take time to just be with your feelings and your emotions. Have a pen handy or even your computer keyboard. Rid yourself of expectations and just write. Stream-of-consciousness journaling provides some of the most useful insights and helps keep us mindful of the fortunate moments we've experienced.

When I go through my own generational gratitude list, I often find that I'm thankful for someone no longer here. For example, I composed this note to Mrs. Johnson, who was my first real boss. My paycheck was for $1.10 an hour, but my real reward was learning from this lovely spirit. I didn't know how much she taught me until I was well into my TV and radio career, and I realized how often I reflected upon her quiet strength. She never lost her temper and was infinitely patient, and her smile opened my heart. I never mailed this letter, as she was already gone when I wrote it, but somehow I know she received it.

Dear Mrs. Johnson,

It's me, Leeza. The last time you saw me, I was just a bit older than that geeky teenager you hired to help you in the Juniors department at Tapp's department store at Dutch Fork mall in Irmo. When I heard you'd passed away, I was so angry. Not at you for dying, but at myself for not making sure you knew how important you were in my life. Did you know, Mrs. Johnson?

When I worked for you, I thought you were impossibly old (and very quiet). I figure now you were probably about 50. Still, it was a conservative town and a conservative time; and you were the epitome of both. I wondered what the managers were thinking putting you in charge of a fashion department when you showed up for work every day in your dress and cardigan sweater. I could see you from across the store, and the sight of that sweater never failed to comfort me. You were security.

I knew you'd never let me mess up. When I rang something up wrong at the register, or when I said something wrong to a customer, you were always there to save the day, never embarrassing me. From you, I learned grace.

One day, a lady was trying on pants in the dressing room and left without buying anything. I went in to clean up what had been left behind and saw a $20 bill on the floor. I took it to you, and after work that day, you went by a few houses and a couple of stores where you thought you might be able to find the woman, because you knew she needed the cash. From you, I learned honesty.

Folding tops on a counter isn't anyone's idea of meaningful work, but you did it with such pride and care. You taught me how to pull the shoulders tight in a square after an intricate series of folds, and then always end with a little pat before putting it on the pile. You'd smile as though you'd just made the final stroke on the Mona Lisa. From you, I learned there's pride in work, no matter how small the task.

At the end of our shift at 9 P.M., you went home to more work with challenges within your family. Even though you wore sensible shoes, you had support hose on to help with the varicose veins. You never complained. From you, I learned sacrifice.

Thank you for encouraging me, for believing in me, for making me do my homework, and for showing me what humility is. Thank you for teaching me that sometimes powerful women are quiet, unassuming ladies with support hose and a cardigan.

Yours sincerely,

Leeza

Have a Cause

I know, I know—I've spent so many pages in this book trying to convince you to put yourself first and that you should prioritize things to make room for you, and now I'm about to talk about being selfless. Sorry for the mixed messages! But creating a spiritual life is a way to focus on yourself while being selfless at the same time. It's easy to get caught up in your own desires, especially when you're on the road to transformation. If you're not careful, you can focus *too* much on yourself and not enough on the needs of others. But if you concentrate on the contribution you're making to the rest of the world, you won't worry as much about your own flaws. This will increase self-confidence and allow you to contribute with maximum efficiency; and the more you give to the world, the more you'll be rewarded with a deeper connection and purpose.

They say one of the characteristics of happy people is that they feel as though they're part of something bigger than themselves. Actually, it's best to take the focus off being happy, which is an emotional state. Think instead of being fulfilled, which is a more sustainable condition whether we're happy or not. Studies have shown that people who have a sense of purpose are happier, healthier, and live longer—by seven years! Pretty good, right? Those who contribute and feel they're valued report that they *are* happier and describe themselves as living the good life, according to best-selling author Richard Leider.

I saw this when I worked with successful people such as Arnold Shapiro and Maria Shriver, whose sense of philanthropy is the stuff legends are made of! My dad taught me as a little girl that if I found a sense of service, I wouldn't find much room for complaining. Well, he was a little off on that one because I can bitch and moan with the best of them, but I've found these words attributed to Eleanor Roosevelt to guide my life: "When you cease to contribute, you begin to die."

From the time my daughter was a young teen, she's been intrigued by the act of giving, too. We went to Africa once and went on elephant-back safaris. We all fell in love with the elephants and were distressed to learn that they die at around age 65 because their teeth fall out and they can't eat the tree bark  and chew the brush that makes up their diet. Well, Lexi was very concerned about the elephants and decided she wanted to start a charity to help. She said she'd call it FEED. I thought this was really great and asked her what it stood for, and she said, "Feed Elderly Elephants Dessert. You know, like tiramisu, cuz it's soft." She was only half joking and subsequently found dozens of other ways she could begin righting all the wrongs we saw along the way. Bless her, she meant well.

That's all we can do—mean well. That is the essence of living with intention spiritually. It's what moves the energy of change.

Have Hope

What gets people through tough economic times, heart-crushing grief, and devastating breakups? What allows a prisoner of war to face unspeakable torture day after day? Hope. This feeling and the faith that comes along with it allow us to believe in something we can't see. They keep us tethered to the possibility of a miracle or a promise of change. Of all the things I want to pass on to my children, this is the quality I want them to possess above all others. It's a self-renewing trait that separates those trusting souls who keep their eye on the prize from the dreary people who are certain that reality requires a dimmer view. It's one of those intangibles that define our existence with much more insight than we can describe, yet it's more real than anything the physical world can measure.

Have you heard about the groundbreaking work of Masaru Emoto, a scientific pioneer in Japan who conducted a study that he said proved that thoughts and feelings affect physical reality? He took two samples of water and exposed one to loving, peaceful words, while the other got negative thoughts and intentions. When viewed under a microscope, he found the loving sample crystallized in symmetrical, bright snowflake-like patterns, while the water with the negative intentions formed asymmetrical patterns and dull colors. The water changed its physical expression based on what emotional energy it was receiving and what words it was being given! We're the same way. We respond to the energy of faith, hope, and love. In it there's a feeling of safety, of belonging, of transcending. It's supportive and nurturing space that's ours for the asking.

We do all kinds of things all day long to try to connect with each other. We look a certain way; we laugh and lecture. We give kudos and applause, hugs and kisses. They're all means to an end. We want to feel something—those intangibles like love and respect, serenity and happiness, satisfaction and appreciation. It's that which we cannot touch that touches us the most.

Living with Hope

Psychologist Richard Lazarus described hope as "fearing the worst, but yearning for better." It's said to keep us creative about finding solutions and is a form of positivity that comes out of despair and failure. The inspirational Diane Sawyer said it best: "Hope changes everything, doesn't it?"

Yes, I think it does, and it's always available to us. The more we feel and believe it, the more easily it will arrive in our hearts effortlessly when we need it.

Diane's friend Robin Roberts, ABC's *Good Morning America* anchor, oozes hope. This woman is such a beautiful symbol of strength of spirit buoyed by faith. First she received the diagnosis of breast cancer, which gave viewers a chance to not only learn more about the disease, but to see her friend Diane show up to shoulder the burden. We saw Robin's optimism, faith, resilience, and humor. Then we celebrated her apparent victory until news came that as a result of the treatment, she'd contracted a rare blood disorder. Once again, she bucked up. And then, before Robin underwent the procedure to gather life-saving bone marrow from her sister, her beloved mother died.

While she was obviously devastated, Robin also said that she didn't want to miss the meaning behind the moment. Her mom had told her to "make your

GET COMFORTABLE AT THE TOP

The cream always rises to the top—it's a cliché because it's true. But to get to the top, you have to separate yourself from the rest of the milk! It might get a little lonely doing the right thing, but do it anyway. It might get scary seeking truth and enlightenment. Do it anyway. If you want to change yourself and the world, it's not gonna happen from nine to five, so put in the time for the things that matter most. Separate from the pack and make your own way. When you get to the top of your mountain, you'll know you deserve to be there because you earned it.

When I get temporarily knocked off my course I adjust my WOW factor. *WOW* stands for "Window On the World." I've talked a lot about how the world is as we see it, so if you find yourself sagging, sinking into a negative space, and abandoning your place at the top, make a mental switch by telling yourself, *Oh, WOW, that's not my window on the world,* and remind yourself who you are.

mess your message." She's done that by sharing her path to wellness, increasing the number of blood donors through her awareness building, and giving all of us who call ourselves part of Team Robin another reason to have faith. Every time I see Robin on camera, I'm reminded of the power of hope. I just love watching her and am always inspired.

Despair is not an emotion I allow myself to have—at least not for long. I say where there's no hope, you make some. That's what Robin's done. Those who face a diagnosis of chronic illness or fatal disease realize that sometimes they have to pull that optimism from nowhere. Our family was frozen with fear when we found out about Mom's Alzheimer's disease. People began to treat us differently, hope was nowhere to be found, and answers were hard to come by.

So we created what we wished we had, and we call it Leeza's Place and Leeza's Care Connection. These are safe, intimate living rooms where family caregivers and their loved ones can get free support while they try to make sense of their lives after the diagnosis of chronic or life-threatening disease. We help our guests summon their courage and call on their strength. We offer education, empowerment, and energy to those husbands, wives, sons, and daughters who need strength and clarity for the long road ahead in their lives as caregivers. The doors are always open, and the coffee is always on, just like Mom's kitchen. It's a powerful way that I stay connected to the legacy of my mother and my family while being privileged to connect with others who are strong and vulnerable, courageous and afraid. I feel spiritually alive whenever I'm there. It's my purpose, my cause, and my connection. (Find out more at **www.leezagibbons.com**)

Your Heart ID

What crafting a spiritual life boils down to is discovering and sharing your essence. Our collections of experiences, the people with whom we spend time, and how we show our love is our heart's identification—what I have been calling our soulprint. Just like our fingerprints, no two are exactly alike. Our true essence is something unique that mostly exists in the stories others know about us and in our own memories.

When my mother got Alzheimer's disease, I saw how fragile this most precious piece of identification is. I watched her lose herself memory by memory, until there was barely a lingering trace of how we'd known her. It was as if her hard drive had crashed and everything had just been erased. Who are you when you don't know who you are? So many of us ponder this question, whether we know someone afflicted with a memory disorder or not. Crafting a spiritual life is the direct line to who we really are, which is why it's so important in finding our story and owning our life. It's essential for Take 2.

Poring over photos and mementos is probably the best therapy you can find when you feel you've drifted. When Mom was sick, I spent nights awake with boxes of photos and letters, some of which became scrapbooks. It helped me make sense of things and start filling in the gaps. Try doing this and sharing your pages. It's interesting: Even though you may forget who you are, when others look at these books, they immediately get an intimate view of what matters to you as they see the people and places that make up your story.

My first scrapbook was created in high school when pom-poms, pageants, and cheerleading were my life. I called my next one *Me: The Early Years*. It was shoulder pads, mile-high hair, and lots of travel with my mother while I was on assignment for *ET*. When we share our lives—with all their drama, turmoil, happiness, and fears—everything somehow becomes more manageable. When we look at our moments of joy, celebration, and private reflection, we can see our very soulprint come alive. My children used to like to flip through the pages of my scrapbooks, and I could see the sense of comfort and security the souvenirs provided. They felt connected.

The Early Years (1978)
Interviewing Sen. Strom Thurmond

Memories matter—it's as simple as that. After all, our lives are made up of recalling where we go, whom we love, and what we care about. The ability to remember and reminisce is one of the sweetest things we know, but memories are funny things. They can creep up on us unannounced and surprise us with nostalgic emotions we thought had long been tucked away.

When someone you love is losing his or her memory, hanging on to those moments and feelings becomes much more meaningful, almost urgent. At least that's how it felt for me when my mother's life story was being rewritten because of Alzheimer's disease. I felt a strong need to preserve it. That's when I found myself alone at night at the kitchen table surrounded by bits and pieces of her story. All the pictures, letters, and mementos became part of my therapy. I was never very crafty, but I found that when I took a memory and lovingly chose a way to showcase it and share it on a page, I began to heal. I also embraced a hobby that connected me to so many other women who elevate moments with their creativity and care.

I made a page honoring my mother's wisdom surrounding a haircut—that's right, a really *bad* haircut. I was a little girl, maybe five, and my mom had me all dressed up for picture day sporting the worst bangs I've ever seen! It looked like someone had taken a chain saw to my wispy blonde hair. When I urged my mother to rip up the photo out of sheer embarrassment, she looked at me and said, "Honey, someday you're going to see this picture and smile. You'll recall this conversation, and it will be a sweet memory."

Once again, Mom was right. The memory comforts me every time I think of us laughing at the picture and the "What were you thinking?" moment surrounding it. You can see from the "family tree" picture on the next page that bad hair is a legacy passed on from Mom to me to my daughter! My friend Hollis framed these for me, and I love them!

Jean Gibbons · Leeza Gibbons · Lexi Gibbons

Honor and Create Traditions

Whenever you can, look for ways to find your place in the circle of eternity through traditions that are passed on through generations. I'm big on traditions in our family. My kids may feign annoyance with my chronic need to celebrate traditions, but I know it leaves an indelible mark on their hearts, and I'll bet they'll do the same things with their kids. At least I hope so.

When we first started doing our annual gratitude hike, it was really a strategy on my part for us to walk off an overly indulgent Thanksgiving meal on the canyon paths near our home. "Let's hike, kiddos!" I said. "We'll head for the top of Runyon Canyon, and when we get there, we can share our gratitude lists."

Eye rolling was a universal reaction, but ultimately this has become one of our most cherished family gatherings. Now we each write out our gratitude letters but don't share them with each other until we settle in with sparkling cider and grateful hearts, overlooking Los Angeles. I'm often overcome with emotion as I hear the words my children have written. Always real, always raw, these aren't censored "greeting card" moments, but rather authentic expressions of truth as they know it on that given day. The depth of what they write and the seriousness with which they approach the hike now shows me how meaningful it is.

Here are a couple of gratitude letters from 2010, one from me and one from a then 12-year-old Nathan. (You'll find video from our hikes and more of our letters at **www.leezagibbons.com**)

Leeza's Gratitude Letter:

Dear Family,

Our worlds move so quickly, blurring the moments into a compound of thoughts that sometimes seem impenetrable and inaccessible. But still, we think they are safe, and that they are ours for the taking whenever we want or need to remember or relive the way we were. The older I get, the more I feel those special times, the painful realities, the bittersweet passages, and all the rest need to be let out more often. They are not meant to be saved, but rather savored. I have found myself being grateful for all the strife and struggle, all the pulling and pushing to get to where we are. This year we have had births in the family, deaths in the family, lots of victories and challenges. But we have had what I always asked you to be grateful for in your prayers at night . . . help-

ful hands and hopeful hearts. It all lines up on the vista exactly as it should, whether we can see it at the time or not.

And so this year, I am grateful for knowing that . . . for (every once in a while) remembering that things come into focus only when we slow down enough to adjust our lens. Every year we take out our letters, go on our little hike, and get a glimpse into each other's souls. This is one of my very favorite parts of being "us." The grumbling about what time we're leaving, the look of incredulous disbelief about hiking to the top, the eye rolling over my picture taking and the flood of tears that invariably accompanies the reading of the words . . . I love it all. I love you all.

I'm thankful that I see who you really are, my family—you are just like me. Flawed, sometimes fearful, often happy, and sometimes unsure of why you are not. You are exquisite examples of humanity in progress—breathing in challenges and exhaling strength. Lexi, it's what you did this summer in Vienna and more recently with your job. You push yourself just far enough so that you bend but never break. I'm thankful for that and for your willingness to always put yourself in the line of fire if it means growing and coming face-to-face with your truth. I'm thankful for your energetic pursuit of life. You are a snowflake in my wide open sky—unique and ever changing as you glide to a landing. This year you bought a home of your own and you continue to find your home in Charlie's arms. I'm grateful for Charlie being such an important part of who we are and for his patience and his joyfulness.

Troy, you stepped up in a big way this year . . . with your academic excellence at school and your commitment to being a great canine parent! Pocket is a nice addition. Your aloof boyishness is still there, but it is tempered now with clear evidence of the man you are becoming. Your emergent responsibility and consideration means so much as I have been able to rely on you more and more. You have really become the authority in your own life this year, and it is impressive to see. You remind me that who we are today is not who we have to be tomorrow as you have chosen to redefine how you approach the world. We are all so happy that Meg joins our circle and makes it stronger.

Nathan, even though you change houses every week, your heart never changes. You are always 100 percent you . . . bright, curious, impossibly funny, and a member of the team, both in sports and in life. We are so excited every time we see you play. I'm thankful for your feisty sense of fun and for your tenderness. You help keep things light and always manage to choose the present moment over anything that came before it or that might come after. Thank you for still hugging me and helping me as you tower over me with size and dominate me with physical strength.

It's both fulfilling and oddly sad for a mother to see her children securely step on the very path she lit for them! It's thrilling and bittersweet to watch you each take one more leap closer to independence, and I'm so proud of your courage and confidence. I choose to hold you in my heart because my arms must let you go, but never too far, I hope. I'm thankful for your academic intelligence, but more than that, I'm grateful for your emotional intelligence that calls upon you to think of other people, to do the right thing even when no one is watching, and to feel empathy for your friends, often being the one to right a wrong or rally for a cause. It's the thing that lets you know, no matter what, you are always gonna be okay. We may get chinks in our armor, we might get rough around the edges, but our core strength is resilient. If I give you nothing else, that is a legacy of which I am very proud.

Steven, my proof of miracles and the manifestation of a lifetime of dreaming . . . thank you for always supporting my growth, whether it means sitting back and waiting or stepping forward and pushing—you always know which choice to make. I'm grateful that we can travel the world together and take in the wonders of the continents and also be alone and take in the wonders of just being a couple of people who can't believe we found each other. Thank you for showing up every day with love, commitment, patience, and intention . . . even when it's hard. Thank you for loving my children and for knowing the place they hold in my life. When you are proud of them and celebrate them and share news about them with your friends and family, I am overwhelmed with happiness. Thank you for reaching out to their dad and for helping us all build such a respectful and supportive relationship. I love your family and am proud to be a part of it as it grows in number and strength.

I'm grateful to you for letting me be as strong as I am, but I'm so thankful for knowing that I don't always have to be, because you are there.

I guess that's really what's most on my heart. You are all there. Every day, living inside me, beyond me, into all that is eternal. This year I have taken a small sip from a stream of calmness that I know runs deep. It feeds into a river of purpose and promise, and that is where I find each of you. It makes sense to me in a way it never has before.

I love you completely—always and forever—no matter what,
Mom

Nate's Gratitude Letter:

This year I'm thankful for my loving family that has always been there for me.

Troy, I'm thankful for you always giving me advice and showing me new music. You've always had my back through everything. Whether it's with Mom and Steven, or Dad, school, and everything in between, you've always been there.

Lexi, I'm thankful for you always being there for me. Although you may not always answer your phone. ;) You've always been available for me. You've given advice with school and parents, and you've helped me understand why some people are the way they are.

Steven, I'm thankful that you've always been understanding of how I feel. Although we may not agree on everything, you've always tried to understand, and you don't get heated. I really appreciate that, and you've always been there for me when I need help.

Mom, you've always helped me with everything, and you've always wanted me to do well in life and do what makes me happy, and I can't thank you enough for that. You always have let me follow my heart and try new things that I might not even like. You've always been supportive of me and always available for me.

Love you all. Happy Thanksgiving.
Nate

Pray

Regardless of how you view God—or even whether you believe—I think you'll find prayer can add meaning to your life. It's been an important part of my spiritual life since I was a little kid, although of course the nature of the prayers has changed dramatically. I used to pray for an extra helping of ice cream and a later bedtime. As an adult and parent, some of my most joyful moments of any day were spent praying with my children before they fell asleep. I loved the innocence and tenderness. When my then-five-year-old said, "Dear God, bless everyone, including the bad guys," I always smiled. My favorite prayer from my daughter at age eight was, "And, God, if I see any homeless people, I'll invite them over to our house to stay; but if they're really hungry, I won't make them eat Mom's cooking."

I pray in my car going to work, during commercial breaks at my show, and in the shower. Anytime I need to feel connection and to recognize that there's a greater power at play in my life, I pray. I talk about everything from peace to patience. Often I ask for strength and wisdom and to have an open mind to recognize God's messages to me. I think so often we pray for something, but we don't like the response, so we deny it. I pray that I will accept the reply and recognize that no is an answer, too.

Wish

My family and I have created a tradition around wishing, which really is a kind of prayer, I think. *A wish is a beautifully simple thing. Anyone can do it at any age, anytime, anywhere in the world. I think its real power is that it takes no forethought, no planning. Children have always known this truth.* When we closed our eyes as kids and blew on a dandelion, we saw those seeds scatter to all the corners of our world. We still can. I think the start of a new year is a great time to unleash the power of wishing.

Right now, each of you reading this has dozens of wishes alive inside of you. Which ones come true? I believe it's all about where we put our attention and how we use our intention. Wishes made for or about someone else hold a special kind of magic. These are the yearnings of our heart, expressing our innate knowledge that we're all connected. Wishes made for ourselves are the most fundamental expression of self-worth, and I'm always on the lookout for ways to unlock their magic. When we moved into our home, there had been a small pond in the front yard. I immediately decided it would become a "wish pond" and that those who visited would be encouraged to throw brightly colored glass stones off the bridge to make a wish. We also end many dinners at home by lighting sparklers by the wish pond.

I believe the problem is that we don't give wishing enough significance and respect. We're usually content to say things like, "Oh, wishful thinking," or "Yeah, you *wish!*" So I decided to create a ritual to give the wish a bigger platform and initiated my annual dressing of the wish tree. Although this tradition takes place in December, it has nothing to do with Hanukah or Christmas, and my wish tree is not your standard evergreen. In fact, I've been known to make the tree out of just about anything. One year, it was a ficus from my office; another time, it was a potted bunch of branches spray painted silver, and it was dazzling.

My inspiration came from a gift I received from a friend. She gave me an ornament that opened and read: "Wishes do come true." I ordered dozens of them, then e-mailed my family and friends and invited them to come over and bring a wish for themselves, someone they love, or for the world. We wrote the wishes down on little pieces of paper, folded them, and placed them lovingly inside the ornaments. Once they were all gathered in a big bowl, the kids placed them on branches of the wish tree, taking time to read each anonymous message.

The first year, this was met with a lot of groans. Now the kids vie for the chance to be the first to read the message inside. This year, ten-year-old Abie read, "I wish I had one more Christmas with my dad." The room got quiet, and even though no names are signed, we thought it had to be from my friend Julie, who'd recently lost her father. "I wish the kids at school wouldn't tease me," another one said. "I wish I had enough money to buy a plane ticket home to visit my folks." Often the sentiments are personal, but occasionally someone breaks the mood with one like this: "I wish Troy would get a haircut!" Okay, true-confession time: Although I *do* wish my son would cut his hair, I swear I didn't write that one!

The thoughts that live in the heart are often too big to be contained, so I like to write them down and say them aloud. Even if you're not up for a full-fledged wish tree, I'll bet you'll find that when you share a wish, magical things happen.

✦••✦

So you're on to me—I do believe in miracles. I do believe that prayers are answered. I do believe that while we have choices in life, there's a master design and that if we release and let the spirit rule our lives we can experience profound serenity. Mostly my prayers are those of gratitude and thanksgiving—I have been truly blessed.

These are my wishes for you, as you call for Take 2 in your life:

• I wish for you an endless supply of optimism—a way to find shooting stars, dandelions, four-leaf clovers, and pots of gold in every situation, all of it summoned at a moment's notice.

• I wish for you days with nothing to do and nowhere to go, being perfectly peaceful without an objective or an agenda, and days jammed with people and purpose, being wonderfully expectant as you make your to-do list ever longer.

• I wish for you a chance to change the world and make a difference, and the opportunity to be changed by the world and to make peace with knowing that some things will never change.

• I wish for you the gifts that come from failing and from seeing the frailties in your own humanity when you fall short of your goals, for it is only then that you can celebrate your successes and the victories that are sweeter because they don't arrive effortlessly.

• I wish for you the love of another so strong that you can occasionally be weak, a love that protects your heart with so much safety that you can afford to keep it open and receive all the blessings that may elude you when you don't feel secure enough to be who you really are.

• I wish for you a chance to be productive, to feel needed. I hope you work so hard and care so much that at the end of the day you're blissfully depleted, yet filled to overflowing with the kind of satisfaction that only comes from knowing you've done your best.

• I wish for you faith that you'll live forever through the lives you touch and the way you love. The memories that you leave behind create a unique print, and the world will never be the same because you were here.

• I wish for you a constant stream of time shared with friends and family, basking in support and gratitude, moments that rest easily in your heart and are retrieved whenever you need a gentle reminder that your life matters and you're not alone.

In my family, we always end our conversations, phone calls, e-mails, texts, and any other communications with: "Love you, AFNMW," which stands for "always and forever, no matter what." We never know, do we? Will we be healthy, will our hearts break, will our children be happy, and will those we love stay safe? Life is nothing if not unpredictable. We may never have seen ourselves in a particular position, but then there we are. If you're open, you'll find others are there, too. Look to your left and your right and know that you're not alone. Find your circle of sisters to support you, cry with you, fight for change with you, and remind you that you're part of history. Meditate, pray, and be awakened to the power of the moment and to your place in the world. Connect and share your soulprint. In doing so, you become a change agent, energy with intention. You don't really have to overthink it.

This is your spirit. Release it and let it *soar.*

Chapter 8

TAKE OWNERSHIP OF YOUR LIFE

"Sometimes I think it would be easier to avoid old age, to die young, but then you'd never complete your life, would you? You'd never wholly know yourself."

— MARILYN MONROE

"Honey, you'd better figure out how to run your own life or someone else will!" How many times did my mom say that? And it's true! As women, we sure can run things. It's why we're so good at being executives—we can create miracles and mark milestones at work and especially for those we love. The real test, though, is how effective we are at running our own lives when we've got to step into the place of ultimate authority. You're an expert on you, and no one else can take control of your destiny unless you get out of the pilot seat and let them. *Don't!*

The minute we get weak and wishy-washy, we run the risk of being relegated to bit parts in our productions. To be a star in your life, you've gotta hit your mark, throw your shoulders back, and *own* the stage.

Sometimes, that's not so easy when things make us feel insecure about who we are. I've never believed in ageism, the idea that people are discriminated against because of how old they are. A lot of us feel that way—that if we're productive, smart, and have contributions to make, there's no such thing as ageism. But then it happens. We have that first experience in the workplace when our ideas are better received because they were filtered through a younger person. I'm here to tell you, this is where perspective is everything.

I always tell my kids that I'm going to live to be 100—and I believe it, too. That means I'm at about the halfway point, and the view from the top of the hill before I start that glide down the back stretch is really great. Like you, I've struggled, climbed, and pulled my way up; and I think we should be pretty proud of that effort. When I made it to 30, it started to feel as if I were inheriting my true womanhood. At 40, I realized that life wasn't over—and in fact, it wasn't nearly as scary as it was made out to be. Then 50 arrived, and I had no idea where that number came from!

Before you even begin to settle into middle age, somebody is going to hit you with the "S word"—*senior*—and I promise you're not going to be ready. I know I wasn't, and neither were any of my friends. But what keeps all us 50-somethings from storming off in what my mother used to call a hissy fit is the fact that there are a lot of big-time advantages to the view from here. I see a lot of things more clearly now, first and foremost being how important it is to take ownership of life. No matter what your age is, you have the benefit of taking the experiences that got you here and letting them launch you forward.

Owning your life can make you feel emotionally naked because it means seeing the parts of yourself that aren't flattering and admitting the things you aren't proud of. It requires hearing criticism from others and actually letting it sink in. Not all of it will seem huge. In fact, most of the moments of truth are small stackable blocks upon which you can build something new.

It took me a long time to come clean about my relationship with work, for instance. I used to feel guilty about working so much, but now I'm not ashamed to talk about how much I like to work. It's my vocation *and* avocation. I overprepare because I like to have more information than most find necessary. That's what makes me feel safe. If other people think I'm neurotic, that's their problem! Seriously, I know this about myself and have admitted it to my husband and family, so they understand when I need to give myself more time for things or when I need to stay up late reading or researching. I've found the right balance for *me;* and even though I still stumble off the path sometimes, at least I know where I'm going.

You have been on a journey to begin anew, and that means taking some risk. Once you admit to others that you're committing yourself to something you care deeply about—aka finding out who you really are—you become 360 degrees vulnerable. When I decided to create Leeza's Place and Leeza's Care Connection, I didn't exactly get cheers and "atta-girls." I was (and am) passionately devoted to helping family members care for someone they love who is sick or dying. I wanted to create what our family wished we'd had when Mom got Alzheimer's disease. I wanted to make sure that caregivers didn't feel alone, and I wanted to make sure that those who are forgetting aren't forgotten.

I said to my talent agency, "I think I can make a difference. I want to start a memory foundation and help families struggling with dementia."

"Are you serious?" is what I got back. "No, don't do it—that's not sexy! It's career suicide, being publicly connected with getting older. You won't be as hirable. Why don't you just stick to your kids charities?"

That gave me even more reason to forge ahead (and start looking for another agent, by the way). I dared to be vulnerable, to talk about my own fears of aging and loss, and in doing so

I took ownership of them. The gifts that have flowed from that choice have been extraordinary.

I have to say, though, that my agent was right in some respects. There's a lot of stigma around getting older, and I guess some folks thought I had already racked up a lotta years. Not long ago, I spoke at an event created by California's then First Lady, my friend Maria Shriver; I was representing the work we do with our memory foundation. Afterward, I was standing around our exhibit booth where people were getting brochures. A passerby looked at the booth and said, "The Leeza Gibbons Memory Foundation—oh, did she pass away?"

Yikes!

My work with my foundation fills my soul

Living from the Heart

Here's the deal: how much can you stand by your choices? How much do you believe in your idea, even if it's not fully developed? Are you willing to let others convince you that they know better about something that's at the core of your soul? I say if the thought inspires you and the very mention of it gets you excited, run toward that energy. Even the very best ideas have to be fine-tuned to perfection and "loved up" to be ready for prime time.

I had *no* idea what I was doing when I decided to start a nonprofit, but I knew enough to trust the process—to recognize that I was a student who was ready to learn and know that the right teachers would show up. Every time I fell down, I learned a little more and recovered from the bruised ego even stronger and more determined.

Failure is the best teacher and always lifts us higher if we let it. In the years since I've been in the charity world, I've been led by a voice stronger than mine, stronger than all the naysayers who tried to dissuade me. It belongs to the spirit of my mother and others like her who have to trust the next generation to build upon their legacies.

I wanted to run my own life and make it stand for the things that matter most to me, so I forged ahead, silencing the disapproving crowd. My dad used to tell me that a leader is willing to make unpopular decisions against popular people; and I wanted to take the lead in my life directly in the direction of my dream, no matter what anyone else thought. My work as an advocate for caregivers and families facing a health crisis has given me so much abundance of heart and richness of spirit.

And what do you know? Jobs haven't dried up, and my career isn't over—but the choice did force me to get real about what mattered. I knew that I didn't want to run away from making a difference because of the fear of fading from the scene in my work. Now I find the opportunities that are born from my health advocacy are much more satisfying for me than celebrity news.

So there's a Leeza Gibbons Memory Foundation—did she pass away? No, she just passed through one door and onto a new, more meaningful stage.

I believe that when I started my philan-thropic work, my publicists and agents failed to grasp some basic truths. While we *are* a culture that is youth obsessed, we're also people who are searching. We spend lifetimes looking for meaning, and it's when we're feeling empty that we obsess about beauty. No one gets this better than my friend Suzanne Somers. She helped me understand the concept when she told me that the physical attributes of youth are momentary gifts to get us through our insecurities. As we mature, we don't need to rely on them so much.

I find that we're actually the most beautiful when our hard edges (internally and externally) have been softened by time. Our unlined faces will morph into the ones we've earned. The surface will fade, but the beauty behind our actions shines on. That's how we get to live forever. It's about what we're doing and how we share our gifts, including our appearance.

Look at what we do in our culture: extreme makeovers, transforming ourselves to be more marketable to our consumer society, eating up sound bites like morsels of real wisdom, and dreading the ravages of time like the plague. I've decided to celebrate my journey, moving ever forward, including lighting the path that's taking me directly into elder status. The real test isn't how long we're able to preserve our physical beauty to match a standard imposed upon us by others; it's about how we use our physical, emotional, and spiritual energy. Ultimately, that can be irresistibly beautiful.

MY TAKE: LEEZA'S LENS

Living Past the "Pause"

I got a call this week from a good friend of mine who is in her early 40s. Janie was very distraught and sad. She had just been to see her doctor, who told her that she was no longer fertile, that she had "dried up" . . . in other words, menopause. This was a jarring call for me because it took me back to the day I faced the fact that I could no longer create life. I was 45. My mom was already experiencing the effects of Alzheimer's disease, so I couldn't go to her for answers to all the questions running through my mind. Janie was in the same situation. Her mother had a hysterectomy at a young age, and so couldn't offer firsthand knowledge to quiet the noise in Janie's head about this unwelcome news.

"The pause" is one of the most difficult transitions for women. We get all excited about starting menstruation, but at the other end, there is no pride, no celebrations, no claiming victory over another milestone in your womanly pursuits. Just confusion (no matter how prepared you may think you are) and sadness. I also felt like a failure whose worth had just declined to rock bottom. I mean, as women we are designed to give life; when we can no longer do so, it messes with our self-esteem. Even those who choose to never have children still feel affected when they find they can't.

Adding to Janie's emptiness was her son telling her, "Mom, I'm so sorry this was taken from you." Janie had always held on to the thought that she may want more children, even though there was no man in her life to father a child and she had her hands full with her one son. I totally understood her feeling that she had somehow been "robbed" too soon. But it got me thinking . . . this is "taken" from all of us, and yet we know it's coming. I'm not insensitive to the grieving process that most of us feel when losing something that ties us to our essence as women. I felt it, too. We view it as another door slamming shut, another option off the table, another way that youth is passing us by . . . but what if we could more peacefully relinquish this moment?

At some point, we have to better express to girls that when their time comes to "hit the pause button," it is just another sign that things are progressing as they should. I think we are poisoning the water for younger women by not letting them know what can happen when they get past menopause. We only seem to focus on the loss, failing to recognize how much we gain—and I think we gain a lot. While it's not necessarily "better," for many of us it is *bigger* than what was on the other side.

Just how big? Well, I was recently at a luncheon with several highly accomplished women. These are the women in whose high heels you'd like to walk a mile so you could experience a life where success, power, and achievement was perfectly complemented and balanced with friendship, love, and family. In other words, they lived the way most of us would like to at the halfway point in our lives. We got talking about this menopause business, and they all said that no one had told them it was even possible that they could feel more comfortable in their own skin than ever before. No one had given them a preview of life beyond menopause that allowed them to see it as a rich, rewarding place. One woman said to me, "I feel freer than I ever have, I'm thinking bigger than I ever did, and I'm owning my life in a way I never could before." We all agreed that if we could have sat ourselves down and had a little talk about the view from the other side, we would have been able to "drop the dread."

I have never felt more powerful in my own life than I do now. I'm not saying the transition is easy; in fact, during what seemed to me like decades of "drying up," I was like a crazy woman! My little sister would take my panicked phone calls and try to reassure me, but it was not an easy feat. She had no answer when I would ask her how much more I could take. I mean, how many tampons could I actually wear at one time while also strapping on a pad the size of a mattress and *still* bleed through?! However, it was the same way when we first began getting our periods, too. It was just much easier to bear when we were all riding the escalator of excitement. Plus, in the days when we first got our periods, we felt like we were joining a new club of women just like us. Well, guess what? It's the same way on the descending end, but we have failed to celebrate the "letting go."

I guess Janie's call to me was my call to action. I am now one of those women who bear the responsibility of setting the scene for what it's like. I told Janie to learn about managing her symptoms and educate herself thoroughly, but mostly to be aware of her emotional journey. Would Janie have felt more ready for "the pause" at age 55? Probably, but no matter when it hits you, there will be an emotional process that goes along with the physical process. Even though it may feel like it will never be over, there is an end and life on the other side, which for me has been fuller, bigger, and more meaningful.

So, for those of you still having your period, try not to complain about it so much. It won't be with you always and you might miss it when it's gone (although I do *not*!). For the rest of us, let's remember to honor and value the fact that menopause is just what I like to call a "pause" in the action so that you can regroup and figure out your next game plan. It's like being on the playing field of life when there is a time-out called. You can get some coaching, see where you're vulnerable, and then start playing offense again!

Lit from Within

Check out this quote by Sam Levenson, from one of Audrey Hepburn's favorite poems: "For attractive lips, speak words of kindness. For lovely eyes, seek out the good in people. . . . For poise, walk with the knowledge that you never walk alone." Don't you love it? Sure, it's easy for one of the most classic, stunning beauties of all time to believe those words, but we all have to admit they're true.

This section of the book focuses on ways to become lit from within. Have you ever seen a woman glow? I'm not talking about the radiance that we say moms-to-be have. I've seen women of all ages walk into a room and light it up.

Now, this doesn't mean that the highlighter a woman used on her bottom lip sends flashes of light across a room or that she has a dusting of shimmering minerals on her décolletage (although I'll get to fun stuff like that later on in the book). She knows something, possesses something, emits something much deeper than what's on the surface.

Have you ever met an average-looking woman who, once you get to know her, you can't help but see as one of the most beautiful women you've ever laid eyes on? We say things like, "She's not exactly a model, but there's something really captivating about her. I can't take my eyes off her."

Most likely that woman is calm, cool, and confident. I'd also bet she's taken ownership of her life, has made peace with her past mistakes, puts herself first, is present in the moment, and doesn't walk in judgment of others. She's self-assured and easy to talk to, not boastful, and never whiny—in fact, she probably has a terrific sense of humor. She's simply a woman who knows what she wants out of life and knows where she's going. Does any of this sound familiar? I sure hope so!

Get to Know Your Goddess Quotient

I've talked about goddesses throughout the book. Let's take a closer look at the term now. If you're emerging in your life; if you're getting closer to your own truth; if you're present and aware of how you feel and how you affect others; if you're an active source of good vibes; and if you own it, share it, and celebrate it, then you're a goddess!

I always say that you have to know who you are before you can create who you want to be. *Real women never run from the realities of their flawed lives, but they sure don't hold up a magnifying glass and dissect each imperfection. Acknowledge, adjust, and move on!*

Goddesses uplift and support each other, always celebrating each other's successes. This is really important. If you have to force yourself to do it at first, it's okay. After a while, you'll be amazed that you really feel it.

If, let's say, you've been jealous of your friend's promotion—or if she gets a job you really wanted *and* she has great hair and the best house on the block, and her banana pudding beats the vanilla wafers out of yours (okay, maybe this is *my* example)—look at it as setting the standard for you. Whatever she can have, so can you.

After a while, you'll discover that you've started feeling actual joy over the victories of others, and you really will become the first to applaud and celebrate when someone wins. Don't forget that you're creating your own trip here. You get to decide how you feel, so choose to feel good! It's extremely attractive to see women who are free of the green-eyed monster as they take potential envy and turn it into appreciation.

No one likes a sore loser, and in the game of life, winners are the ones who know how to allow others their fortune. Keep in mind that there's enough of everything for everyone—enough material things, successes, and relationships. If those around you are getting what they want, that's perfect. It means that their energy is dancing with yours, and your wishes are also on the way.

A goddess lives without limits. She sees herself as an endless source of possibility and creation. She nourishes herself—mind, body, soul, and spirit. If you're a true goddess, you aren't constantly depleted. You aren't in a time tailspin, breathlessly arriving late to everything. You don't feel overscheduled, burdened by your commitments, or hassled by your day-to-day realities. This is the chapter in my own goddess primer that I have to read over and over again.

A goddess looks for solutions rather than focusing on the problems. And sometimes the solution is as simple as just saying no. This woman is gracious and giving, flexible and forgiving—especially with herself. She's at peace with who she is and enjoys her own company.

It all comes down to this: A woman isn't a full-fledged goddess unless she loves herself.

MY TAKE: LEEZA'S LENS

A Gold-Star Goddess

If there is a more powerful example of transformation, I don't know where you'd find it. Jamie Lee Curtis stands as a female force of *facing* change, *creating* change, and *going through* change. She has managed to be in-your-face authentic while not only accepting aging but being actively seduced by it. "I want to be older," she told *AARP The Magazine.* "I actually think there's an incredible amount of self-knowledge that comes with getting older. I feel way better now than I did when I was 20. I'm stronger, I'm smarter in every way."

I've interviewed Jamie Lee a bunch of times. At first I viewed her mainly as a famous movie star with a pedigree. As the daughter of Janet Leigh and Tony Curtis, she has always known what it's like to be in the spotlight, yet somehow her life as the wife of director/actor Christopher Guest and mom to Annie and Thomas has been very low-key and incredibly "normal."

Jamie Lee does not like artifice. That's what I noticed as I had more chances to report on this gutsy woman. Then I became aware of the driving force for Jamie Lee—her activism and commitment to various causes. She shows up for service and stands up for change every time. Even while onstage, accepting an honor given by my foundation as someone who "Dares to Care," Jamie Lee lovingly took a moment to encourage me and let me know that my work mattered. She has always found time to support women and their dreams. That's true goddess goodness.

Every time I see another project, another interview, another book, or another cause embraced by Jamie Lee, I do a little happy dance. She is just the ultimate in cool. Once she was known as film's "scream queen," or simply "the body." Turn the page, and she's gaining credibility and fans as a children's book author who has now revolutionized the genre. She is a world-class mom who tackled that role with everything she's got. Flash forward and she makes a bold move to promote yogurt that makes you poop better. And while I'm sure she must get paid well, she didn't do it for the money; it was for the access to change lives.

See, that's why Jamie Lee is a gold-star winner at the top of my list of goddess go-tos. The woman takes on change and flows with it. If I ever need to see how it's done, I look to her; it's all there. She shares what she knows and puts everything on the line for the lesson. How many of us would do photo shoots with no makeup or pose for magazine covers without airbrushing? Jamie Lee does it to make a point. Getting older is inescapable, so we may as well approach it with our heads held high, shoulders back, and focus on where we're going, which, she says, is to take our place along the chain of our ancestors.

"In America, we celebrate youth and all of youth's indiscretions and follies," Jamie Lee says. "We cling to the shiny new thing, we stare at altered photographs and wonder why we don't measure up." But the fact is, we *do* measure up. And because of examples like Jamie Lee, we get to see what it's like to really claim our life, run our own show, and call for as many takes as we want to become our best self.

Get on with It, Goddess Girl!

They say in love relationships that if you don't have it, you can't give it away; that if you don't first value who you are, you won't attract someone of value into your life; and if you don't know what self-love is, then you really can't love anyone else. We've talked about a lot of themes and issues, but the thread that holds it all together is the underlying message of self-love. We can't embrace change, replace fear with courage, set goals, and accept setbacks unless we care for ourselves first.

Having self-love and self-compassion are the cornerstones to a glorious Take 2. I hope you're there now, and that you feel like the goddess you deserve to be. When you're able to claim and own this as your identity, you'll find the rest of the world will follow your lead and treat you better, valuing you more.

Of course there will always be days when, as in any relationship, you find you're disappointed, angry, ashamed, and ultimately not feeling very lovey-dovey with yourself. Allowing these emotions to hit home is a healthy thing, because that's what taking ownership entails. You accept the bad with the good and become accountable. That's where change and growth come from. But remember that these are emotions, not facts. Don't confuse how you momentarily feel about yourself with reality, and don't let a fleeting circumstance dictate a norm or pattern.

This is where I've found it helpful to go back and read old journal entries where I see my continuing themes of self-doubt chronicled. I'm able to notice that when I wrote things like, *I wonder how I'll make it through,* I always did. I may have anguished over a breakup and written, *I'll be crushed if it's over,* but now I can see how it all served my growth. When I look at past doubts, they're barely footnotes in my story compared to the main themes of success, accomplishments, and fulfillment.

To find self-love means that you take yourself for better or for worse. If so many of us can make that commitment to a life partner, then why not turn it inward? When you dip into the dark side, you might find it helps to acknowledge that you're living with the shadow of yourself. Sometimes I'll say out loud, "Okay, doldrums, why are you here? Who invited you, and what have you come to teach me?"

Sometimes I'll even continue the conversation in my mind, where the blues remind me that they're back only briefly because I never let them stay long. They tell me that as soon as I give them what they want, they'll leave—and what they want is to be acknowledged. They are, after all, expressions of me, and I need to love my entire being, for better or worse.

All the self-help gurus tell you that what you resist persists, so as soon as you can come face-to-face with your shadow side, you can accept these feelings as part of you. They may not be the biggest or best part, but they're yours just the same. Ultimately, you get to decide what to do with them.

If you find your Goddess Quotient (GQ) is low, then it's time to go on a search-and-rescue mission. It might be time to reboot your main drive. To find out what's keeping you from radiating strength and love, ask yourself a few basic questions:

- *Am I trying my best and being honest with myself?*

- *Have I opened up to allow myself to see who I am and what I need?*

- *Am I filled with faith and hope?*

- *Am I taking care of myself and prioritizing my own agenda in my life?*

If you answer no to any of these question, it means that who you *want* to be is out of sync with who you actually *are,* and that causes stress. Guess where it shows up first? It appears on your face, which is also the last place to recover. Stress is an equal opportunity destroyer, and it will systematically move in until you look old and depressed. This is not part of your Take 2. So as with everything else, you need a plan.

EAT SMART

In addition to using my diet to mitigate stress, I try to eat smart—more literally than you might think. Again, because I have a history of Alzheimer's in my family, I incorporate into my diet as many foods as I can that are known to boost cognitive functioning. Broccoli is a terrific choice that's been shown to improve memory and slow down the aging process. With that promise, I'll buy it by the bushel! Dark chocolate is antioxidant rich and helps with concentration and focus—what a yummy reason to add some shavings onto a nonfat latte or treat yourself to a candy bar once in a while. Blueberries, mixed nuts, flaxseeds, and avocado are all great brain foods to enjoy on the fly; whole grains, including oatmeal, increase circulation to the brain. Eggs and fish (eat wild instead of farm raised for a real brain boost) top the list for omega-3s and choline—both incredible assets for improving memory and overall brain functioning.

Stress: The Ultimate Beauty Suck!

Let me just give you the bottom line: Stress makes you ugly—inside and out. It can put creases in your face and dog-ears on the pages of your story. It's impossible to take ownership of your life if stress is holding it hostage.

I've experienced these real and damaging effects firsthand. You see, my daughter, Lexi, is a dancer and has been blessed with the opportunity to travel to several countries to study her art. Last summer, while she was taking some dance courses in Vienna, Austria, I got a call from the U.S. Embassy in Hungary. They told me that they'd opened a missing-person report on Lexi. *What?*

She was last seen at a hostel in Budapest, where she failed to come back and retrieve her passport. It's a long story that turned out fine, but I was beyond stressed—literally sick with worry. I could see myself on the nightly news in a panic of pain trying to urge the public to somehow help me. I'm telling you, it took me weeks to recover. The anxiety made me grayer; my skin was dull, my hair fell out, and I got unexplained bumpy patches on my neck.

Stress can also cause breakouts, weight gain, brittle nails, sleep disturbance, irritability, and more! It's not our friend when it comes to health (or our looks), but the truth is that we're never going to get rid of it. When asked if stress was a major factor in their lives, 80 percent of men and 79 percent of women said yes. So since you can't eliminate it, mitigate it. Here's how:

• **Control stress eating.** *While all food is energy, all food energy isn't the same.* Junk food and processed snacks tend to fill you fast but bring your blood sugar crashing down soon after—these things actually make you more tired in the long run. To combat stress, you need fuel that fights fatigue. Make choices that will keep your blood sugar stable, provide lots of energy, and help your mood stay even. These include lean protein; whole grains (such as oats); foods with omega-3 fatty acids (like salmon); and lots of plants, including fruits, veggies, and nuts.

I wish I had some magic formula to give you, but it simply comes down to this: The better you eat, the better you feel and look. This is an inescapable truth. Listen, no one has more of a love-hate relationship with sugar than I do. But for my brain, it's like cocaine; and for my hips, it's like the ghost under the stairs that I have to continually exorcise! When I back away from this drug, the rest of my life works better. I look better, cope better, and have more energy; and my complexion is better, too.

My brain doc, Daniel Amen, has scanned my brain so I've actually seen what a difference it makes when I fuel it with the right foods. Since there have been two generations of women in my family who died from Alzheimer's disease, I'm always interested in what I can do to make sure I don't get it. At the top of the list are three items: manage stress, exercise, and eat well. Historically, women have enjoyed a longer life span than men, but the stress women experience threatens to change that. And we don't do ourselves any favors when it comes to what we eat. Broccoli, onions, leafy greens, beans, and wild salmon have been targeted as some of the foods we should eat more of, especially when it comes to preventing brain drain. Read more here: **www.readersdigest.ca /food/healthy-food/6-foods-help-prevent-alzheimers**.

• **Rely on shortcuts to make healthy eating easier.** Chop up fresh veggies once every few days and place them in plastic baggies. Make leafy greens a part of salads and sandwiches, or serve them cold with a little olive oil. This is a surefire way to increase calcium in your diet, as well as an array of other impressive nutrients. Just adding diced onions to salads and sandwiches all week long helps add essential micronutrients and provide antibacterial, anti-inflammatory, and cancer-fighting properties.

Stick to simple recipes with minimal ingredients. For example, fish, a steamed veggie, and brown rice take only a few minutes to prepare. Freeze blueberries and eat them as snacks. Keep almonds handy; they give you sustainable protein and omega-3 protection, and satisfy your need to crunch. Preparing a three-bean salad at the beginning of the week lets you have a great side dish that helps meet the daily recommendation for protein, folate, fiber, tryptophan, protein, iron, magnesium, and potassium. Beans are terrific if you're in a time crunch because they come ready-made. They've also been linked to a reduced risk of type 2 diabetes, high blood pressure, and breast cancer. Cut up power or protein bars, put them in zip-top plastic bags, and throw them in the freezer. It's not a Snicker's bar, but we do what we can!

• **Make double portions.** Save and freeze leftovers for a quick meal later, or arrange a meal swap with a friend so that you cook once but get two different dishes. Gwyneth Paltrow says she spends an hour or two on Sunday prepping meals for the rest of the week. If she has time, I figure I can make time, too!

• **Get a massage.** In addition to eating healthy every day, I have a full-body message about twice a month. The benefits are endless, so it's not really an indulgence, but a wellness strategy. I light my aromatherapy candles and put on my favorite music, and a professional visits my home for an hour or so and works the tension out. Sometimes I also go to a local spa. I used to imagine doing this when I was a college student who couldn't find money for books! Now that I manifested it into my life, I always start the session with gratitude and by congratulating myself.

Easy Ways to Even Out

I always say an unnamed enemy has way more power than naming and claiming your nemesis, and that's how I think about stress. It's a sneaky little thief, an adversary creeping up when you least expect it. It's time to take the mask off and learn more about how it zaps your energy, peace of mind, and health. Then I'm going to give you a security system to take the thief out before it takes you down.

As I've said, stress is inevitable; and a lot of it comes from good things: getting married, taking a trip, moving, getting a new job, or having a baby. Then there's the assault on our senses: loud and crowded places, traffic on freeways, and lines at airports and in grocery stores. Stress often accompanies fear, so if someone rear-ends your car or you're being chased by a barking dog, most likely you're not only scared, but also stressed out as you wave down some help. But the types of tension I'm most familiar with and feel most qualified to discuss are the internal strain that comes from worrying and the physical and emotional anxiety that come from working too much or too hard at anything!

A lot of stress comes from feeling overwhelmed and overtired and just not knowing how to manage your time. We're talking about serious health risks here—mental and physical. Stress can cause or contribute to stroke, high blood pressure, heart disease, alcoholism, obesity, and more. Three out of four of us say we're seriously stressed a couple of times a month, and some experts warn that if we don't deal with it, we'll have a recipe for metabolic disaster.

No doubt stress is a part of your story, but unless you address it and learn to mitigate it, this nasty customer will become the main character. You simply can't call for Take 2 or even watch from the wings if you're tied up in knots all the time. So here's a recap: Stress is real, it's dangerous, but it can soon be run out of town with its tail between its legs. Or at least we can take the bark down to a whimper by following these tips:

1. Get a good night's sleep. This is the first weapon against stress or anxiety. It provides the resilience and recovery you need to maximize your efforts during your waking hours. You can't be fighting any demons if you're too tired to keep your head up. Plus, when you're mentally and physically fatigued, you tend to exaggerate the problems at hand. They seem less controllable and worse than they really are. If you ever see me making a mountain out of a molehill, most likely I didn't get a good night's rest.

Make this strategy a routine, since sometimes you have to signal to your body that it's time to sleep. Chamomile tea and warm milk really do work to take the edge off, and they also regulate your body clock, cuing you to wind down. Although it's tempting to use the television and computer as pacifiers to drift into dreamland, sleep scientists tell us that they don't make for a restorative night. Brain waves are too engaged to really downshift into recovery mode when electronics are on.

2. Harness the power of a nap. It's too bad our culture doesn't really embrace the benefits of napping. The truth is that cats know something we humans don't—it's not necessarily best to get all of our sleep at one time. A good 20-minute nap can increase alertness, improve memory and learning, and create a better mood, along with boosting your intelligence and productivity. A lot of the greats took great naps, including Winston Churchill and John F. Kennedy. If you have the option, do it! It's a great way to manage stress.

3. Chant. This technique could be the best two minutes in your day—yep, just two minutes can do wonders. People who chant are healthier, and I'm not making this up—it's a fact. Let me break it down simply: Chanting can increase oxygen intake, and decrease carbon dioxide in the body. Getting more oxygen to your brain (as much as 10 percent more) and emitting more carbon dioxide means you concentrate better, learn more easily, and handle stress more effectively. Chanting really doesn't have anything to do with religious practice but has everything to do with lowering your heart rate, reducing your blood pressure, and managing your tension.

Start with the tried and true *om,* which should be chanted as three syllables that sound something like this: *ah-uh-mm.* Think of saying "home" without the H. Draw out the final syllable and let it resonate in your sinuses, like a humming sound. That's it! If you want more help, and just because I know you're gonna love it, check out these YouTube videos. The first is a basic "How To" and the next is Tina Turner chanting from her home! How cool is that? Check out **video.about.com/hinduism/How-to-Chant-Om** and **youtube/PRr3zTzoVhk.**

4. Meditate. I talked about this in the last chapter, and I hope that if you don't meditate already, you'll see there's no mystery or secret to it. You can choose to do this anytime, anywhere. It's just about dropping into yourself and finding your natural state of relaxation and consciousness. If you're planning and worrying, you're *not* meditating. We get so used to being in a state of frenzy that it's hard to let go of that addiction.

Start with these activities:

- Take a warm bath.
- Do some gardening.
- Swing.
- Paint.
- Sit quietly with an elderly friend.
- Hum.

If you're doing any of them, pat yourself on the back. You're meditating! As you can see, lots of daily activities are gateways to this practice, so don't overthink it! So many physical ailments come from inner turmoil, and calming your mental state should vastly improve your physical state.

5. Take a walk. This has been proven to be better medicine than any drug or other treatment out there for stress and diseases of the body and mind. Your digestion benefits, your brain gets oxygen, your skin improves, your mood lifts, and you'll live longer! There really is no excuse.

6. Phone a friend. Everyone needs a go-to person who will be the glue when she cracks. This isn't someone to fix things or to swing into intervention mode, but someone who will be a safe place to temporarily deposit your doubts, insecurities, fear, foibles, confessions, and concerns.

Usually, my friends can tell if something is up by the sound of my voice when I say, "Hey, it's me." That tone is the signal to stand by for an avalanche of grievances as minor as, "I can't believe I paid full price for those shoes and now they're on sale," to something as major as, "I'm worried—the doctor called and said some of my tests didn't come out great." A good friend will resist the urge to fill in the blank space between breaths. She'll just allow you to empty it all out.

I used to tell my friends, "We're gonna put that in a pink bubble and let it float and follow you around for a while. It's there if you need to open it and talk some more, but you can always just pop it away when you decide you're ready." There's something about knowing that what you say will be received without judgment and that it won't precipitate any action that allows you to release and move on. Whether you chat for 30 seconds or 30 minutes, this tip never fails.

7. Have a primal scream. I used to have a padded recording room where I taped my radio shows at home. It was just a space with a thick layer of soundproofing and my audio gear on a table. The kids used to joke that it was my screaming room, where I could go when I got frustrated—and they weren't too far off! Just like an audible exhale or a few rounds with a punching bag and some jumping jacks, sometimes a good scream is just the ticket to release and recharge.

8. Pray. You can interpret this in any way you want, as you learned in Chapter 7. It's really just a private conversation between you and your Creator, your center, or your source energy. Pray for others, for strength, for great abs . . . I'm sure not gonna be the one to tell you how to do it or what to ask for. What I will say is this: Prayer is powerful. It's an articulation and recognition of what's etched on your soul.

9. Do something creative. Blog, journal, sculpt, or sing, especially when you feel a dearth of creativity! Most of the time we don't feel inspired simply because we haven't given space to it. Slow down, open up, and wait. You are a creative spirit. When you express that, it triggers your essence. Don't skip this.

10. Cross-train your brain. Our minds are made to expand; and new knowledge is always a healthy pursuit, no matter what you learn. Take up a hobby and make it a habit. Our brains are meant to cross-train. Many people say that once they learned to knit, they got better at math; playing piano helped them learn new languages; and completing motorcycle maintenance led to a more productive business! So decide to knit, juggle, paint, dance, collect stamps, learn a language, or join a club—whatever it is that will expose you to new and different energy and ideas.

11. Have a belly laugh. My dad is always my best source for this one. I'd share one of his jokes with you here, but none of them are PG rated. Suffice it to say, put a premium on people who can help you laugh it off.

12. Find a good therapist. We often think we're so complicated and different that no one can understand us, but opening up to a good professional is life changing. It can release us from the burden of trying to figure everything out and open us up to a process of self-discovery we might have never pursued otherwise. What's more important than knowing ourselves? I've sought therapy for myself, my children, and our family over the years; it has been a bridge connecting us to a new level of being.

13. Make a list. This simple strategy can offer a great reprieve from the enormous overwhelm that can threaten our sanity. Somehow, seeing everything written out always helps me be more comfortable with the mountain of things to do. I usually make lists in the notes section on my phone. The truth is that I rarely look at the list, but knowing it's there keeps me from worrying about it.

14. Speak your mind. You'll eat yourself up with stress if you have something on your mind or in your heart and fail to release it. If someone upset, offended, hurt, or wronged you, learning how to take steps to go on the record with your feelings is one of the best things you can ever do for yourself.

We used to say that my mother could take someone down and not even mess up the shine on his shoes—she was that good at speaking her mind without making a mess of things. I think those of us who aren't quite at Mom's level hold back out of fear that we're going to make things worse if we dare to stand up for ourselves or own up to our feelings. While that's possible, I've found it almost never happens. Don't let things fester or stew.

15. Expect challenges. Smart people are never naïve about the journey. They often expect bumps in the road, and they know how to navigate them. If you anticipate detours and curves along the way, you're less likely to let them trouble you. If you can train yourself to see those junctures as gateways to solutions, you'll speed right through them. And when you can't do that, you'll fail and learn. We discussed this a bit before, but it can always stand to be reinforced.

Those who acknowledge their missteps almost invariably say that the challenges gave them a bigger platform, a stronger lesson, and a better story. My mom told me, *"You don't fail when you fall. You only fail when you don't get back up or when you blame someone else for pushing you."* Bottom line: Take ownership. Your life is your creation. As Benjamin Disraeli said, "We are not victims of circumstance; we are creators of circumstance."

When you mess up or get kicked to the curb, you'll really see who you are. That's when you get to develop the emotional fitness that will take you the distance. For the longest time in my marriage to my children's father, I tried and tried and tried some more to make it work. When it ended, I was destroyed by the notion of not being able to create a home for my kids with their dad. I was heartbroken for myself, of course, but even more devastated by what I thought was hurting my children. I spent years focused on what I'd "lost" and the damage I was doing to the kids. I felt like I was in that Whac-a-Mole game—every time I popped up my head, it got hammered back down.

Our relationship's demise was due to a clash of worldviews. More than a question of who was right or wrong, it was just different ways of seeing most everything. When careers are on fire and kids are underfoot, there's little time to question our essence. We were too busy trying to get through it all. My ex and I both knew what we were doing (or not doing), but mostly we ignored the issues or delayed dealing with them. I mention this because it's easy to let the years of your life add up while you play the waiting game—waiting for the right time or the right opportunity to push you out of your false sense of security. It was really arrogant of me to think that if I could just hang on longer and try something else, I could make it work.

The decision had been made for me. I was emotionally betrayed, and I had not been chosen. That was a huge bash to my ego, and it took my sister and several others a long time to hammer that point home. *During those dark days of questioning everything, I sat with my pain, walked with it, gave in to it, and ultimately let it be with me until it no longer served me.* Emotion drives behavior, and those actions determine your quality of life.

Your own power lies in your decisions. I had to decide that I deserved to be happy. I had to decide that my heart might build up some scar tissue, but it would keep beating even stronger than before. I had to determine that I was doing all I could to protect my children and that they would be secure in their dad's and my love for them, even if we weren't a single parenting unit. Mostly I had to make the choice to let go and move forward. Only then could I begin the process of healing, forgiving, and rebuilding. Now their father; my husband, Steven; and I all respect each other and work well together toward our children's best interest. It's a long way from hurt and anger, and I'm proud of how much we've all grown. I think life is about beginnings, and that means it all comes alive when something else ends. I said this earlier, sometimes things fall apart so you can prove to yourself that you can put them back together again. Luckily, I had a bit of experience with disappointment before.

MY TAKE: LEEZA'S LENS

Adapt. Adjust. Move On.

If you never fail, you probably aren't taking big enough risks. No one gets to the finish line without the privilege, the blessing, and the gift of falling on her face multiple times. Guaranteed, every successful person you know with a mantel full of awards and walls lined with accolades also has closets and drawers filled with missteps, misfires, mistakes, and screwups. Smart people know how to view those failures. They're the portals, bridges, tunnels, and tethers to success. The trick is to recognize that when they're happening.

One of my career "kisses"—that is, of being allowed to climb up because of falling down—came in New York. When I moved to the Big Apple in the fall of 1982, my "New York state of mind" was a combo of panic and intimidation. I was full of swagger and confidence on the outside, but I was freaked out by even the thought of the city. I had pictures in my mind of sophisticated dinner parties populated with urbane literati discussing deep topics over fancy food and pricey wine. Witty banter peppered with French phrases and oblique quotations, informed discussions about global issues, and insightful observations into art and commerce were, I was sure, part of a routine evening in NYC. I was never going to be able to keep up.

Now there was no reason for me to feel apprehensive, no matter what waited for me. My parents had always been beyond supportive and never made me feel like there was anything I couldn't do. Still, I figured it was a fluke that the producers at *Two on the Town* wanted to consider me. When I was asked to audition, I treated it like a goof. I'd never seen the city and it was the station's dime, so what the heck.

1982. My shoulder pads weren't big enough to hold up NYC!

I'll never figure out why they offered me the job. Everyone around me was wearing the requisite black, while I auditioned in my favorite denim ensemble with roughed-up leather trim. They all had severe Sassoon hair, while I was doggedly dedicated to my Farrah flip. They were ghostly pale; I had a mahogany tan. Maybe it was my beyond-hip fringed boots that tipped the scales my way—well, that and my metropolitan, "Hi, y'all! How ya doin'?" That showed 'em I was their uptown girl. Whatever it was, I was offered the job and took it, figuring they wanted me for me.

Uh, not exactly. Within minutes of saying yes, the show unleashed a brigade of hair people, makeup artists, stylists, and voice coaches intent on transforming Daisy Mae into Audrey Hepburn. My Aquanetted hair fell in sheets to the floor, makeup was blended, racks of black clothes were wheeled in, and hot-pink nails were toned down to misty pearl. I was lost and alone. Lucky for me, I soon met a producer who changed my life: Andrea Ambandos. She was a woman who knew what she wanted and went toe-to-toe with the boys to get it. I'd never met anyone like her—gorgeously pulled-together with cutting-edge style. Oh, there were strong women in the South, but their battles were fought with charm, heart-melting grace, and warm wit. I'd seen my mom, sorority sisters, and belle-like girlfriends move mountains without a ruffled feather or anything close to a confrontation.

Andrea thrived on confrontation. At work, she expected on-time perfection with no excuses. Interns burst into tears. Technicians cowered in their dark edit bays, and frightened field producers performed miracles to keep her happy. But before you start equating her with *The Devil Wears Prada*, know this: She was truly interested in helping everyone be their best, and we all knew that underneath her tough exterior was the most loyal heart of gold. Through Andrea, I realized what it meant to own your life. She spoke her mind, meant what she said, and backed it up with action. She expected people to respect her, and they did.

As the weeks flew by, my relationship with Andrea became more sisterly—if the sisters were separated at birth, with one being needy and the other busy redefining independence. But Andrea covered me with her blanket of cool, and she kept me in the game when I was unsure. Along with my cohost, Robb Weller (still one of the nicest people I've ever worked with), we tore up the five boroughs of New York. We would be out in the field and get word that the research showed we should be more urbane, so we'd rewrite the copy. Then we'd find out viewers wanted us to be more accessible and less metropolitan, so we'd do that. I guess it was a great lesson that you can't be all things to all people, but we sure tried. And as hard as we kept pushing, we still got the call from the execs: "Don't hurry home; we put your stuff in a box by the door." The news came while we were on location in Rio: "The show is canceled."

And that was that. Even Andrea couldn't stop it.

It was the first time I'd been fired, and the ink wasn't even dry on my contract. The brownstone I just bought was still filled with moving boxes. I did the only thing I knew to do; I pulled my fringed boots out of the closet and my pink lip gloss out of my purse. Boots and lips—I was armed and ready, locked and loaded. Next!

I love this quote that's attributed to David Brinkley: "Lay a firm foundation with the bricks that others throw at you." I'm living proof that a bend in the road is not the end of the road. Walk with the hurt, but not for long. Adapt, adjust, and move on. I know it sounds simplistic, but for decades this has been the technique that has kept me afloat in the stream of life.

Andrea has always been there for me

Today, Andrea is one of my closest friends. The job didn't last, but the friendship did. Robb Weller became my cohost again on *ET,* and we've always liked and respected each other. The point is this: Commit to your work ethic, invest in your relationships, and guard your reputation. These are the things that last.

The way you exit a situation is perhaps more important than the grand entrance. Your integrity is your calling card for what's next. It's easy to be the queen when you're wearing the tiara, but your Goddess Quotient is really measured by how you react when you're dethroned and have to take off the diamonds.

Okay, great work! Taking a deep dive into growing your spiritual life, owning who you are, increasing your Goddess Quotient, loving yourself, eating well, and reducing stress are big factors in a successful second take. Now I think you're ready to move on and make sure you see yourself as the fabulous face of your own show!

Chapter 9

KNOW WHERE YOU'RE GOING, LOOK GOOD WHEN YOU GET THERE

"Beauty without grace is the hook without the bait."

— RALPH WALDO EMERSON

The title of this chapter has always been my mantra. I think it takes care of both sides of the coin of our experience as women. To be fulfilled, I believe we have to have a road map, a mission statement, and a plan of action, or else we'll always feel lost. So knowing where we're going is the basis for reinvention of any kind. Then we sure as heck want to look good when we get there, right?

As women, we gain so much as we age: wisdom, perspective, confidence, security, resilience, and on and on. But none of that stuff really seems to rock our world, does it? We don't wake up on our 50th birthday, throw back the curtains, and rejoice to the world: "I am a strong woman who knows where she's going! And that's beautiful!" Why isn't this enough? It's because most of the time, our age-earned attributes have nothing to do with physical beauty, so with the culture we live in, we end up feeling less and less valuable with each birthday.

I wish I could tell you that your skin is going to tighten over time by itself, or that your eyelids are never going to droop, or that you'll never feel bad about your neck (to quote the late Nora Ephron). None of that is going to happen, but here's the deal: We know beauty is in the eye of the beholder (in this case, that's you), and *you* need to decide that at every age, you are a wonderful sight to behold! I've chosen to redefine what I think beauty should mean at any age: *A fierce combination of strength and grace wrapped up in the best possible physical package.*

Don't misunderstand me. While a woman is beautiful when she embodies strength and grace, it doesn't mean that she goes down without a fight—and that includes challenging time and gravity! You should absolutely do what feels right for you. What I most want to get across, though, is that you can't be or feel completely beautiful (to yourself and the world) without first being lit from within by the knowledge and fulfillment of knowing who you are and being firmly on your own path (know where you're going). Then you must channel that energy to present your inner beauty and strength in the best physical package (look good when you get there).

So, since we've been talking throughout the book about owning your life to make sure you chart a course to get where you want to go, I'm going to use this chapter to focus on outward beauty: the products, tips, and tricks to help you unlock your best self.

Redefining Beauty

Maybe it's because I work in an industry where looks are a commodity, or maybe it's because I developed a makeup line, but I'm fascinated by beauty and the business of being beautiful. After interviewing gorgeous women from Faye Dunaway and Bette Davis to Angelina Jolie and Scarlett Johansson, I've seen the power that comes from appearance. I've also seen how really remarkable women have used that to make their "beauty mark" in the world. It's the way they influence others, effect change, and commandeer the spotlight to shine it on social injustice.

My strong Southern mother always told me, "Pretty is as pretty does," and a woman of strength is always beautiful. As I shared in the "Be a Woman of Strength" poem earlier, a strong woman has confidence, while a woman of strength has grace to go with it. The most stunningly beautiful creature loses all allure if she hasn't found how to use her looks for something more lasting. How many of us know drop-dead gorgeous girls who are hard-pressed for an answer to hello? After a spellbinding initial meeting, it's rare for these folks to get a callback out in real life. It's one of the essential truths: Women who have graciousness and goodness always win out over those who have a physical package without any of the spiritual essence to give it value.

What is beauty anyway? Well, if you believe the images from the fashion and entertainment worlds, it ends at size two, doesn't go beyond age 30, and usually involves lips that are pumped so full they create a "trout mouth" of seduction. But what if we had a world where women didn't have to shrink to fit in and we appreciated beauty in all its forms? What if we forgave ourselves for our physical imperfections and for what we lack, and then focused on embracing and improving what we do have? If you look at the science of beauty, it talks about symmetry and the spacing of our features. I think it's more about having a certain quality that isn't necessarily inherited and has nothing to do with winning the genetics lottery. I believe true, lasting beauty is something that can be developed and learned. *And as Martin Buxbaum says,*

"Some people, no matter how old they get, never lose their beauty—they merely move it from their faces into their hearts."

I've traveled all over the world—Fiji, Europe, Africa, Thailand, China, India, Morocco, and beyond—and I can tell you for sure that the most beautiful women aren't the ones with the most symmetrical features or whose figures are proportionally perfect. The most attractive women all have one thing in common: They're lit from within. There's a confident security about them that causes you to look past the size of their breasts and the texture of their skin.

A New Perspective

We tend to fall into the trap of believing that we *are* our bodies; and when we think of ourselves, that's what rushes front and center in our mind. We never stop seeing ourselves through the external packaging, but at a certain point, we begin to experience something new. As we move forward along the age continuum, we can begin to separate the physical from the spiritual. We realize that our spiritual aspect isn't dependent upon the size, shape, and firmness of our bodies; we can appreciate our physical gifts while not being desperately attached to them. I don't think of this as a loss, but rather as a release from the struggle.

Look at those pictures of yourself from high school when you were thinking, *I am so fat! I wish I were prettier!* Now you realize just how hot you really were. So my question to you is this: Why would today be any different? Ten years from now, you'll no doubt look back at this moment and wonder why you didn't get just how great you were. You are beautiful and sexy *now*, so what are you saving it for? Enjoy it, flaunt it, *use* it!

This chapter will show you how to maximize what you've got. A little disclaimer before we dive in to some of my favorite beauty techniques and shortcuts, though: No one has made more hair, makeup, and fashion mistakes than I have. My advantage has been that the learning curve has been escalated by seeing those goof-ups on the air or in countless "What Was She Thinking?" editorial roundups in magazines.

I've had decades of sitting in the makeup chair while some of the industry's best and most skilled artists brilliantly applied paint, paste, and pencil. Keith Crary, my friend and makeup artist from my days at Paramount and Telepictures, remains my favorite. I studied his artistry in the mirror for years; and while I've picked up some tricks along the way, I'm no professional. I figure you probably aren't, either. But when I developed my makeup line, I became a dedicated student of all things beauty and have reached millions of women worldwide through the rare privilege of being in touch with them and sharing ideas, worries, and secrets about skin care, makeup, and beyond. Beauty is a universal touchstone for us. For better or worse, it's part of being female. I say for better, because while we talk about the makeup that's on our face, we get to talk about the things in our hearts and on our minds, as well.

So, it's cool if we can be loyal to the face we've made, but that doesn't mean we have to "go gentle into that good night." Aging fearlessly and gracefully doesn't mean that we shouldn't take advantage of every product and tool out there to help us be our best. So, with apologies to every beauty professional out there, these are my own life-tested, red-carpet-reviewed tips and tricks. Let's do it!

MY BEAUTY DISCLAIMER

Love my GlamBand! Julie, Dean & Keith

Many of you (like me) have all the latest cosmetics, accessories, and fashion must-haves. I often buy them online, through in-home parties, and at high-end boutiques. Imagine my excitement when I moved to the Glamour Capital of the World and had instant access to the best of the best! We're talking *me,* a recovering redneck from Irmo, South Carolina, getting tressed and dressed by the industry's most sought-after "glam squads." I have spent 30-something years being like an apprentice; just opening up while all that style and taste poured through the vast wasteland of my parched, deserted sense of how to put myself together.

Does this make me a beauty professional? Absolutely not, but I *have* learned a thing or two at the hands of my favorite beauty authorities—my longtime friends and personal GlamBand, Keith Crary on makeup, Dean Banowetz on hair, and Julie Kozak on wardrobe. We have worked together on *ET, Extra!,* my talk show, live events, and about 5,000 photo shoots. That's a lot of lip gloss and leg-cover cream, not to mention worry, celebration, support, and friendship. We often get the band back together, like on the day we did a shoot with our favorite photographer, Ron Derhacopian, for the picture that ultimately became the cover of this book.

Many of you could write this section of the book in several languages while filing your nails and tweezing your brows. I didn't write it for you, so feel free to skip it, skim it, or see if you agree with it. But

With photographer
Ron Derhacopian

I didn't think we could talk about reinventing on the inside, where all the emotional work is done, without talking about the outside, which might need its own Take 2.

Disclaimer: Keith, Dean, and Julie still have to wrestle me down and fight against my urge to revert back to my "shopping mall hair," my "raccoon eyes," and my "Sorority Sue" style. Hey, you can take the girl out of the South, but you can't take the South out of me!

214

This is the artistry of my friend
Christian Scott, whose brilliance
could transform anyone!

MY TAKE: LEEZA'S LENS

"We've Got a Fatty!"

I remember first coming to Hollywood by way of Texas after my brief stint in New York. This was in the 1980s, long before zero became a size on the clothing rack. Still, it was the *Flashdance* era, and we all got the message.

To that end, Marie Osmond spent her teen years disappearing on her TV show—all behind the perfect on-camera smile and backstage threats telling her to lose more weight. I had no idea then that I'd grow to be friends with Marie, and she probably had no idea that she'd later inspire a nation to get real about their weight, starting with her appearance on *Dancing with the Stars*.

As you learned from what I shared about my experience, I found every aspect of the show to be challenging, and I've never been more aware of my shape and size. My biggest fear should have been about learning the dance steps, but instead it was, *Oh my God, I've got to wear those costumes!* Everyone on the show looked like they just stepped out of a St. Tropez advertisement, all bronzed up and glistening with the kind of tans that we think should cover cellulite and any other sins of the flesh. The problem is it doesn't work like that—at least not for me.

I recall resisting at first, saying I didn't see why I had to tan. There were gasps all around: *Oh no! The lights are way too strong* not *to tan.* So there I stood with my legs spread and my arms over my head, getting sprayed down buck naked next to the world's most perfect dancer bodies, silently repeating my mantra: *My body is strong and healthy, my body is strong and healthy.* I was trying to hang on to what really mattered when all I wanted was one day of those cellulite-free thighs and a butt that's lifted so high it starts at your waist.

It reminded me of an experience when I was a new reporter at *ET*. I was doing a cameo appearance on a sitcom, and when I went to the wardrobe department, the stylist took one look at me and announced, "We've got a fatty! Get out the size sixes!" She cackled, threw her head back, and put her hand on my shoulder, saying, "Don't worry, honey. We're gonna find you something nice."

Wardrobe departments have plenty of zeroes, some twos, a few fours, but not a lot of sixes. No matter who you are or how your body looks, there's always someone or something to give you the impression that you're not enough. No matter how we see it, someone else will have a different view.

This point was brought home to me courtesy of my son Nathan. One night he was watching an episode of *The Fresh Prince of Bel-Air* on Nick at Night. He said, "Mom, you never told me you did that show. I saw your episode. Your hair was so short—and then they were talking about your legs!"

"Well, everyone doesn't see me as an old lady like you do!" I quipped. "I used to kinda be known for my legs."

Pause.

"Mom, that's disgusting!"

Skin Care

Never, ever skip cleansing or you will pay the price. I cleanse and tone in the morning and again at night. When I remove my makeup in the evening, I like to use a gentle foaming cleanser. Leaving makeup on and not cleansing thoroughly can clog pores and lead to breakouts.

I am careful not to dry out my thin, combination skin, never using hot water and exfoliating only once a week. I use a moisturizing mask at least once a week as well. But every day I put moisturizer with SPF 15 on my face, neck, and décolletage; and I apply the moisturizer all the way down to my cleavage. Age spots and discoloration don't have to happen in these areas if we protect ourselves well enough, early enough.

I use serums around my eyes at night and a heavier neck cream. When we sleep, our bodies go into recovery mode, and I want to give my skin what it needs most—moisture! I use SPF moisturizer on my hands, too, since that's where age begins to show the earliest. Driving exposes the tops of your hand to excessive sun, so don't skimp on the sunscreen.

Regardless of skin type, avoid soap, which can strip your natural oils; and pick a moisturizer or makeup that contains a low level of sunscreen, such as SPF 15. It keeps your skin soft and smooth while preventing the negative effects of harmful ultraviolet (UV) rays. I never go bare, and I usually wear mineral powder foundation with a natural SPF 15 every day, even over another base.

Enhancing your beauty means understanding how to work around your features and accentuating your assets. Knowing the shape of your face is as important to putting on makeup as knowing the shape of your body is to choosing the right clothes. There are six basic face shapes: oval, round, long, square, heart, and diamond. To find your shape, visit: **www.eyebrowz.com/faceshape .htm,** or figure it out the old-fashioned way: Put on a headband to reveal your entire face. With eyeliner, draw a few dots around the periphery of your face (or imagine them). If you connected the dots, what shape is formed? I have an oval face; but when I was younger, it tended to be on the round side because I had chubby cheeks. Oh, how I wish for those now!

Experiment and play with lots of products. Samples are available at most cosmetic counters, so try something new. Take on another role, if just for the night.

Inspect the Tools You Use

When we think of skin care, we think about cleaning, moisturizing, and SPF. But when was the last time you paid attention to your brushes? Bacteria can build up, get into your pores, and irritate your skin, so clean your brushes once a month by washing them with a mild cleanser. I use baby shampoo.

Before we get into specifics about makeup itself, it's important to make sure you have the right tools to apply it. Investing in a good set of brushes can enhance your look by giving you the right brush for the right product.

I've found that I like natural bristles best, but you can find good synthetic options, too—even at the drugstore. If you can, rub the brush over your hand a few times to see if it's losing bristles. If it's not and it's reasonably soft, I think you're good to go. The trick now is to make sure you're using the right brush for the right application. I've found that this can help even the least expensive makeup look like a million bucks. You can go crazy with choices, but I basically use just six brushes.

• For eyes, you need these:

1. A flat brush with firmer bristles. Use this for picking up color packs on shadow overall.

2. A soft, domed brush. This works for making the outer V shape and contouring the crease. A rounded end helps with blending and creating a smoky eye.

3. A flat liner brush (or a super-thin pointed brush). Usually, I use cream eyeliner, but I can use these brushes with liquids and cake liners, too. I like to have both brushes to dip, wet or dry, into powders or creams to go on top of the line or smudge it out. Because I wear false eyelashes so often, this brush allows me to cover up a goof if I ever make a mistake putting them on. I start with the outer corner of the eye and kind of wiggle my way in with the brush.

A BEAUTY BASIC

Your skin is thirsty, and so is your brain. Staying hydrated will help your complexion and your performance, and keep you from overeating. All of your organs function better when you're properly hydrated; and being that your skin is your largest organ, remembering to drink water will offer a beauty quick fix that's fast, cheap, and effective!

Dehydration can wreak havoc on your hand-eye coordination and decrease your mental sharpness. Here are some basic guidelines: Before you work out, drink 16 ounces of fluid. While you're working out, drink 5 to 10 ounces every 15 to 20 minutes—I always just remember 10 in 20. Afterward have more—16 ounces for each pound of body weight—thanks to all the moisture lost during the activity through sweat. In other words, drink more than you probably think. On a day with no workout, that means 48 ounces. If your urine throughout the day is clear, you're good to go; if not, add more water.

• For your face, you need the following brushes:

4. A foundation brush. I find liquids and creams to be messy and offer unpredictable coverage. I only use mineral foundation, so brushes are important. I like a big, rounded one that's full but not too dense to sweep on the mineral powder and blend softly. Many women use a flat-edge, soft, "Kabuki" brush for this, too.

I dip the brush into the pot of minerals, then tap it on the countertop to remove the excess and work the product into the bristles. Then I just brush it on, "layering" the mineral foundation in the places where I need more. I also use this brush for my setting powder, which I put on after everything else is done. I love it— it's like airbrushing.

If you use cream or liquid foundation, an angled brush that's tight with pretty stiff but flexible bristles is good—certainly better than mixing your fingers with the makeup and getting pore-clogging oils on your face. The angled brush also gives a prettier application than a sponge does. It will help you blend around your chin and prevent streaking.

You might also experiment with a flat-edged "stipple" brush for an airbrushed finish with these types of foundation. Either way, it's best to put the foundation on top of your hand and dab your brush into it.

5. A blush brush. Get an angled brush that's not too big and is designed to work around the apples of your cheeks. Smile, finding the roundest part of the cheek, and in a circular motion, apply color from the cheek rounds to the hairline. Don't use your powder brush for blush because it could cause too much color and streaking.

6. A "spoolie." This is that small spiral brush that you can use on brows or lashes. I like to put a little hairspray on mine to tame unruly brows, and I also de-clump my mascara with it.

Nails

I have an incredibly low-maintenance, high-efficiency lifestyle when it comes to my beauty regimen. While I'd love to indulge in twice-weekly trips to salons for a pamper-fest, with my work and family, I simply don't have time. Chances are you don't, either! The one thing I can't go without, though, is my manicures. I get one every two to three weeks. My natural nails are weak. They peel and don't grow, so I have acrylic nails, which makes polish stay on longer. It doesn't chip between salon visits, something that's important because of my production schedule. I've also found I get long-lasting results with gels. When I don't have time to get to the nail salon, I have found that I can do it myself at home with a kit by Nailene that is surprisingly easy for do-it-yourself acrylics! Either way, to keep my cuticles from drying, I use argan oil every night.

Makeup

If I were sent to a desert island, I'd probably take along my moisturizer with sunblock and Binaca breath spray! Seriously, people joke with me about it because I always have it with me—fresh breath gives me confidence! Beyond that, probably a tube of mascara. I have really wimpy lashes. How about you? Luckily, we're not stuck on a desolate sandbar somewhere, so we have a few more options, but let's start with the basics.

Beautiful, glowing skin is always your best asset. If you're tired and stressed, though, you probably don't have it naturally. I could go bare skinned when I was younger; but since I passed 35, I've found it necessary to use foundation to even out dark spots, conceal blemishes, and just give me an overall even look.

Foundation

I like the goof-proof easiness of a mineral powder foundation, and I've never found one I love more than my Sheer Cover that I helped develop years ago. It's super blendable, and I love that it contains natural minerals that cause light to shine *away* from your flaws, deflecting the things you don't want to show. It's what keeps skin looking luminescent and youthful because the structure of the minerals causes them to overlap on your skin, giving great coverage while still looking sheer and dewy. For me, some of the liquids and creams or sticks can enhance the look of enlarged pores around my nose and they don't last as long. Some days, I'll put on a tinted moisturizer or a natural tinted liquid and then brush mineral powder over the top. But the way makeup looks and feels is such a personal thing, and your preference will probably change over time. It's a good idea to experiment; and when you see someone wearing something that looks amazing, ask her what's she's using! Don't be afraid to change it up.

Regardless of what you use, if you aren't using a primer, do yourself a favor and try it. The job of the primer is to act as spackle before you apply the paint! It smooths the surface, fills in lines, and preps your skin for foundation. It's especially important if you have enlarged pores. Look for one that will do double duty and give you skin-soothing repair or treatment ingredients as well.

It's best to apply makeup in natural daylight; when I'm traveling, I always take a magnifying compact to check my look by the window before heading out. The worst is in fluorescent lighting, which tends to give off a greenish tone. That's probably what you have in your office, and it's what you'll find at most department-store cosmetic counters. It makes everything look worse, so you'll tend to put on too much concealer or blush. That's also how you end up buying something that looks one way in the store only for it to look nothing like that at home. Coated or halogen bulbs are the best lighting for makeup because they're softer.

So make sure you check out what kind of lighting you're using before you apply any of your makeup. You want soft light from all sides, like you get in a round, lighted, magnifying mirror; overhead light isn't helpful because it casts harsh shadows. Plus, most household lamps are yellow light, and they don't show enough detail. Invest in a well-lighted makeup mirror that magnifies at least ten times. Mine has settings for office, daylight, evening, and home, and it is indispensable.

Blending is everything when it comes to foundation. I always blend my mineral makeup into my neck and décolletage; and in the evenings, I brush on a little bit of highlighter on my cleavage for a bit of extra intrigue. Use anything that shimmers very sparingly; but a little highlighter under your brow bone, just off the apples of your cheeks, and even down your shins can catch the light and make you feel confident and radiant.

Concealer and Powder

Concealer is your best friend. Use it right after you moisturize —in fact, I often combine the two steps. For under your eyes, choose a color that's a shade lighter than your skin. Most women will want a hint of yellow to correct dark circles, which tend to appear blue without it. But whether you have that challenge or not, I think everyone benefits from a slightly lighter color around the eye to open and add interest.

When determining the right color concealer for your face overall, go for a close match. I always use this product on my eyelids, too. It provides a great base for shadow and evens out any skin-tone issues. I put it under my eyes; down the center of my nose,;and on the outer corners of my mouth, which tend to cave in. I like a creamy concealer because it won't tug at the delicate skin around my eyes. I'm not fond of the sticks because they often drag across the thin eye skin. Even if you use a concealer that comes with a round sponge applicator or something else, you'll probably want to use a brush for precision application. Remember to blot it on, using circular motions rather than rubbing.

I set it all with a finishing powder. This acts like airbrushing for the canvas of your face and helps blend the concealer, blush, highlighters, and shadows. I use it after I've applied my cheek color and eye shadow, but before mascara. The powder helps coat lashes, which primes them for maximum mascara application. Mascara will glide on, do its job, and stay put until you take it off. You can check out videos of some of my makeup demonstrations at **www .leezagibbons.com**.

Eyes

Nothing makes a difference in a face more than eyes that look alive. Before we get to the tricks that make your eyes alluring, let's start with how you wake up. If, like many women, your eyes are puffy, then we have to deal with that first. Overnight, fluid can build up under your eyes in the sockets that may be covered by looser skin as you age because of standard muscle sagging. If that's you, you're just gonna have to give yourself a little more time to get out the door. To reduce puffiness, get a bag of frozen peas or corn and rest it on your eyes for ten minutes or so. Then take some cold chamomile tea and dip a thin cloth in it. Ring it out and place that over your eyes for another five minutes, followed by an eye cream that has caffeine. The caffeine will help reduce the swelling, too.

All right, now that we've leveled the playing field . . . you know those inner corners? Well, I call them "the cave," because most women are dark there. To open up my eyes, I add a light shadow or powder to the inner corner and then a lighter color on the lid, just below the crease. A chocolate-brown shade is my favorite to apply in the crease, up to the brow bone on the outside of the eye to give a wider look. Then I use a warm highlight right under the brown to finish. Light reflects off the lighter parts and makes my eyes appear larger and more alert, more interested, and more alluring! I often use a white pencil to line the inner rim (waterline), just above the lower lashes. This does wonders on camera and also opens the eye in real life. For a dramatic effect for evenings, do this with a dark brown, black, or navy pencil.

And speaking of evenings, you can't beat a smoky eye at night. It's fun and glamorous and breaks up the monotony of daytime makeup. You can always create a mysterious look by applying a dark color to the outer edge of the eye in a V shape, or take the color from your lash line all the way through to the crease. Then smudge color along the lower lashes for a sultry look. Day or night, unless you have perfectly shaped almond eyes, it works to extend your liner with a slight flick upward at the outside of the eye to "lift" it.

I laugh and call myself a pack-a-day addict when it comes to false eyelashes. It's no joke that each of my kids could apply a full set before they reached the age of five. I often got ready for events with my lashes in one hand and a baby on my lap. The kids used to call it "planting corn," because I dip each lash (mediums) into the glue starting with the outside, gradually moving to smaller ones (shorts) toward the middle of the eye until I get close to my nose.

I prefer dark-brown eyeliner, typically using a cream liner before the lashes go on. After they're secure, I often use a soft pencil or liquid to line the top of the lashes at the lash line, starting with the outside corners and narrowing as I go inward. I usually apply a very light coat of mascara, except at night, when I really layer up the outer edges. If you've never used false lashes before, know that it takes some practice; so while I do love lashes and think almost every woman looks good in them, don't try this for the first time right before a big event.

I order my lashes by the case (is that pathetic?) and wear the short ones for daytime and mediums at night. For on-camera work, I always use mediums on the outer corners with a light coat of mascara. I've tried the products that claim to grow your lashes, and they do work for me, but I found that the new growth came in stick straight. I could never get the look I wanted, so I've remained loyal to my falsies.

Cheeks

If you want a natural blush of color, use a powder blush, which I think is much easier to blend than other types. Apply it with a natural-bristle brush that's rounded on the sides or angled, and don't use one that's bigger than the apples of your cheeks. This will help you make sure you don't use too much, and you can avoid that clown look. Regardless of your face shape, for a flushed look, smile and apply on the apples of the cheeks and blend up and back toward the temples to soften. If you need to narrow your face or if you want a more sculpted look, put a deeper color blush just under the cheekbones and use your brush to blend, blend, blend.

I also have lots of wedged sponges on hand, which are great for blending after your final touches. Remember that applying cheek color lower than your nose can make your face appear droopy.

If you're fair, go for rosy or soft peach colors; medium skin tones can experiment a bit more. But unless you have darker skin, I'd skip the intense options like coral or magenta! Highlighters are a personal preference. If you use one, go with warm tones and use small amounts. A little light reflecting from this product can work on the outer edges of the cheeks, lightly on top of the apples, and even under the cheekbone, depending on what look you're going for. Remember, you can always put more on, but it's really frustrating to try to take it down if you've put too much on.

Lips

It's true that after your mid-30s, your lips begin to lose definition and color, but a luscious look doesn't have to be a memory. I use a liner, but again, blending is everything; I use a lip brush to make sure the lip color and liner don't give that "Oreo cookie" effect of two dark lines sandwiching the light middle!

I use a soft liner in a nude shade; and I usually continue the liner color all over the lip, too, as a base. That gives me a solid shade to start, and it really helps my color last longer. Plus, it keeps my lipstick from feathering.

Next, I apply my lip color. I don't like the really wet or sticky glosses, so I normally go with a tube that's a natural, soft matte pink or peach. I make one pass on the lips directly from the tube, and then I dip my lip brush into the lipstick and finish the application with more precision. I use a gloss or wand highlighter on the middle of my bottom lip to plump and add attention.

Normally, I choose the same lip color no matter what clothes I'm wearing, since it's neutral. I have lots of glosses and highlighters, though. One of my favorite looks is to take a Sheer Cover

Lip-to-Lid Highlighter in pink and dab some of the loose minerals right in the center of my bottom lip. Then I use the same color under my brows and on my cheekbones near the temples.

Eyebrows

Eyebrows can make or break a look. They frame your face, enhance your eyes, and can even change your expression! I say that after cleansing and moisturizing with SPF, seeking advice about eyebrows is the next most important thing you can do for your face. Hey, eyebrows are complicated, so it's no wonder most of us mess up here big time! Thick, thin, long, short, threading, waxing, tweezing —what's the look? What's in vogue? We've all attempted the arc, but for many of us who aren't artists with tweezers, it proved a futile effort, if not disastrous. I've made the mistake of overtweezing and undertweezing; I've had them too dark and too light. One day before a live event, my hairdresser put something on my brows to lighten them. It must have been a potent mixture, because within five minutes my skin had bubbled up and my brows disintegrated! Now I'm very sensitive about this feature.

I prefer to apply pressed brow color with a stiff, angled brush, but pencils are good *if* you have enough thickness in your brow line. Your brows should provide a beautiful frame for your face and interest for your eyes; they should *not* be overdrawn, sparse, too thick, or too dark. Use a sharp angled tweezer and tweeze right after a shower when the follicles are open, and it will hurt less.

Your brows should begin right above your tear duct and the arch, or peak, in line with the outer side of your iris. If you hold a pencil from the base of your nostril to the outside of your eye, that is the angle at which your brow should end—about 45 degrees from the outside corner of the eye.

Even if you are overtweezed or have a unibrow right now, you're not beyond help! There are good kits out there, but seeking some professional advice is easy; most of the time, free consultation services are offered at makeup counters. Try spending time on one of the free online virtual sites where you can try everything from brow shapes to hairstyles: **www.modiface.com** and **www.taaz.com** are two of my favorites.

Hair

Look at a woman's hair, and you might be able to tell her mood since it's another way of expressing herself. Appearing on television every day, there's an argument to be made for consistency, but too much standardization is boring. I've kinda settled down with my hair now, although I have to admit that it's gotten me into trouble more than anything else over the years. After I arrived at *ET,* I was sent  to a beauty consultant, and the man promptly dyed my hair red and cut it. I was miserable for a year. It might have looked good on Bette Midler, but it did not look good on me!

Just past my shoulders is probably the best length for me, as I find it goes with more clothing styles. It can easily move from trendy to classic, from casual to sophisticated, without much of an effort. I also find it's easy for me to pull it back or throw it up. I've tried many variations with length before settling here: bobbed, blunted, shagged, lightly layered, heavily beveled, and everything in between. I've had it cut in angles so that it has energy and moves when I walk through the audience; and I've had it pulled back, put up, and swept to the side.

Why is hairstyle so tied into our psychological state? When I used to tape two shows a day, I was known for cutting my hair between the first and second episodes because I needed a psychological lift. Now I sometimes give myself a "bang-dectomy" before going on air at HSN. I must confess, though, there have been times when I've suffered from haircut hangover—that day after a trim when your hair is in shock and you still haven't figured out how to work with it. Thank goodness now there are extensions to cover the damage!

I've been lucky enough to work with the best of the best in the hair and makeup world. As I mentioned, I've learned a lot being in the chair getting ready for shows and events. Now I color and cut my own hair (except for once a year); do my own highlights; and have even developed my own hair extensions, which I wear often. I have an entire wardrobe of extensions in various lengths that I cut myself. No one ever knows when I'm wearing them because they're designed to cascade along your hairline, mimicking the shape of your head.

Here's the coolest thing about them: Because they're synthetic (even though they feel like natural hair), you can apply heat from your normal styling tools up to 350 degrees. While the hair is warm, you give it the shape you want, and then when it cools off, it's set. So in 30 seconds or less, you get a style that stays in even when it's wet! I say that's better than real hair, which often gets limp and falls. With my extensions, I save my natural hair from heat damage from dryers and styling tools, and I get a set that lasts until I apply heat again. Go to **www.leezagibbons.com** to see tips on applying, cutting, and curling hair extensions.

If you've been wearing the same style and color since you graduated high school, make a bold move and *stop it*. You may find that some variation on the same theme really is best for you, but chances are you'll discover other sides of your spirit by unlocking different aspects of your look. Go try on wigs in colors and styles you'd *never* consider and see how they make you feel, or have a virtual makeover. You can upload your picture on one of these websites to try lots of different styles: **www.instyle.com/instyle /makeover** and **http://makeovr.com/hairmixer**.

Remember, your hair responds to your lifestyle; so staying hydrated, eating well, not smoking, and getting enough sleep will affect your hair just like it affects your skin. Here's my short list of basics:

• **Shampooing and conditioning.** I really like WEN products because they don't have the typical soapy lather that strips hair of its natural oils; but sometimes I just like suds, so I mix it up. I found that periodically rotating what I use works because hair will respond differently to various products. No matter what you choose, resist the urge to lather more than once; if you have oily hair, it will only stimulate more oil production.

• **Drying.** What you dry with does make a difference. If you can invest in a higher-end blow-dryer, you won't be sorry. With cheap dryers, the heating element may be plastic or metal that can burn your hair with uneven heat. Over time (and it doesn't take much time) your hair will look dry, frizzy, and brittle. Look for ceramic heating (often it is infused with tourmaline) that delivers a more gentle, even heat. You may hear about ionic heating—that's a good thing. Inexpensive dryers can send positive ions into your hair that opens up the shaft and makes it look frizzy or damaged. You want negative ions (tourmaline does this) to close the shaft and trap in the moisture, leaving hair shinier. Why else do you want this? It can dry your hair 70 percent faster!

Overall, I say if you're paying for the good stuff, the higher the wattage the better (1,500 plus is my suggestion). But regardless, don't leave the blow-dryer in one spot for more than a few seconds; keep it moving and at a good distance away from your hair. Gently use your fingers or a pick to untangle any knots while your hair is drying.

• **Combing and brushing.** Use a brush with bristles made from natural animal hairs because it's softer and more flexible, which means it's less damaging. I swear by my Mason Pearson brush. Plastic brushes and combs can cause static in your hair. Choose widely spaced bristles or teeth and smooth tips. Sharp-tooth combs can damage your hair, cause split ends, and scratch your scalp. To keep your brushes and combs clean, wash them weekly using soap or shampoo.

When you can, comb your hair to remove any tangles before brushing it. Start at the ends so you can gently get tangles out as you work your way up. Hair is most fragile when it's wet, so wait until it's almost completely dry before brushing it to avoid a lot of damage and breakage.

Down-Home Beauty

I love experimenting with new ways to pamper myself. As a child, I became a believer in homemade beauty treatments when my mother used to wrap my hair in mayonnaise and eggs. I had stringy, limp locks, so Mom whipped up this concoction and wrapped my head in plastic wrap for 30 minutes. Well, it worked. The mayo softens, acts like a moisturizer, and stimulates growth. The egg is antibacterial and will make your hair grow quicker. Now I often add olive oil and take another couple of eggs and separate the whites. (While my hair's getting treated, I use the egg whites as a facial mask to shrink pores.) Try this, but be sure to wash your hair afterward with a clarifying shampoo.

I love home remedies; and if you have honey, almonds, and avocados, it seems there's nothing you can't do! From washing my hair with beer to making oatmeal exfoliants, I'm still a down-home girl from Irmo, South Carolina. Here are some of my favorites:

• **Olive oil tub-side.** Add a tablespoon of olive oil to your bathwater to instantly turn any soak session into a dry-skin treatment. Just be careful stepping out! It gets a little slippery.

• **The power of green.** Avocados have a really high fatty-acid content, which makes for a mega-moisturizer. Mash and apply to a freshly cleansed face, then let sit for 10 to 15 minutes.

• **The itch fix.** Adding a cup of oatmeal to bathwater will soothe itchy, dry skin, and other conditions such as eczema and psoriasis. Use the colloidal oatmeal, which is just oatmeal that has been ground to a fine powder. (You can buy it like that or use your coffee grinder.) Also, regular old oatmeal is a great exfoliant and pore cleanser for your face; I mix it with olive oil. Oats contain lubricating fats that help plump your skin, and olive oil is loaded with nutrients and antioxidants. This mixture can also help detoxify. If you'd like to amplify this facial, just add one egg and two tablespoons of olive oil to a cup of oats.

• **Grow your own.** Aloe vera has saved me from many sunburns. It soothes while it starts to regenerate and moisturize even the most sensitive skin. It's like nature's hydrator. If you grow your own potted aloe vera plant, just crack one of the leaf spikes open to apply pure aloe-vera gel directly to skin. There's nothing like it.

• **Yogurt facial.** You don't have to scrub to get rid of dead skin. Just a few minutes of yogurt will do the trick because of its gentle lactic acid, which ex-foliates and works to close large pores. This beats more abrasive granules and other over-the-counter exfoliators. Make sure you're using plain yogurt, and leave it on about 15 to 20 minutes. Do this two to three times a week.

• **Cucumber hair conditioner.** This is great if you swim in a chlorinated pool and good even if you don't! Just take one beaten egg, one half eggshell full of olive oil, and one peeled cucumber. Blend 'em all together, apply evenly to your hair, leave on 15 to 20 minutes, then rinse.

If you want to see videos of more of my home remedies and share your own, check out **www.leezagibbons.com.**

Fashion

I like to keep things basic but not boring. I enjoy having fun with my fashion. I don't want to run the risk of being too trendy, though, so I incorporate a sense of liveliness through color and accessories. For work, I lean toward monochromatic suits with detail and interest above the waist because that's most often how I'm seen on camera.

I'm also all about a solid-colored dress. Aqua and shades of blue are my favorites, almost always with a narrow waist. I have a long torso, and I love dresses that are sleek around the middle and forgiving in the hips. When in doubt, I always reach for a dress. I feel ladylike and powerful when it's cut just above the knee. I don't wear mid-length jackets that break at the hip; I like them either short or below the hip. I think in between is an awkward and unflattering line for many women.

Boots are my fashion staple. I have them in all heel heights, in velvets and leathers, round toe and square toe, from Victorian to funky. I'm tall enough that sometimes I can carry off a little drama with my clothing, but I try to keep it proportionate.

One of my favorite ways to layer is with a sheer blouse and vest under a jacket. I love interesting, sizable pieces of jewelry and find that the best canvas for those is usually something simple and clean, but I especially love to feature a long dress with a sweater, or a sweater dress. I never wear boxy clothes and stay away from raglan shoulders.

I have lots and lots of blouses in my wardrobe, many with great colors and oversized collars—they're a wonderful way to get more mileage from a basic suit. I love luxurious fabrics, and I like my clothes to have a feminine flair, but I have to be careful of fads and trends to avoid looking dated in reruns or reprinted pictures.

Let me just say there are some shots out there that are so plain wrong, they make you wonder if I looked in a mirror when I walked out the door! I have no shame and have posted some for your viewing pleasure at **www.leezagibbons.com**.

Beyoncé, Can You Feel Me?

One of my favorite fashion moments came at the Soul Train Awards. I was presenting an award for the show and my hairstylist, Hollywood Hair Guy Dean Banowetz, and I decided to go all out. (Remember I talked about Dean earlier and his gig with the In Styler.) I love working and playing with Dean—he always inspires me to reach and stretch my limits of prefab beauty. For this ceremony, we figured, *If not here, where?* So he whipped out some magenta-colored extensions along with some colorful feathers for my waist-length hair—mind you, this was way before extensions became de rigueur and before feathers were a common accessory. Julie Kozak, my longtime wardrobe stylist and dear friend, had me in a pair of leather pants and a long duster coat over a sequined halter top. Yep, my dream of becoming one of the Supremes had come true. I got mixed reviews from the fashion brigade. But backstage, Beyoncé (who was then part of Destiny's Child) told me my hair was fierce, and I felt redeemed!

Weight

I've been on every lame diet ever talked about—I used to do all the trendy, goofy plans. There was one called the TWA Stewardess Diet (that's how long ago this was, back when they called flight attendants stewardesses). You would eat a grapefruit one day, then the next day you were supposed to have cottage cheese and hamburger patties, and the following day something like peanut butter. It was this ridiculous, all-over-the-place diet—but I did it religiously for two weeks, lost a pound, and then moved on to the next thing. I've pretty much been into all of them: low carb–high protein, low fat–low carb, and high carb–energy building; fruit diets, rice diets, and liquid shakes. Yet I never stay with them for long. I usually go back to intuitive eating, which is just all things in moderation and letting your body control what your mind is telling you it wants.

When I run down the list of women I most admire for their sense of style and commitment to fitness, they're not on the list because they've achieved physical perfection, but because they make the most of what they have. Most of the women we see on magazine covers and hip TV shows are genetic freaks. I mean, that look is not achievable for most of us no matter how hard we try, so it's counterproductive to obsess over the pursuit of an unobtainable goal. I cheered at the recent news that *Seventeen* magazine had made a commitment to stop airbrushing the girls on the magazine's covers, deciding that it was important to show young women as they really look. Finally! My friend Jamie Lee Curtis made a similar point when she posed for the cover of *More* in her bra top and spandex shorts without any retouching to smooth things out. I always liked Jamie Lee, but after that I loved her even more! She's also a great example of a woman who works out her brain as well as her body. The brain is a muscle, too; and we often forget to keep it properly fueled and challenged. With a strong mind and a fit body, you can really be dangerous.

Winning at staying healthy requires a plan, so here are some tricks that can keep you on track and focused on not sabotaging any weight- or health-related goals you've set:

• Never, ever go to a cocktail party, open house, or any other kind of social function without eating something first. That way, all the delectable goodies won't be nearly as tempting, and you can have just a taste.

• For every glass of wine or cocktail you drink, have a full glass of water. It will keep you from going over your limit and save you calories.

• Buy a couple of new outfits for the season, making sure they're fairly snug. When I do this myself, it makes me less likely to do anything to jeopardize my ability to wear them.

• When you're entertaining, send your guests home with the leftovers (always have plenty of Tupperware on hand), take the surplus to a homeless shelter, or feed it to the neighborhood dogs. Do anything other than put the food back into your refrigerator, where it will call out your name at 2 A.M.

Nutrition is important to me since I want to fuel my body and eat foods that I know can boost my cognitive abilities at the same time. Salmon is my favorite—I like it best grilled with a little olive oil, but basically, I've never met a piece of salmon

I didn't like. When I'm on set, low-fat cottage cheese and oatmeal are my standbys. They're filling and tend to stick with me throughout the day.

I love crunch, so I also toast everything! I get the "skinny" bagels and toast them before adding peanut butter and banana. Protein is so important for mental power and energy that I look for ways to work it into meals. Eggs are an excellent source for me (I don't have cholesterol problems), and I like them boiled, scrambled, fried, whatever. I can chop a hard-boiled egg on a mixed-green salad, add a mug of soup, and be a happy girl.

When I keep sliced apples in the fridge, I'm much more likely to eat them rather than chips; and frozen blueberries are great by the handful or on top of most anything. I'm crazy about tomato soup and love the prepackaged cups that make it so easy: Flip open the top, pop it in the microwave, add pepper, and I'm out the door! (These are not so good if you're monitoring your sodium, though.)

I gave up diet drinks a while ago; although my husband went cold turkey and never looked back, I do occasionally love to have a Diet Coke with lots of ice. Now that it's on my "rarely" consumed list, it seems like a true indulgence. Artificial sweeteners can mess with your metabolism and create a host of other health issues. Mostly I keep soda water around and squirt fresh lemon, lime, or orange juice in. One of the things I love most about living in Southern California is that I can walk right out my kitchen door and pick my citrus.

Like a lot of people, I have other items on my "rarely" consumed list. Besides the obvious—sugar—cheese is one of the things I can't seem to resist (at least, happily). I love cheese. When I was growing up in the South, *gourmet* meant adding more cheese. I still love to put it on grits, toast, pasta, eggs, everything—but that's not good for my sinuses or my thighs! Even though I try not to have it but once or twice a week, to me, cheese is the ultimate comfort food.

I usually want my comfort foods when I get overwhelmed and my days seem tight. I can start to panic just from pulling up the calendar on my iPhone and find myself thinking about indulging in something—usually something sugary or crunchy. Before I know it, I've crammed chips, nuts, cookies, and goodness knows what else into my mouth without even being aware of it! Now I keep frozen blueberries and other fruit on hand so I can get the crunch satisfaction without my hips swelling up in protest!

Exercise

Since high school, I've always exercised, but back then it seemed effortlessly incorporated into my lifestyle. Not so much at college: When I moved into the dorms, I gained the Freshman 15. I know that some make do with the Freshman 5, but remember, I'm an overachiever! My solution then was the same as now. I had to increase three things: my water intake, the amount of movement in my day, and the amount of sanity in my life. When life feels out of control, so does my eating.

Now I look for ways to incorporate isometrics in the car, in the elevator, anywhere that I can get in some repetitions of "squeeze and hold." Being mindful of good posture also helps me keep my core tight. Doing something every day is the goal. I was fanatical for a while, but now I'm pretty much into maintenance. I found that it was stressful for me to obsess about my workouts and diet. I became testy and anxious—the very things exercise is supposed to help you manage.

I've learned that, as with most things, fitness is achieved by taking small steps consistently. My target is 150 minutes of cardio a week, along with strengthening and stretching. My little dog, Biggie, and I love to walk and play, so that's a handy reason for me to keep moving. But I love walking with my husband best of all—we can cover a wide range of life's most challenging topics before we round the corner to head home. We also have an exercise bike, an elliptical, and a treadmill, so I have no excuse for not getting my time in. I'm so lucky that at this point of my life I have a full gym at home, but I still rely on two inexpensive pieces: my Pilates ring and my resistance bands. With just these items, I can work on every muscle group. They are the first things in my carry-on bag when I travel.

Stretching is also an important part of my routine. It's good for my body and helps me meditate as well. I stretch five days a week, do cardio four days, and work on weight resistance and isometrics three days. I try to mix up the cardio because I know "muscle confusion" is good to maximize my efforts. The body adapts to routine, often making it less effective if it becomes too repetitive.

I love to be on the treadmill or bike while watching the morning shows, and whatever can be done to take the drudgery out of exercise is worth it. I always enjoy the workout once I get into it, and I'm always proud, energized, and more resilient afterward— but many days I have to push to get there. When I slip up, I may beat myself up for a little bit, but I quickly forgive and get right back on track. It's never too late for a do-over!

Fast Fixes

In every woman's second take there's a little bag of tricks—the things she knows and the things she does to look good, feel good, and keep it all together. A woman who has truly transformed has learned or borrowed ideas, and she uses what works and tosses the rest. Here are my quick tips and fast fixes:

• **Eyes that go the distance.** If you want your liner to last and last, trace over it with a stiff brush dipped in your favorite powder. This is a great freshen-up at the end of the day. To pump your lashes, after you curl, wedge the volumizing mascara wand at the base of the lash and wiggle it as you go toward the tips, then use a waterproof formula on top which will hold the lash curl. Also, use your ring finger when you are applying anything in or around your eyes, as it's the gentlest touch. I always warm up my hands before applying any concealer because it will thin the texture and melt it on more smoothly.

• **Sleek hair.** Use a root-boost and/or a heat-protection product before blow-drying, flat ironing, or curling your hair. It will keep you from overdrying your ends and give your hair a lively lift without teasing. Work in small sections and make sure the roots are dry before moving on. Sprinkling a bit of setting powder along your part line at the scalp can do wonders in between washing. It dries up the oil and works like a dry shampoo!

• **Smooth skin.** Exfoliate your face and body regularly. Dull, dry skin and dead cells can make you look old and tired. Once a week, I make sure to invigorate my face with an exfoliator, and I do my entire body twice a week in the shower with a salt scrub.

• **De-frizz.** Overworked hair can really take a beating. When I need to tame my frizzy and dry split ends, I reach for my argan oil. It's basically a vegetable oil and comes from a tree native to Morocco that's rich in vitamins D and E. I'm telling you, I use it for everything. For hair, I squeeze a little bit into the palms of my hands, rub together, and work it through the ends. I also leave it on wet hair overnight after washing. I use it on dry cuticles, cracked heels, and dry elbows. I also use it on a Q-tip to clean up makeup smudges around my eyes, and I keep a small bottle in my purse and even in my glove box.

• **Smell sweet.** I never feel fully dressed without my fragrance. I spray it into the palms of my hands and rub it underneath my hair near my scalp. It seems to stay with me longer that way. Never underestimate the power of smell. Animals live according to scent, and it triggers strong physical and psychological changes in humans. Like your jewelry, shoes, or bag, your fragrance says a lot about you. My mother wore Norell; it was her signature scent. Sometimes when I miss her most, I splash on her fragrance—it was *that* synonymous with her. I tend to go with floral scents that are classic, feminine, and romantic. Lately I've been wearing Dolce & Gabbana Light Blue and Marc Jacobs Daisy.

• **Get sleep.** I love linen sprays and find that when I use a lavender one, it does wonders toward making sure I get a restful night's sleep. A few spritzes on my pillowcase, and I feel pampered. Lately I've been using verbena, which is a plant with a great fresh scent that's said to have a range of healing qualities, from easing sinusitis to acting as an anti-inflammatory. But I love freesia and gardenia, too. Use linen sprays as part of your process to create a sleep routine, signaling your brain and body that it's time to shut down!

• **Pore power.** I do a facial steam once a week at home to open up my pores and keep my skin soft. A home steam kit is a good, inexpensive investment in your health. I also use it on my kids when they have sinus or allergy problems.

• **Refresh.** During the last part of the day, I spritz my face with a freshener and lightly sponge over my mineral powder. It instantly gives a dewy freshness and leaves me good to go for the rest of the night. This little pick-me-up gives an added dose of moisture and smoothness.

• **Hydrate.** Up to 60 percent of the body is made up of water, and the brain is composed of 70 percent. If you're feeling low, lethargic, or hungry, or look a little dim, drinking some water will give your brain and body exactly what they need, quickly and accessibly. It's the easiest beauty and health solution around! For external hydration, moisturize after a bath or shower when your skin is damp to lock in moisture. I always keep Neutrogena Light Sesame Oil in my shower, and since baths are my indulgence, I often squeeze several drops in my bath water.

• **Move.** Even just ten-minute spurts of activity in between meetings, from the parking lot to the grocery store, and so on, will change your mood, help you meditate, and get your heart pumping. Make a commitment to move your body more—it doesn't have to involve a formal gym membership! Activity outside is even better, as you'll get the vitamin D that so many of us are deficient in; however, don't discount the power of stair-climbing, chasing after babies, or housecleaning.

I'd love to hear what's in *your* bag of tricks. Get in touch at **www.leezagibbons.com** or through **facebook.com /officialleezagibbons.**

Here's the bottom line: You're doing the most important work of your life through your process of self-discovery and growth. For heaven's sake, look the part! You know where you're going (you're headed nonstop toward the destination of a better you), so look good when you get there!

Chapter 10

UNDERSTAND THE BUSINESS OF SUCCESS

"The best thing about Leeza is that the glass is always half full; the worst thing about Leeza is that the glass is always half full."

— JEFF COLLINS (FRIEND, FORMER
EMPLOYEE, NOW TV EXECUTIVE)

I'm often asked about my secret for making it in the entertainment business. There is no secret, but I have to admit that in three-and-a-half decades of high heels and business deals, I've gathered up some tips. This book speaks to many of my beliefs; but in this section, I'll give you my top 20 strategies.

Everyone likes to win, and some of us like to lead. They say that if you're not the lead dog in a pack, your view never changes. Well, I've learned that too many lead dogs can mess up anything and being a great follower or lieutenant is an undervalued skill. Regardless of where you're playing on the field, be well rounded. Being great at business is wonderful, but it's more important to excel at growing as a person, friend, wife, lover, mother, daughter, or student. The more you acquire mastery in one area, the more likely you are to smooth out the bumps in other areas, too.

Basically, you should never be afraid to play out of position. If you're going to be successful in today's world, you have to be adaptable and flexible and think like an entrepreneur. To do that, you need to know what it feels like to be the other members on the team.

When I first started out in TV, I learned how to shoot using a film camera (dark ages, I know!). I wasn't very good at handling my little Bell and Howell "Scoop It," and I was notorious for "up-cutting" my audio for news stories to run on the six o'clock broadcast. See, in those days, you took magnets to literally erase the audio from the strips of film, which you taped together. If you messed up, you were screwed, because there was no "undo" command, and it wasn't saved anywhere. Through that experience, I learned to value and respect the crew, editors, writers, and producers. And when I finally had the chance to be in charge, make the assignments, and call the shots, I often chose to play out of position. Leaving my executive producer title behind to cater a lunch, taking a lighting course, or being a gopher on a field shoot empowered others to show up in a way they might not have otherwise. I learned a few things along the way, and sometimes I get asked about it.

Younger women usually want to know how I managed to climb the ranks and have a family along with a nice reputation. Reporters often ask the balance question (which I talked about at length in Chapter 5), and most everyone else just wants to know celebrity gossip and the insider scoop. After all, I spent more than 15 years on *Entertainment Tonight* and *Extra!*

ET started when MTV did, and these two changed everything. Since I was one of the first hosts of *ET,* I became synonymous with the new entertainment-news culture, and I was right there when that whole tsunami hit. It was a phenomenal ride, and I had the time of my life, but I have nothing to share in the star-stories category. Truly, I was never comfortable with the more scandalous side of celebrity, and I was often scolded by my bosses for not hitting hard enough with a tabloid approach. I'm fortunate that I was building my career before the walls of perceived appropriateness came tumbling down. Let's be real: I started as a TV journalist before computers and videotape—much less social media, reality shows, and the omnipresence of digital cameras!

I remember we had interns at *Entertainment Tonight* transcribe our videotaped interviews by hand before they went into an actual hard-copy file (unfathomable, right?). After one interview, I was reviewing the transcripts, which should have included a reference to Nikita Khrushchev, who led the Soviet Union during part of the Cold War. I scanned the notes a few times before I discovered the poor intern had no idea who Khrushchev was. She'd

transcribed the name as "Niki, the crew chef." Life before Google was pretty scary!

While I suppose I do know some secrets of the stars, I have no desire to ever share them—not here, not anywhere. And they aren't secrets of the kiss-and-tell variety, anyway. I'm blessed to have had the residual halo effect of building a career off the backs of celebrities; and I'm respectful, grateful, and discreet.

Can you believe I actually sang with
Patti LaBelle and wore my version
of her legendary "fans"!
Must be when I got into extensions!

Leeza's Top 20 Tips for Success

"Write what you know" is what they say, so that takes me to my self-taught, trial-and-error business strategies for work-life satisfaction. I do have some good tips on how to build a career you're proud of, a family you love, and a reputation that honors you, and still manage to be sane and grateful as you move ever forward. I preface them by sharing my definition of success, which is: *having a choice about how I spend my time, contributing something of value that makes me proud while not compromising my standards, and honoring my need for putting my family first.* I've been ridiculously lucky. I know my mom would be happy to know that after 30 years of working in a competitive, public business, I think I still have my feet on the ground. But as Oprah says, now I just wear better shoes!

As I've emphasized, there are no secrets, just these strategies:

1. Be flexible with your dream. I thought when I started working that I'd be in charge of my destiny. I brought to the workforce my "fondness for being in control," as my mom used to call it. Imagine my shock when I started my journalism career and I wasn't running the newsroom or covering world events like my Barbies had when I played reporter as a girl. Instead, I was called the newest *anchorette.* They said I was cute as a speckled pup, and if I'd wear tight sweaters and peroxide my hair, I'd probably make it. No one ever said that to my Barbie! I wasn't in charge of anything, not even the way I looked. I had to change my thinking. I decided to be flexible on my dream and find another way in.

Enter *Entertainment Tonight,* where my motto became: Don't fight it, light it! And they did. My legs were featured next to Mary Hart's, buffed and shined up and made to look miles long. I'd never expected to be second-string; but I was second to Mary, and it actually gave me a place to stand out. I kept my eye on the prize and tried not to block the blessings along the way. After ten celebrity-crammed years as cohost of *Entertainment Tonight,* I got my own talk show where I could call the shots, book the guests, and run the format—a control freak's paradise!

The lesson here is to know your nonnegotiables, but be as flexible as you can. The road to the top of your mountain probably has detours, bends, and even a few dead ends. This is the sign that you're on the right path.

2. Don't get bitter, get better. This is different from flexibility. It means get ready to have the rug pulled out from under you and master the change by facing it down. I can't tell you how many times I've had new bosses come on board, contracts that didn't happen, opportunities that went belly up, and promises that weren't kept. You either get bitter or you get on with it and face the change. Why do you need to be a master of change? I think it's because the quality of your life depends on the decisions you make and your willingness to embrace progress. You don't sit around talking about how hard the change is or whining because it's different. You just step up your game and get better.

Getting better means forging ahead with fearlessness. Being afraid keeps you in your comfort zone, static and immobile. It helps to think of how fear decreases as value increases. You may be deathly afraid of public speaking, but if I paid you a million bucks you might get over it. I'm terrified of snakes, but if my child jumped into a pit with vipers and boa constrictors, I'd be the next one in without a second thought. So would you.

In business, focus on the value you get from the change. There's always an upside.

3. Prepare, prepare, and prepare some more. With all due respect to the "naturals" out there and to those who thrive on the pressure of deadlines (myself included), there's really no shortcut for being ready. Learning your lines, doing the research, reading the reports—whatever your job entails, make sure you've given it proper respect. Of course there will be times when you'll have to wing it and do things on the fly. However, if you look behind the curtain, you'll usually find that successful people have prepared for success, so when it arrives, they recognize it and open the door.

4. Be an optimist. This is where my friend Jeff says I get into trouble. It's my natural view of the world, and he'd also admit that it's worked for me. Even if you're a cynic who believes that "just because you're paranoid doesn't mean they're not out to get you," hear me out. You have a choice in how to view things—always. I'm not saying that you should be unrealistic or too much of a Pollyanna; rather, when you choose to look at the positive side, you tend to save time and energy. Being a pessimist just muddies the water longer.

People like those who think positively. It inspires others to reach higher, too. Yet the optimistic black hole is what you want to avoid, and where my friends have seen me lost. That's where you continue to see the best in a person or situation long after they've proven you shouldn't.

5. Be grateful and gracious. Eckhart Tolle says, "Acknowledging the good that you already have in your life is the foundation for all abundance." I believe that 100 percent. If you can't be thankful where you are, you'll never get where you want to be. Maybe it's not the "end of the rainbow" job for you—so what? Show gratitude. This is the foundation upon which you build more. Not showing you're grateful makes you miserable, jaded, jealous, and petty.

It's not a sign of weakness to be nice. There's an honorable way to say no, walk away, conclude a relationship, disagree, or even be in litigation. When I have a choice on whom to hire, I always tip the scales in favor of those who were grateful and kind and who are known to show respect. It's the secret weapon for getting things done. Give encouragement and show gratitude through texts, e-mails, notes, and other offerings that demonstrate your graciousness. Cheer on others—really root for them. You'll be part of their jet stream of success.

6. Work harder (or smarter) than anyone else. I don't care how much you know, people are more interested in how much you *care*. That means you can be the smartest, best-qualified candidate for anything, but if you haven't shown how much you're willing to work and demonstrated how much you care, you won't last long. Going the extra mile never goes out of style and is a strategy that has worked for me over and over.

When I was in college, I used to do the local "cut-ins" for a National Public Radio show, which required me to sign on at 5 A.M. Our studio was at the far end of campus from my dorm, so I made friends with the custodian who locked the building at night. I got him to agree to let me sleep in the lobby with my little alarm clock so I'd be sure never to miss my shift. I used to tidy up at the studio, ask for feedback, stay late, and offer to help with anything. Years later, I found out that the big bosses (whom I did not know at the time) were aware of my work ethic, and they opened the door for my next move.

7. Know the room. Whether you're trying to sell TV shows or pharmaceuticals, it's the same rule: Take the time to know who's going to be there. Have an understanding of what they're up against and the demands on their time and budgets. Get a feel for the culture and how they play the game. Find out the backstory about what might influence their decisions.

I made an awkward mistake one time when I was making a pitch to host a program. My agents had already laid the groundwork, so it should have been a slam dunk. But because I didn't know who was going to be there and hadn't taken the time to investigate their backgrounds, I talked about how weak I thought the current host was and how much better I was for the format. Silence. It turns out that the current host was the girlfriend of the executive sitting in front of me. I clearly didn't know the room!

8. Don't apologize for your lines in the sand. Be clear with yourself and others about what's important to you. It if matters to you, it must be meaningful, so don't apologize. Business is all about the terms, so be very comfortable with yours. Make sure you're prepared to sacrifice a deal if a line is crossed. If not, refer to point one: Be flexible. There's no time in a deal when you have more power than before you sign or commit. You lose credibility if you're all over the place, so be clear on what means the most to you, whether it's taking Fridays off, having the flexibility to job share, getting a parking place, the amount of money you're paid, or the title you receive. If there's a point of no return for you, own it, communicate it, and don't apologize.

When I needed to work my production schedule around breast-feeding times for my newborn, I didn't say to Paramount, "I'm really sorry, but it would be great if we could work out a way for me to feed my baby." I said, "If you want me to continue to produce and host the show while my baby is breast-feeding, we'll have to change the schedule."

9. GROW. Get Rewards by Opening Windows—that's how I think of it. If you aren't moving forward, you're in decline. I sign all my notes "Ever forward," because it reminds me of how I want to live my life. There's nothing more annoying in business than crotchety old veterans who think they know better. While I'm the first to respect experience, there's no excuse for being close-minded. Stay current with the latest information in your industry. Follow the thought leaders and decision makers who set the pace.

Open yourself up to doing things differently and letting go of what you know in order to learn something new. Above my desk, I have a quote attributed to C. S. Lewis: "You are never too old to set another goal or to dream a new dream." Keep 'em coming.

10. Take bold action. When the door opens, walk through it. If it doesn't—kick it down. I've never known a successful person who didn't do this. If you have a great idea but fail to act, it's not great. If you don't take action when opportunity calls for you, then you don't deserve it. Being timid when it comes to your business decisions means you aren't in the right business. I believe what T. S. Eliot is reported to have said: "Only those who risk going too far can possibly find out how far one can go." Take chances, take action, and be bold. Answer the question *What's the worst thing that can happen?* and you'll probably see that the worst case is often being embarrassed, overlooked, or taken for granted.

You can't be outstanding if you don't *stand out.* Do it by taking bold action.

11. Strengthen your strengths. If you're good at something, work at it until you have no equal. If you have a skill that's paying off, utilize it more. Whether it's raising our kids or trying to improve ourselves, human beings have a tendency to focus on overcoming our deficits.

Parents say, "Johnny's good at history, but he really struggles with math, so we're getting him a tutor to help." I've done the same thing with my kids. We try to level the playing field, but what if instead we gave Johnny more support to get even better at the things he loves? Chances are he'd find his place in the world more easily.

In business, notice what's working. You're good at customer service, developing new products, employee morale, innovation, interviewing—whatever it is, put your time and energy on getting better at those things. Acknowledge your weaknesses and let them go; then become known for your core competency. Become an expert, an authority, and *the* definitive source by strengthening your strengths.

12. Be on time. Ugh, this one continues to challenge me. Yet when someone is late for a meeting with me or I'm held up because of another person's thoughtless tardiness, I make a mental note about whether I want to do business with that individual again. Someone who's chronically late or habitually unprepared is basically saying their time is more important than yours. Not only is it rude, it's arrogant.

Now I know there are lots of legitimate reasons why things may not run on time occasionally, but as much as you can, honor your time commitments. Leave early enough to arrive ahead of your scheduled appointment. Bursting through a door, regurgitating apologies while fumbling through a purse or briefcase, is not the way to get respect.

13. Be future focused. While it matters what a person has done in the past, more times than not, that's merely the price of admission. Once you get in the door, you must deliver *fresh* victories. As Babe Ruth said, "Yesterday's home runs don't win today's games."

Talking about the way things used to be or how you did it before can be a red flag showing your reluctance to adapt. I'm not saying that experience doesn't count—it does—but mostly it will get you a callback or a chance to prove what you're gonna do *now.* Everyone wants to know: *What's in it for me?* Make sure you have an answer.

14. Eat, play, sleep. I know this sounds like that Elizabeth Gilbert book *Eat, Pray, Love,* but hang with me on this one. To be at your best, you have to fuel up. Many of us pay extra at the pump to make sure we're giving our cars the best quality gas to run most efficiently, so why would we cheat ourselves? If we don't eat well, our brains don't kick into high gear, and we lose information and energy. If we don't counterweight our work with play, we lose imagination and enthusiasm. And if we don't sleep, we lose the ability to cope, and stress threatens to derail our days.

The most successful people I know recognize that eating right, exercising, sleeping well, and playing are all important to the final product, no matter what the business. Paying attention to these core needs means you can deliver peak performance in your career, job, or family.

15. Accept praise. I know, I know: The usual advice is to learn to accept criticism, but I think most of us get that part. Oh, we may push back a little or get a bit defensive, but usually we come around. On the other hand, think about the last time you got a compliment. For me, it was my husband telling me a room I'd been decorating looked really nice. "Oh well, it will be nice once I finish with the painting," I said. "I think it looks great now," he insisted. "Nooo, there's not nearly enough light, and I still need to change those drapes . . . but it's coming along."

Poor Steven probably felt terrible. I managed to completely dismiss his compliments and then negate his opinion! It's the same in business. Countless times producers or directors have praised my performance in a show or interview, and I immediately zeroed in on what had gone wrong.

When someone gives you credit for something, accept it. Be thankful for it and let that moment have some air before you suck it all up with a deflection. My mom always said that "It's a poor frog who doesn't praise his own pond," so be proud of your efforts and allow others to compliment you, for goodness' sake!

16. Never look back. The exception would be gazing over the distance to see how far you've come—no regrets, no excuses.

When I was building my career, I had some amazing opportunities. I'd established myself and created some successes, and doors were opening wide. We all know the future is based on choice, not chance; and I (like everyone else) had to choose which doors to walk through and which roads to take.

Some of the exits I decided on sent me on detours I hadn't expected. I saw other people step into shows I'd been offered but turned down, and they became huge hits, yet I've never had a moment of regret. What's done is done, and I'm certain life always unfolds exactly as it should. Petty jealousy, revisionist history, and whining aren't the hallmarks of successful people.

17. Know that *I will* is greater than IQ. Brilliance is no substitute for dedication. Time after time, the person who gets hired, promoted, or given a raise is the one who didn't give up. Even if you're up against genius-level Mensa types, *you* can be the one to win. In a showdown of skills, most people prefer those who have the right attitude versus the right aptitude. Nothing wrong with having both, of course!

18. Show respect. I know sometimes we work with and for those we may not like or approve of. But I feel if you can't show respect for the individual, then show it for the position or the project. I had more than a few executive producers who were screamers and bullied others to get what they wanted. I don't respect that approach, but I believed my choice was to get into it or get out of it. In other words, if I chose to continue to do the job, I should find a way to be respectful.

People in positions of authority usually paid a price to get there—most often through lots of hours, education, and hard knocks. Veterans at anything usually command respect because they've kept moving forward. Honor their tenure, if nothing else. Unless your name is on the door, give props to the person whose name is; and until you're writing the paychecks, show proper respect for those who are.

19. Surround yourself with brilliance. Many business leaders talk about how important it is to pick your team. Each member reflects on you, just as you reflect on the person at the top when you're part of the group. It's been said over and over: When you hire people who are smarter than you are, you prove you're smarter than they are.

Never insist on being the sharpest person in the room, on the board, or in the company—always make room for those who can teach you something or make you look good. And when you get those smart people around you, for goodness' sake, let them shine! Give them credit and acknowledge their contributions. As Mary Kay Ash advised, look at people as if they have a sign around their neck saying, Make me feel important.

20. It's all personal. It doesn't matter what business we're in, it all comes down to personal relationships. We all want to work with people we trust, who make us feel good, and whom we believe in.

Cultivating your relationships is the wisest investment you can make in your life and career. That means being impeccable with your word. Call people back, and respond to requests. A quick no is always preferable to a long maybe. Listen. Be unfailingly courteous, respectful, and interested. I often have a choice about whom I want to work with. I choose character over skill every time. Skill can be taught; character delivers, no matter what.

What Really Matters

I love business. I adore my work in TV and radio. I cherish my opportunity to make a difference in the lives of others as a social entrepreneur, and I plan to keep contributing where I can till my last breath. *But* on their deathbed, no one wishes for one more day at the office. No one cares about that last report, those sales numbers, or the one client that's never happy. My family, friends, and relationships hold a bigger, stronger, and more satisfying place in my heart than any job, career, or work assignment. Our lives, in my opinion, are always about who we loved and how we cared for them. That goes on forever.

Maybe we get our final emotional growth spurt when we write the concluding chapter in our lives. How sad that it is only then when we tend to see what to value, what to prioritize, and where to focus. We can benefit from the words, wisdom, and wishes of the dying to jolt ourselves into the proper perspective.

You already know how important I think family caregivers are. The husbands, wives, sons, daughters, and friends who take care of those who are sick and dying are simply the glue that holds a fragile moment together when it seems all hope is shattered. I also respect the paid professionals who care for others in their greatest moment of need. Australian palliative-care nurse Bronnie Ware is one of those people. She wrote a blog post that got a lot of attention a while ago, giving a summary of the many bedside conversations she'd had with those who were ready to transition.

The blog later became a book, *The Top Five Regrets of the Dying*, but her message is actually quite simple yet powerful. Here are the top five regrets of the dying, as witnessed by Bronnie:

1. I wish I'd had the courage to live a life true to myself, not the life others expected of me. (This was the most common regret of all.)

2. I wish I hadn't worked so hard. (Interestingly, this came from every male patient Bronnie nursed.)

3. I wish I'd had the courage to express my feelings.

4. I wish I had stayed in touch with my friends.

5. I wish that I had let myself be happier.

Don't those five wishes accurately reflect the things we've been talking about? Being authentic and happy, connected to those we love, living a life where we can celebrate who we really are regardless of what others want us to be. The people Bronnie interviewed had regrets because they either didn't know how to re-create their lives or they didn't know they could call for another take.

Don't wait until you're in the December of your life and cast your gaze over the years gone by wishing you had played it differently. I suppose we expect people to get wise toward the end of life and then espouse all that inside information for mass consumption, but you're alert and awake *now* and this is your moment.

We learn so much about ourselves along the way, and any time is a good time for a check-in to make sure we're on the path we intended, and if not to do a U-turn toward a new direction. Right now, not at the end of our life, is the time for an inventory of lessons learned and love lost, a gathering up of what works and a letting go of what doesn't.

I've hit the reset button a few times so that at the end of my life, if I'm ever asked about my wishes I will be able to say, "I wish everyone could have a life as wonderful, fulfilling, fun and meaningful as mine!" That's what Take 2 is all about.

Chapter 11

BOOKMARK IT

"I'm still learning."

— MICHELANGELO

You arrived at your future a moment ago . . . now what are you going to do? Well, you picked up this book, so that's a darned good indication that you plan to step into your next act as the ruler of your destiny. It's never too late to start over. Have a recall election and vote yourself "most likely to create a fulfilling life of meaning and joy." Throughout this book, I hope you've been encouraged to change the way you look at things and get curious about the operating system that drives you. Achievement or accomplishment is a science—it's quantifiable. We can study it, dissect it, and see how it's done and who does it right. As you do these things and learn something through the process, "bookmark it." That is, remember it. Keep coming back to use it, and let it help you keep turning your pages and writing your story as you claim your second take. What's the use of putting in all the work if you don't stop at the teachable moments and allow them to make an indelible mark on your journey? You can hit the reset button on your life at any point. At any age, on any day of the week, you can start over; take inventory; and get smarter, stronger, and sexier with no looking back in your rearview mirror.

You've heard me talk about how life is a series of holding on and letting go. That's how you keep the pages turning. The secret is to know when to do which. *Do I hold on to this relationship that's suffocating me? Do I let go of this go-nowhere job? Is there meaning to this career? Am I fulfilled?* The questions barrage us. I have to admit that this constant cycle of self-doubt, anxiety, and fear of the unknown is an ongoing challenge for me. I'm always comforted to know, however, that it's the same for everyone else.

I've thought a lot lately about how I personally bookmark information that nourishes me, people who inspire me, and situations that challenge me. Over the years, I've come up with what we've talked about in this book. But I hope my children will arrive at this skill much younger than I did. From the looks of things, they will. This year, Lexi graduated from college and Nathan graduated from junior high, so this idea of another take is resonating everywhere in my life.

Commencement is a great concept, really. It's all about a beginning, a new start, and is a great inspiration for how I think we should look at life. There's a starting gate wherever we want to put one.

For Nathan's transition to high school, he had to lead a session with his parents and teachers in which he analyzed his progress. They call it a "gateway." As his dad and Steven and I sat there, we were astounded by Nathan's self-awareness. "These are my strengths," he said, as he rattled off things like his compassion, leadership, kind heart, and humor. Then he went through an even longer list of the things he was working on, including being distracted, making jokes during class, and disrupting others! He shared with us his plan for improving those areas as we sat amazed by his perceptiveness. When he was done, I was so impressed by his personal scorecard and how he'd become an open vessel for feedback. Talk about the perfect opportunity to hit the reset button!

We are always graduating from one stage of life to another and basically getting a new schedule of classes with new professors and teachers to get us through. Nathan's commencement made me realize that anytime is a good time to create our own scorecards as we become aware of our gateways in life.

MY TAKE: LEEZA'S LENS

From Holly to Hollis

The most powerful example I know of restarting your life belongs to Holly. She actually transformed so much that I now call her Hollis, because the woman formerly known as Holly is gone. Whenever I think I'm stuck, whenever I feel as if the deck is stacked against me, I consider Hollis's story and realize that starting over is possible for anyone, at anytime, if we just make it so.

Now this may sound far-fetched, even unbelievable, but that's why it's at the top of my "bookmarked life lessons" for me. It was the 1990s and I was hosting and producing my talk show, *Leeza*, on the Paramount lot in Hollywood. Holly, a young girl in England, watched an episode of my show that was an update on teens we had helped to overcome their addictions. The topic of the show is less relevant than the fact that it ended up changing her life. Holly had been suicidal, and something about that show made her believe that she didn't need to end her life. She later told me, "I had no one to turn to for help and nothing left at the end of my dwindling path of suffering except an intricate plan to die."

Without saying a word to anyone, Holly boarded a plane to L.A. to find me because she thought I could somehow save her life. Not because I was

famous or on television, she says, but because when she watched that show, "a flash of intuition" swept through her. She had enough money for a few days' expenses, one change of clothes, and a map of L.A., which she'd scanned at a library in England.

Well, actually she had more than that. She had a secret of childhood emotional trauma and abuse that weighed so heavily on her, she took the biggest gamble of her life to escape it. As Holly put it, "I was scared of my memories and scared of living another day reliving my past. The flashbacks were debilitating. It's impossible to outrun what's trapped in your mind. I knew I had to get to America to find Leeza. I hadn't thought beyond that, not even what I would say to her, but it didn't matter."

I didn't know any of this when a solemn-looking girl showed up in my audience, with braces, glasses, and short hair that made her look a bit like Harry Potter. It was miraculous that she made it to the city, learned to use the bus system, and figured out how to get tickets to the show on the lot. She came for several days; each time, she was making a pact with herself, building up the courage to reach out to me and dare to ask a question as a member of the audience.

After one of those shows, my assistant gave me a very neatly handwritten letter that had been left for me on one of the audience chairs. It simply said "Leeza" on it. For reasons as unknown as what prompted Holly to respond to a TV show hosted by a woman she didn't know, and despite the fact that I often received hundreds of letters a day, this one compelled me to open it right away.

The letter was from Holly, telling me her story. Before I read that letter, no one on the planet knew where Holly was. No one knew she was living alone in a rough neighborhood in Venice Beach, where drug dealers waited outside the door and roaches waited in her bed. I was so moved by her story that I immediately decided to call her. I left her a message to come back to another show taping, and later that week, she did.

On show days, when I first entered the stage from my dressing room, the warm-up guy usually had the audience whipped into a frenzy. I'd walk out to a sea of cheering people all on their feet ready to engage. This day, I hadn't thought about Holly being there, but as soon as I scanned the crowd, I knew. I walked right up to this geeky-looking girl and asked, "Are you Holly? I'm Leeza. Nice to meet you."

I still don't understand what it was about Holly that prompted me to engage, but there was something that touched me in her story of courage growing from fear. Even though she struggled with the challenges of mental illness brought on by nightmares no kid should face, Holly managed to get by. Ultimately, she went back to England to get her visa so she could return to America as a student. She was just 20 years old, and she was hell-bent on reclaiming her life.

While she was in England, I sent Holly a letter, which she says held a key for her. I told her that she had learned something at a very young age, which many people don't learn in a lifetime—to ask for help. Holly says, "There are two types of people that ask for help . . . those who ask thinking the work will be done for them, and those who ask for the tools to help themselves." She was the latter, and that was the basis for Holly to become Hollis and to own her life.

She knew she was "broken." I knew I didn't have the tools or credentials to help her. The people on my staff were leery of this disturbed young woman from halfway around the world who seemed obsessed with me. I knew she was only "obsessed" with her own sanity and salvation; I was merely the conduit. I put her in touch with a youth counselor who had appeared on the show she saw that day, and helped her get admitted into a psychiatric hospital for two weeks, which she says saved her life. It led to nine years of intensive hard work and therapy that delivered her to a healthy place, free of her demons. "I put in the work," Holly said. "I didn't let my past dictate my future, and I was accountable to myself all along the way."

When Holly graduated from UCLA, I was there to see her in her cap and gown. Getting a degree from that institution is a remarkable accomplishment, but getting free from your past and reclaiming your life is an even bigger deal. I don't know why two souls oceans apart would find themselves on the same playing field in life. I don't know who's pitching and who's swinging the bat. I only know that, at 20 years old, a wounded girl wanted to change her life and she did. Honestly, I know that, regardless of whether she'd been able to find her way to me and my show, Holly would have saved her own life; but I saw something in her that made me want to step up to the plate.

Holly is now 35. We are friends and see each other all the time. She has found forgiveness and closed the door on her childhood wounds. She is close to her family and loves being in England, but only as a visitor. I still find strength in her ongoing battle to be true to herself, and inspiration in her unfailing efforts to lift others along the way. I have bookmarked her story, and I often return to it as the ultimate example of a happy ending and a new beginning.

Personal Power and Basic Needs

When I moved to L.A. to begin work at *Entertainment Tonight*, one of the first things I did was to order Tony Robbins's *Personal Power* tapes from an infomercial. I remember watching late at night (of course!), seeing Martin Sheen talking about what the program did for his life. Then when he said he wasn't being paid to endorse it, I almost got whiplash as I dashed to the phone to order!

With Tony on the set of *Get the Edge*

My cassette tapes (that's how long ago it was) arrived, and I did my work following Tony's guidance on how to unlock my own power.

I remember listening to the tapes while driving on the way to assignments. When I'd arrive at my destination, I wouldn't want to leave the car because I was so swept up in what I was learning. I'd shifted the momentum in my life, and it was powerful and exciting.

That's where I hope you are, and this is where the laws of physics work in your favor. A body in motion tends to stay in motion, so there's no stopping you now! I love what Will Rogers said: "Make progress: Even if you're on the right track, you'll get run over if you just sit there!"

In those early days, I was not about to just sit there! I did my homework, recorded my progress in the workbook and basically became aware of what I was doing (and not doing) to create my life. After I did that investigation into who I was and what I wanted by using Tony's tapes, I took my journals, put them in a box and moved forward.

Years later, I got a call from my agent asking me if I would meet with Tony about interviewing him for a new infomercial—talk about manifesting your destiny! In the years since I'd listened to the tapes I'd developed a solid relationship with myself because I knew more about *me*. Mostly I learned that I was the one and only person responsible for where I was, who I was, and where I was going. When I was asked to interview Tony, I came to it as a student and a seeker. I still am.

Over the years, Tony and his advice (and that of others who are experts at human behavior) have helped me tremendously. I'd never imagined when I was writing in my little workbook way back when that I'd one day be on shows with Tony and Oprah—and be friends with both of them!

I love all things Oprah, and because of her generosity of spirit, we're reminded often of her ongoing struggles to find her true self. She was recently doing a story with Tony where she attended one of his Life Mastery seminars. Tony was talking about the six basic human needs and how once we identify them, we can learn a lot about why we do things and what motivates and drives others, too. We all have the same requirements but in differing amounts and times in our lives. Tony says these aren't just wants and desires, but rather needs that give insight into everything we do. I think this is among the most valuable lessons he offers. Read through the list and then ask yourself which of these core needs are the most important in your life. This is the code to why we act the way we do.

I watched Oprah go through the list on the air and apply each one to her life, just like the thousands of other people who'd gone through Tony's seminar that day. Oprah? Really? After decades of analyzing human behavior, wouldn't she know this stuff? That's one of the cool things about Oprah, though: she constantly holds up the mirror to herself and is genuinely curious. She seeks knowledge and bookmarks it.

This segment with Tony helped remind me that, just like Oprah, I have the need to contribute and a need for growth. Those are the two dominant forces in my life. They're what shape me, and it's been the same two things ever since I can remember. In fact, they're what pushed me to write this book. I really wanted to pass on what I've learned and what's been shared with me. I wanted to contribute. When I feel as though I'm offering value to someone's life, I feel significant, and so do you—so does everyone. Knowing this about myself has been tremendously valuable because I can use these qualities as a metric to measure my choices and evaluate my actions and reactions.

Tony's Six Basic Human Needs

1. Certainty/Comfort. We want to know we can count on certain things to happen because that makes us comfortable. It feels safe and comfortable to know with certainty that night follows day, that school starts at the same time every day, and that our dog is always going to love us, for example.

2. Variety. This seems contradictory to the need for certainty, but it's a great paradox that makes us interesting. We want to mix it up. We want enough *un*certainty to give our lives some spontaneity and adventure.

3. Significance. This is one of my big ones, but everyone has this to some degree. Basically, we want to know that we matter. It's like my mother having a desire for her story of Alzheimer's disease to count. That made her feel significant. We want to be significant to our spouse, our kids, and others who matter to us.

4. Connection/Love. This one is at the core of all human existence, I think. We need to connect; we want to be part of something. It's why we join things, start clubs, communicate through social media. We want to give love and get it back.

5. Growth. Every time we try, or whenever we seek to learn or understand something, we demonstrate this need. We all want to become better. True, it's hard to find in some people, but it's always there, even if they are afraid to admit it about themselves.

6. Contribution. The desire to make the world a better place, or at least improve our corner of it, is universal. From sweeping the walkway in front of the house to running a homeless shelter or helping someone cross the street, we all have a need to offer something of value, to help others.

The Need for Certainty

While writing this book, I came to realize that for all the talking about change that I do, for all the teaching and preaching, I still have a real need for certainty along with my deep desire to contribute whether my contribution is wanted or not! I was on my way home from my beach trip with my girls Zaidee and Terri this year when I got a message from my sister that Daddy was on his way to the hospital. He'd been out working in the yard when he was attacked and stung multiple times by a swarm of yellow jackets. Cammy said, "Can you meet us at the ER? Dad was gasping for breath and in a lot of pain." Before I could call her back, she was ringing my cell again: "They've sent him to a cardiac unit."

Our father had never spent the night in a hospital and had never had any ailment that a jar of Vick's VapoRub couldn't fix. (I smile as a write that, recalling seeing him nursing a headache with his head wrapped in a cloth slathered with Vick's.) I don't remember *ever* seeing Daddy sick. He's always been incredibly fit; at age 83, he was wearing the same size he did when he was a young soldier.

I arrived on the scene at the hospital expecting the measures to have been taken only as a precaution and that Dad would be released in the morning. True to form, he managed to flirt with the nurses and even snag a few phone numbers! Bless him, Daddy has always shown us what confidence can do.

Overnight, his condition declined and our concern rose. My brother, Carl, and his wife, Anne Marie; Cammy; Steven; and I were all stunned when Daddy had to have a heart catheter. I, of course, flew into my usual take-charge-and-fix-it mode, telling him that they'd probably put in some stents and he'd feel much better afterward.

I believed it, too, until after the procedure when we were told by the cardiologist, "It's bad. There was too much damage for us to put in stents. Your father needs quadruple-bypass surgery." Of course, the docs had no way of knowing that our dad was as stubborn as he was tan, and getting him to agree to surgery wasn't going to be easy. I tried to leverage everything I could to get him to see that he could probably live to be 100 if he had this procedure; that it is done successfully very often now; and that he could be the king of rehab afterward with lots of captive listeners for his joke-telling and poem-writing. I tried guilt, conspiracy—everything—but Dad wasn't having it. All I could do was get him to agree to having a medical alert mobile system put in so he could continue to live independently without me calling every hour to make sure he was all right.

I was lamenting about this on the phone with my friend and colleague Bonnie, who observed that this situation played to my weaknesses. She noted that I wasn't comfortable with standing by. She said, "You have always had a need to know; this time, you just don't know, and you really can't." She was right. I could offer my support and assistance all day long. I could intervene and interject for a month of Sundays. But in the end, it was Daddy's call about having surgery—and even if he agreed, the outcome couldn't be guaranteed.

Here's the part of my Take 2 where I always get stuck. Remember, my driving forces are the need to be significant and to contribute, and I felt that I could do neither with my dad's health right then. Daddy has been resolute in his decision not to have the bypass surgery. So far, he seems to be doing okay; in fact, he uses his wellness to say he should be exonerated about not going under the knife. His stubbornness is part of what makes my father who he is, so I have chosen to recognize and honor that and allow him his authority over his life, without my driving desire to contribute or interfere.

Sweet Bonnie's core needs are love, connection, and support, so she managed to help me find some peace with doing what I could and letting go of the rest. She helped me realize that I could learn to be okay with just "standing by." We're better when we know where we each come from emotionally and can make our choices from there.

Looking Forward

What drives *you?* What's at the core of your story? I hope that now you have a better understanding of who you are—or at least an idea of how to learn more. More than that, I hope you're passionately interested in the process and empowered to call for a second take, confident that at any time you can create new beginnings and happy endings.

This is your moment. Everyone talks about the future like it's some big "save up for it" point in the distance, but that whole notion makes no sense to me. Don't wait for some far-off time when the alarm will ring and you'll suddenly know to step out of the shadows and into the spotlight. Remember, emotions fuel actions; so I say, don't save them but spend them freely. I always have—sometimes to my detriment and at great pain—but I'd do it all over again in a heartbeat. You'll need that emotional reservoir to create the new story of your life, so open the floodgates.

My philosophy about emotions is this: Use 'em up as if your life depends on it (it does). Spend them today, share them tomorrow, and give them away freely, because unlike interest on your money, your emotional investments only grow when you take them out and spend them. I learned that from my mother, big time. When someone is losing his or her memory, you discover the power of a moment pretty quickly. This is *your* moment to dive into your second take.

Have you ever heard someone say, "I just have to get my ducks in a row" before they get going? Do you ever feel you have to get things set up or have your schedule cleared before you start something? It's a delay tactic. To help you avoid this trap, think of this: When a mother duck wants to gather up the ducklings and lead them somewhere, she never waits for them to get in a row. She just starts walking, and then they fall in line. It's the same with each of us. All we have to do is take the first step and keep moving forward. I send you this as you begin.

My Wish for You

My wish for you is that you're valued and loved for being exactly who you are at this moment. I wish for you a deep connection to the knowledge that you have custody of your life and that you can change, adapt, and alter it as you see fit. I wish for you a chance to breathe in strength and exhale hurt so that only acceptance and serenity about the life you live and the choices you make are left behind. I wish for you meaningful moments that rest easy and gentle in your spirit and allow you to radiate love and forgiveness, knowing it's all unfolding exactly as it should. I wish for you the quiet validation that comes from always giving your best and from investing your highest intention every time you dare to care.

My story led me to you, and now our lives have intersected. Knowing that you've explored my ideas and allowed me to share some of myself gives me tremendous joy. We've danced to the same music for a time, which gives each of us a common experience that feels safe. But when that music stops or changes (and we both know it will), dance anyway. If you don't have a partner, just start the steps; the music and the people will show up. Move away from the stage of who you were when you were younger, single, married, successful, happier, skinnier, richer, poorer, or whatever, and step into the spotlight of now. Owning this moment can be the greatest adventure of your life, and you've already started. So call for a second take, and enjoy every moment!

❦

PreSCRIPTions: TAKE YOUR WEEKLY DOSE!

While working on your Take 2, no doubt you'll stumble upon challenges that threaten to sabotage your hard work. That's why you'll need to take your PreSCRIPTions—action steps that act as a weekly antidote to fear, anxiety, self-doubt, isolation, depression, or any other emotion you might feel along your transformation journey. The following are 52 weeks' worth of ideas to keep you on your path to fulfillment; these are all things I've found helpful in my own life. When you feel off track, just rewrite the script with these PreSCRIPTions!

Week 1: Make a Plan

If you feel like you're beginning your journey alone, it's because you are. Nobody can do this but you. That can feel pretty scary, but you can get a grip on the fear of the unknown as you get started. You know I'm all about seeing yourself as successful, so make a plan. Expect that it will work, but also know that there may be bumps in your road ahead. So this week, close your eyes and actually imagine yourself failing or something not going your way. How do you feel, what do you do, how do you respond? This mental imagery will help you adjust to the worst-case scenario *before* it happens; then *if* it does, you'll be well equipped to react in a more functional way. If you plan for potential setbacks, when they arrive, they never set you back. This is your permission to briefly preview the worst so that if it does come to pass, you'll recognize it as the chance to bring in your backup.

Week 2: Show Your Cards

Early in your journey, tell someone—maybe a member of your goddess circle or even a co-worker—that you're going after your dream or making a big change. Telling people will make you feel accountable, and you'll gain the support and encouragement of those who want nothing less than to see you succeed. So when you decide to go for it, be proud and be loud.

Week 3: Figure Out Your Skill Set

You feel ready to make a change, but don't quite know how to get started? Figure out your skill set. Knowing your strengths and then activating them is a good first place to start. If you know you're organized, then start your transformation with a daily itinerary or list of things that you need to accomplish by that evening. If you're a little competitive, setting a weekly goal might ignite the champion inside by giving you something tangible to strive for. You're good at something—probably many things—so put them to use as you begin the next take.

Week 4: Pay It Forward

You're rounding the one-month mark, and you're hopeful the changes and progress you've made will stick. This might be a good time to pay it forward and inspire someone you care about to make a change, too. Sharing the wisdom you've gained and the success you've achieved thus far will remind you of the guts, faith, and strength it took for you to take the first step. By inspiring another person, you'll reinforce your own inspiration and keep your confidence going.

Week 5: Keep a Journal

Over time, I've written in a lot of diaries. I've seen my attitudes change, my Achilles' heel continue to plague me, and a cast of thousands move in and out of my life. Journaling puts me face-to-face with what and who was important along my path. It's not only a terrific way to preserve memories; it's also a critical tool in tracking progress. We're ever changing, and that means our thoughts and ideas about ourselves and our worldview change, too. As you keep motivated on your transformation journey, read entries from your former self and see how far your confidence and abilities have come. Then relish the idea that your best is still yet to be written.

Week 6: Write a Gratitude Letter

It's important to keep an attitude of gratitude. Write a letter like the one I wrote in Chapter 7 to Mrs. Johnson, my employer back in high school. Even if the person is long gone, do it anyway. It's a special way of finding the importance in details about our lives that we thought were lost. What I love most about this is that it helps us identify the attributes of people we'd like to embody. Gratitude letters also remind us that we're not alone, and our paths cross and connect for good reason.

Week 7: See What Others See

Try looking at yourself the way other people see you. We have this ability to not treat ourselves the way we treat others. In fact, we're often kinder and more forgiving toward strangers than to ourselves. This week, imagine you're your child, your friend, or your mother. How do they treat you? Do they express love, admiration, or gratitude? Well, turn those feelings on yourself! If this seems too difficult at first (and it probably will), pull out some old letters or cards from loved ones and read their thoughts. Make their opinions and attitudes a part of how you view yourself. Seeing yourself through their eyes can awaken you to how much you're appreciated and cherished.

Week 8: Stop Looking at the Past

We discussed this a lot through this book, and it's important to consciously remind yourself once in a while to live in the present and not judge yourself against an old version of yourself. As we age, it's common to grieve the loss of who we once were or the way it used to be. Your re-creation attempts will likely come to a screeching halt when you look back rather than forward. This week, try to surrender the former versions of yourself. Release them with love—they've served you well.

Week 9: Accept Anger

To combat any feelings of resentment or anger you may feel toward yourself, whether from past mistakes or present ones, allow yourself to experience the emotion. A good cry always works for me, but find your own outlet. Scream it out, work it out, talk it out, whatever—but create a safe way to feel. Then put it aside. The idea is to learn more about yourself through your emotions and ultimately find the peace of mind you need to move ahead.

Week 10: Connect

Isolation is a problem that consumes women all around the globe and in every stage of life—whether a new college grad, a first-time mom, an empty nester, a single parent, or a caregiver—so many women are so overwhelmed that they shut down or avoid friends. Navigating a busy schedule can cut people off from spending quality time with friends and family members and is a big factor in veering off the path of self-improvement. This is a tough one because isolation breeds more of the same. In this case, you'll have to fight hard to stay connected. Find just one person with whom you can sit in silence if you're too overwhelmed to talk. Or reach out to a friend you suspect might be going through a similar phase. You'll be surprised by how many other women feel exactly as you do right now.

Week 11: Have a Check-In Moment

At the end of this week, check in on the good things and the not-so-good things that happened. How did you handle the situations? What caused the good or bad to occur? Who was around you when it happened? The daily grind can be so consuming that you might forget the small achievements and chances for improvement sent to you each and every day. Checking in to review these very moments will help you come to terms with emotions, review strategies, and make adjustments where needed. Your hindsight will actually become a *proactive* way to ensure improvement and accomplishment in the coming weeks.

Week 12: Fuel Your Body

You're busy planning your transformation, walking through the door marked *change,* but have you forgotten anything? Nutrition is vital to staying on track mentally and physically. Keeping fresh foods around and avoiding processed meals must be a strategy this week. Prepare go-to items, such as chopped fresh veggies or frozen fruit and low-calorie snacks, to nourish your body this week. Incorporate one superfood into your meal plan a day (for a list of superfoods, try these sites: **www.anrhealth .com/category_s/45.htm** and **www.betterfitnessdaily.com /amazing-super-foods-for-better-skin-fewer-wrinkles**).

Attempt to eliminate one or two sugary drinks or processed foods. You'll see a difference in your energy level, which will inspire you to keep making healthy eating a priority throughout the rest of your journey.

Week 13: Adopt a Mantra

This week, remind yourself that you're doing your best. Make up a mantra such as, *I love myself, I am doing the best I can.* When you walk, do your chores, and drive to work, say your mantra out loud and become a cheerleader for yourself. Lately I've been using this one: *I try hard, I care a lot, and I always mean well.*

Week 14: Create a Bedtime Ritual

Sleep deprivation has become an epidemic for men, women, and children alike. We're wired up, plugged in, and logged on 24/7. With the demands of family, work, home, and community, it's no wonder we're fatigued, depleted, and prone to illness and emotional issues. This week, try resetting your body clock and cuing yourself for sleep. For the first step, get off the computer. I take ten minutes to decompress at night by stretching. I also signal to my body that the day has ended by drinking chamomile tea or warm milk—they really do work. Rituals tell your brain and the rest of your body, *You've done your best today, but it's time for rest. Tomorrow is another day and another chance to begin with your best intention.*

Week 15: Breathe

Take purposeful breaths when you're anxious. Deep breathing helps you gain control of your physical space, which allows you to better control your physiological response to stress. Once you calm your body, you will be able to better target your emotional space and handle the obstacle more productively. This week, be aware of how often you engage in shallow breathing. Just ten deep, conscious breaths can slow it all down so you're back in charge.

Week 16: Compartmentalize

It's inevitable that you'll become overwhelmed. You're trying to stay true to the path you've forged while taking care of the other responsibilities in your life. To avoid burnout, break down your responsibilities one by one so that you gain better perspective and set priorities. Then recruit team members who can help you. Maybe these people won't be in your immediate family or even close to you geographically—just be sure you look for allies who know you, have patience, and have experienced what you're feeling and trying to achieve.

Week 17: Follow Your Heart

Listen to your yearnings, desires, truth, and natural inclinations. To do otherwise means that you'll always experience friction in your day-to-day existence. Being true to your core is the only way to feel content. There really is no other choice if you want to be authentic, be impeccable with your word, and show integrity through all your actions. This week, be aware of things you may be doing (or thinking) that go against your heart. Why do you think you're doing them? Steve Jobs spoke about this very thing when he gave the commencement address at Stanford in 2005. He said: "Remembering that you are going to die is the best way I know to avoid the trap of thinking you have something to lose. You are already naked. There is no reason not to follow your heart."

Week 18: Confess Something

This week, look at what skeletons may be in your emotional closet, and admit the truth about yourself. Finally reveal a hidden secret. Come clean about a situation with your family members, friends, or colleagues that has haunted you. It doesn't have to be a scandalous admission or a riveting revelation, just something that makes you accountable and releases a part of you that's been beholden to the thing you keep private. I promise that you'll feel emotionally lighter and will probably develop closer bonds with those who receive the information.

Week 19: Jump Ship

What can you close the door on this week? Is there a project or assignment that's been hovering for the longest time? If you're devoting time and energy to something that's either a dead end—or worse, an energy-siphoning hole of distraction and waste—let it go. Here's what Warren Buffett is credited with saying about that: "In a chronically leaking boat, energy devoted to changing vessels is more productive than energy devoted to patching leaks." Know when to cut your losses and move on. (This applies to relationships, too!)

Week 20: Ask for a Lift

Be aware of how often you choose to go it alone. Pay attention to what it feels like to carry the heavy burden of your responsibilities. This week, ask someone to carry you. Maybe it's just for this one day or this particular project, but see what it feels like to let another person shoulder it with you or for you. I'm not asking you to fall apart or collapse totally, just to drop into the strength of another who can offer you a wonderful gift. (Be aware of when you can provide those strong arms for someone else. It's the ultimate give-and-take.)

Week 21: Don't Take Crap from Anyone

Every time you do, you get a little smaller and respect yourself a little less. This week, expect respect from others; and if you don't get it, walk away or change the game. By the way, this includes your kids. Being patient and understanding is one thing, but letting them run all over you is not okay with the new you.

Week 22: Give Back

Look at what talents or resources you have. How much time can you spare? Can you make phone calls for a cause, serve meals, or bathe dogs at the shelter? Can you give a business suit to a battered woman who finds it hard to summon the confidence to go on a job interview? Maybe you can just let someone cut in front of you in line or pay the toll or parking fee for the person in the car behind you. Whatever it is, be aware of ways you can pay it forward this week.

Week 23: Gather Up a Team

Who's on your side? Whom can you count on? This isn't the time to be shy about asking for support. This week, put out an APB and enlist some help. Just sharing your goal will lighten the load. Get clear with yourself about what you want and need, and then go tell it on the mountain, honey! Ask your team to send you encouraging e-mails and voice mails or to join you in your reinvention.

Week 24: Honor Where You Are Today

Declare and trust that today and *every* day is a new blank page. This week, wake up every day and celebrate the parts of you that serve you well. Your body works, you have a sharp mind, you're funny, you have good friends . . . whatever you can find to praise, do it. So what if you still haven't lost the weight or still don't have the dream job or the right partner? If you can accept your starting position and love yourself now, you're in a much better place to create the changes you may want to make.

Week 25: Put Your Game Face On

Mental preparation is the better part of victory—all athletes know this. Most of them rehearse running the track, making the dive, or scoring the goal over and over in their minds before they show up on game day. You're at the starting gate of the rest of your life, so make sure you put your game face on. This week, mentally see your life going the way you want. Walk out the door every day wearing a look of confidence. Many people have started over with less.

Week 26: Commit Yourself to Commitment!

Stepping into your second take (or third or fourth) requires that you stay with it. Every day, several times a day, you're going to be asked to put other things ahead of you and your goals. This week, continue to be flexible, but be aware of how easy it may be to fall off your mark. Don't let that happen. Just pay attention to any wishy-washy behavior and get it in check.

Week 27: Value Your Reputation

If you've called for a redo on life as you knew it, you can build your new reputation on the blocks of your past. However, if there's nothing of value that you want to resurrect (although I really doubt that), then you'll need to be very aware of how your words and actions are setting the tone for the way people feel about you now, and you'll have to be bold.

As you know, I'm not one for going against your heart and your values just so that you can be well thought of or popular, but a solid reputation is a huge investment in your future—mostly when it comes to your opinion of yourself. It's impossible to have self-esteem if you aren't proud of your behavior. When you put your head on the pillow at night, you'll be the only one who knows if you deserve your own admiration.

Week 28: Declutter

Chances are that if your desk is messy, your dresser drawers are chaos, or your kitchen is a wreck, then your emotional space is likely to feel cluttered, too. There's something very satisfying about letting go of things. It psychologically prompts us to stop emotional hoarding as well. This week, see if you can free yourself from some of the pileups that bog you down. Even if it's just organizing your computer desktop, take a step toward clutter-free bliss!

Week 29: Practice Self-Care

I know this really is the frame for everything we've been talking about, but this week, schedule some time for your self-care practices. Your physical, mental, emotional, and spiritual health is up to you; and you need to keep yourself nourished to run at maximum capacity. Meditate, do yoga, get a massage, take a hike, chant—whatever it is you find that fills you up, focus on setting it in your schedule in stone.

Week 30: Open Up and Bloom

If you're disconnected from who you really are, it makes sense that you may start to feel unworthy. If you've attempted to restart your life but have fallen short, that's stressful. No one performs well in those circumstances. But stress is simply having desires and no plan; it's having more problems than solutions. So this week, start to break that down. Think of yourself as a flower: You need light, water, and food to grow. For your soul to thrive, you need friends, compassion, and love—that's what makes you blossom. So open up and restore your capacity to receive those things. That's the plan to connect to your core energy so you can flourish.

Week 31: Take the Limits Off

Just for this week, try dreaming beyond your wildest dreams. Think of what you'd ask for if the dream fairy flew by and sprinkled magic dust all over you. What would you do if you knew you could not fail? Imagination isn't meant to be stifled, and limitless living always starts with a thought. So spend time cultivating your ideas without concern for their practicality. When you give yourself permission to move a thought just a few more yards down the field, who knows what players may show up to take it across the line?

Week 32: Find the Heart-to-Heart Connection

At the center of your physical being is your heart, that amazing organ that beats inside your chest. At the core of your emotional universe is your spiritual heart, that incredible compass of feelings that beats inside your soul. This week, focus on taking care of your emotional sanity as well as your physical well-being. There must be a heart-to-heart link that drives everything you do. One without the other falls short.

Week 33: Drop Your Security Blanket

Chances are, there are certain things in your life that make you feel safe—people you call, things you eat, clothes you wear, and even the route you take to school or the office. This week, see how you feel when you change it up. Do things out of sequence, wear what's hanging in the back of your closet, and give up your rhythms for a few days to see what steps into that space. When life becomes too predictable, you forget to value every part of yourself. Use this time to become reacquainted with your resourcefulness, playfulness, and resilience. As André Gide said, "Man cannot discover new oceans unless he has the courage to lose sight of the shore."

Week 34: Listen More than You Talk

This is one of my tips for success in the business world, but it applies to life in general. As women, we make sense of our world by talking. It relieves our stress and helps us feel safe. No one gets this one better than me! But this week, be aware of how often you chime in without really needing to. What would happen if you didn't feel the need to go on the record, share your opinion, or break the ice? When you're an active listener, you give others the simple joy of knowing that they intrigue you and that you're interested in what they have to say.

Week 35: Fight Procrastination

We can find all kinds of ways to justify the things we put off, but if you come right down to it, lack of self-worth drives a lot of it. This week, since you know you're worth it, make the hard call, start on that creative project, and cross off whatever difficult thing has taken up permanent residence on your to-do list. Give yourself the relief that will follow—not to mention the stress off your heart and the self-pride that will take its place.

Week 36: Smile

Yep, that's it for this week . . . except I'm asking that you smile even when you don't feel like it. Research shows that the mere act of smiling has a positive impact on your emotions and consequently your heart health. It also helps keep your facial muscles nice and toned.

Week 37: Find the Hero in You

Whether it's an astronaut, a firefighter, or anyone in between, a hero looks to serve others. So this week, I want you to figure out how to best serve yourself right now. Start with defining what makes you original. (Think about what kind of cape you'd wear!) What are your talents? Where do you contribute? If you could hide behind a mask like Spider-Man, what would you do that you aren't doing now? The odds are that you go above and beyond every day, but you don't give yourself credit. The best way to answer the call for heroism is simply to be the best version of yourself you can possibly be. You're on your way.

Week 38: Ask Questions

Don't worry about looking foolish, and don't give up until you have answers. This week, ask questions of everyone about everything and take your natural curiosity out for walk. A good interviewer knows that the key to getting more answers is to listen and capitalize on a nugget of information in order to formulate the next question. You might be surprised where an innocent line of questioning can take you.

Week 39: Never Give Up

When the project is *you,* the stakes are as high as they come, so you must never, ever give up in your pursuit of growth. When you're so frustrated that you could scream (and you will be) and are certain you can't do it, that's the time to remember the words of the White Queen in Lewis Carroll's *Through the Looking Glass:* "Why, sometimes I've believed as many as six impossible things before breakfast." This week, push through what's difficult for you and remember that you'll grow in proportion to the challenge.

Week 40: Face Your Finances

Money matters. Whether you have extravagant desires for expensive things and experiences or you just want enough to get by on, the reality is that money can cause you stress and damage your relationships if you don't have a plan and a budget. This week, gather up everything you need to get honest about money. Learn what you don't know, and seek out a financial planner if you can. If you've never done this before or think you're so far in the hole that you can't climb out, get over yourself and just handle it.

Week 41: Banish Blame

You and you alone are creating your reality—right now. You're the one who can take all the gifts you've been given and all the challenges you have and answer the question, *Now what?* It has nothing to do with how your parents treated you, how many times you changed schools, or how many boyfriends made you feel like dirt. If you don't have enough money or if you were overindulged, make peace with where you are now and be accountable for moving forward to where you want to be. Dragging anyone or anything behind you as you go will just weigh you down.

Week 42: Celebrate Your Sexuality

If you already adore your body and enjoy intimacy in a safe, loving environment, then you really have a reason to be happy and celebrate! If not, take a long look this week at how you can reclaim this important part of your life. It's not an add-on or something to deal with later. Your sex drive is an integral part of who you are as a human. It's part of your DNA, and I think it should be everyone's birthright. As a woman, not only is your body hard-wired for pleasure, but sex is also tied in with feelings of comfort, love, value, naughtiness, and companionship. You may need to work with a therapist to sort out these feelings and explore ways you can have a healthy sex life. When you do, watch other parts of your life suddenly work, too.

Week 43: Tame the Green-Eyed Monster

It's natural to want something someone else has. In fact, I've talked about how valuable it can be to use that longing as inspiration for you to get the relationship, business savvy, body, or patience of one of your role models. But real jealousy is another thing. It will eat you alive and prevent joy from finding its way to you. When you feel "less than" because of what someone else has, when you feel like a failure because of another's achievement, flip that around. Whenever you start to feel envious this week, catch it and say to yourself, *Good for her. I can have that, too,* or *There's enough for everyone, and this time it goes to her. There is plenty of time for me to shine.*

Week 44: Don't Settle

We give up on ourselves too quickly sometimes. For all the right reasons, we often give in or let ourselves be talked out of our boundaries in an attempt to keep the peace or make things nice for everyone. The problem is that we know better, and we begin to slump a little in shame. Look at people who demand the best—very often they get it. They receive it from others, and they demand it of themselves. This week, be aware of how quickly you may be swayed or how often you throw in the towel. Being cooperative and flexible is great; settling for anything less than you deserve is not.

Week 45: Be Your Own Therapist

I believe in professional counselors and therapists for sure, but I also think there are things that you can do to heal yourself. One of them is to break down and cry. I don't mean happy tears that trickle in dainty little rivulets down your cheeks; I'm talking sobbing, chest-heaving, "ugly" crying to rid yourself of whatever needs to come out. It's something in your emotional toolbox that may not be used often because you feel embarrassed, out of control, or manipulative. This week, create a safe place to let it all go.

Week 46: Link to Your Legacy

Where did you come from? What's your history? This week, connect with the fact that you belong to a bigger picture that started before you were born and will continue long after you're gone. While there are many sites online for researching your family tree, try to do it the old-fashioned way, by interviewing distant relatives, neighbors, or friends of your parents. Drench yourself in the family stories and myths. Keep the flame burning for your kids or the ones who will come after you.

Week 47: Switch It Up

How long have you parted your hair on the same side? Have you had this color for decades? When was the last time you changed your eye makeup, lipstick, or blush color? Having a look is not a bad thing at all—the cool thing is that you learn what works for you and tend to stay with it. Knowing your style sometimes takes a lifetime, and perfecting it is a victory. But this week, shake it up. Wear false eyelashes. (Personally, I do this every day. I already told you that I'm a pack-a-day girl when it comes to this product!) Cut your bangs or throw on a headband, a scarf, or hair jewels. The point is to surprise yourself and keep others on the alert that you're a dynamic force of nature!

Week 48: Plant Something

It could be big or small, indoors or out, decorative or functional. The idea is to use your hands to give life to something that needs your touch. My foundation threw an Oscar-party fund-raiser one year, and we decided to create a carbon-neutral environment for our guests by planting a tree for each attendee. We worked with the nonprofit group TreePeople and planted seedlings in one of the canyons in L.A. It was such a magical experience, knowing that decades from now those trees will be supplying oxygen, beauty, and shade for people I'll never meet. You can easily forget that you *are* nature, so connecting with it can make you breathe easier, literally and figuratively.

Week 49: Say Thanks to Your Ex File

When Steven and I were married, Lexi and Troy were ordained so they could perform the ceremony (Nathan handled the giving of the rings). It's a good thing, since there were no other attendees. Lexi sings beautifully, so we asked her to contribute the song "Bless the Broken Road," famously interpreted by Rascal Flatts. As she sang, I think the kids really understood the message about how every broken heart and every lost love had paved the way for Steven and me to find each other. We're so grateful for our former loves, because they each helped us learn more about who we are and what we have to give.

This week, be glad for the ones who loved you and left you, turned you down, stepped on your heart, and sent you packing. They prepared you for where you are now. You don't need to call them, confront them, or send any kind of communication. It's done. Just whisper a prayer of gratitude and know that they served you well.

Week 50: Don't Block the Blessings

This week's dose is something Patti LaBelle always said and the title of her memoir. In this moment, look at how much goodness is aimed right at you that you're just not receiving. You're either too stubborn to see that you need it, too busy to recognize it, too proud to let it in, or too dumb to know that blessings often come in disguise! Remember how you used to pray that a certain boy would like you? After you grew up and saw what he became and how he lives, you feel like that Garth Brooks song—and thank God for unanswered prayers! Your blessings are out there waiting for you, so open up and let them in.

Week 51: Put Up with the Rain

I have a necklace with a quote on it from Dolly Parton: "If you want the rainbow, you have to put up with the rain." Isn't that simply perfect and perfectly simple? This week, look at the price you have to pay for anything worthwhile. You want to grow and evolve as a person; you want to make sure your life counts for something, and that your story doesn't suffer from that awful "sagging middle" syndrome I talked about at the beginning of the book. Well then, you have to put in the time and make hard choices and sacrifices to get there. The difference between extraordinary and ordinary is that little something extra. Your rainbow is on its way.

Week 52: Find the Time

Everyone says it: *I just don't have enough time.* Yes, you do. Own up to that reality this week. When you whine about time, you're really turning over your power to the clock. Everyone has the same number of hours in a day, and everyone makes time for what she thinks is important. Stop the excuses and be accountable. Exercise, visiting with friends, focusing on family—whatever is at the top of your list, don't sacrifice it. Tell yourself, *This is important to me, I'm going to find time,* or *I'm working on making sure the things I care about are always at the top of my list.* Make a chart, use an app, or do something else so that you can see how you're spending your time. If there are more withdrawals than deposits, it's time to balance the books!

BREATHE, BELIEVE, RECEIVE

I'd like to end this book by talking to you about the importance of three seemingly simple things. It's time to breathe, believe, and receive (BBR).

We've talked all about change, and this is a great way to change your reaction to stress within you and change coming from the outside. You can either react or respond, and knowing how to manage it can save your life. We all know CPR can save a life, and I think BBR can, too!

• **Breathe:** Take ten purposeful breaths, expanding your lungs and breathing in through your nose. On each inhale, breathe in with the certainty that you're doing your best. Exhale all the negativity that weighs heavy in your head and on your heart. Just breathing like this can change your physical and emotional state, slowing down your heart rate, aiding your digestion, and reducing your stress so that you can cope with the very challenging and exciting journey you're on.

• **Believe:** How come circumstances drown some of us, while others are buoyant? I think there's a way of looking at things that makes a difference. The lens through which you create your world affects everything. No matter where you go, there you are—you, with your own approach, temperament, and expectations. This is where those glass-half-full kinds of people have the advantage, so now is the time to be an optimist, to believe. Whether it's because of shooting stars, four-leaf clovers, Buddha, God, or unicorns, take time to believe that good things are coming and that you're part of something bigger than yourself. Have faith that no matter what, it will all be okay. Optimists really do fare better in warding off everything from the common cold to gastrointestinal problems and sleeplessness. Know that you can do it and that your efforts will be enough. Believe that you can be empowered by others who have achieved this before you. Draw strength from them, and realize that what you learn on your journey will also lift those who come next.

• **Receive:** Everyone has limits, and there will be days when you feel that you just can't do it anymore. That's why it's so important to be surrounded by an encouraging community and to explore your resources. Sometimes you need to stop achieving and start receiving. Understand that real strength comes from knowing your limits and asking for help. When someone asks, "Do you need anything?" get comfortable with saying yes, and be prepared to provide a list! It can include everything from walking the dog to bringing dinner and listening to you vent, but don't be afraid to let people know what's helpful to you.

The following was written for guests at Leeza's Place and Leeza's Care Connection to help them ground themselves in purposeful connection every day. I hope it reminds you to seek out support on your journey, too.

Breathe, Believe, Receive

Today I will take a deep breath in as I move forward. I come to gain strength and to offer it. I know that I am on a path that I cannot walk alone, so I will find ways to connect and communicate my needs. I give myself permission to be vulnerable, recognizing that my fear is just courage looking for a way in. I know that even when I fall short of my hopes, I am enough because I try and I care. When I am overwhelmed or frustrated, I will connect to the community of support that is my family of choice. There is wisdom in our connection, there is hope in our hearts, and there is strength in our togetherness. Today I will exhale, knowing I am not alone. Breathe, believe, receive.

AFTERWORD: HONORING CAREGIVERS: FAMILY FIRST RESPONDERS

With this book, I honor all those brave souls whose life stories are painfully rewritten when someone they love is sick or dying, beginning with my own family: my dad, Carlos; my brother, Carlos Jr.; his wife, Anne Marie; and my sister, Cammy. As we cared for my mom, Jean, while she battled Alzheimer's disease, we became part of a group of family caregivers who face a moment of truth that changes everything. As I write this, I see Steven's family struggle with the pain of losing their patriarch, Frank, to Parkinson's and Alzheimer's. His mom, Judie; his sisters and brother; and their spouses are all trying to form a shield to try to protect Frank and also to protect themselves from a gaping wound of sadness that seems to grow bigger every day. They are reluctant recruits to this new world.

Being a caregiver is not anyone's version of happily ever after, but it's reality for more than 65 million people who never thought their lives would come to this. These are the husbands and wives, sons and daughters, who have been tested in a moment of truth.

How can we ever offer enough respect, gratitude, honor, and validation to those family members and friends who give hundreds of thousands of hours of unpaid care and who often don't get a thank-you, a pat on the back, or the comfort that comes from knowing they're making a difference?

For most, becoming a caregiver is like being recruited into a group you don't really want to belong to. At least it was that way for me—I went kicking and screaming. Like most, I was resentful and resistant. After a long period of doing everything I could to deny my new reality, life changed the instant we got the diagnosis that Mom had Alzheimer's disease. Our boat could no longer stay moored in the safe harbor we'd always known, and our family was about to set sail into uncharted and often treacherous waters. I wish we'd known then what we know now. We were afraid. Afraid of what we knew was coming next, and afraid of what we didn't know about how we would manage our way through it.

Over the past decade, I've tried to share what I learned about the physical, emotional, spiritual, and financial assault that families face when this thief pulls up a chair at their table. I've seen families ripped apart by this diagnosis, simply unraveling at the prospect of the devastation to come. My mother's descent into darkness took more than ten years as she journeyed through the disease, and we tried so hard to make it better. My dad, my siblings, and our extended family all dealt with it differently, each of us coping in our own way. But we were still a unit, a team. How blessed we have been.

With caregiving, there's strength in numbers, and I became very proud of being able to join the troop that showed up for duty every day.

I promised Mom that I'd take our story and share it, so in 2002 I founded the Leeza Gibbons Memory Foundation, and we began offering free support services for family caregivers at Leeza's Place and now through Leeza's Care Connection. Since then, I've learned that millions of us have faced or are facing something so daunting that it can't be managed alone. I've realized that when we reach out and lift each other up, we can not only survive but thrive through our new reality. It's like a powerful connection of care, and it works!

I think you *can* create a new beginning. All it takes is closing the door on what came before. *With this book about starting over, I honor all of those who were sucked into their next act without the luxury of choosing it. But caregivers, most of all, can find the value and the promise of creating a fresh start.*

Many of us were inspired to call for a second take when we learned someone we loved was sick or dying. I know what tremendous gifts I received because of this. Caregivers are masters of change whose courage, dignity, grace, and resilience have taught me much of what I convey in these pages. They often face a long, dark hallway that seems to have no end. It's like playing a game where the rules switch from minute to minute, and only when we team up and coach each other along can everyone win. That's what we do at Leeza's Place and Leeza's Care Connection. We encourage our guests to summon their strength and call on their wisdom.

Through my interactions with the caregivers whose lives I've been privileged to share, I'm finally able to really understand the wisdom spoken by Christopher Robin in A. A. Milne's Winnie the Pooh stories: *"You are braver than you believe, stronger than you seem, and smarter than you think."* Because these people are forced to look afresh at most everything, every day, theirs is a story of transformation like no other. It has been a beacon for my path to be a witness to their journey.

Whatever your story is, it's not over, and I sure hope you're ready for your second take. As it evolves, as *you* create the future, honor it, tell it, and make it count!

GRATITUDE AND LOVE FOR MY FRIENDS, FAMILY, TEACHERS, AND GUIDES

"Acknowledgments" is typically what this section of the book is labeled, but to me that seems like such a generic or lame term. I mean, I can recognize that someone performed a certain function or was involved in a certain way, but there's no love in that! And here's the deal: this entire book is about valuing our growth process and being open for coaching and teaching, so for me just to "acknowledge" those who have guided my path doesn't seem right. So I'd prefer to think of this as a love letter, sent with the deepest gratitude and respect to those who taught me, encouraged me, supported me, nudged me, and set me straight during this process.

My amazing husband, Steven Fenton, did all of those things and more. Baby, I love you for believing I had a voice and a point of view that was valuable. Thank you for often pushing me out the door and standing me up at the starting line with that unshakable confidence you have in me, saying, "Just get started and you'll see." To my children, whose love is my life jacket, thank you for helping me grow up and show up, because I want to be the best mom I can be to the best kids I can ever imagine.

They say when the student is ready, the teacher will appear, and this project was a big-time validation of that philosophy. I love to share what I've learned, and I love to express my thoughts and ideas. What I don't love is editing them, researching them, rewriting them, and organizing them. Luckily, I have Hay House with its team of experts in my corner. I like to think of the folks at Hay House as always being on "soul patrol" because not only are they top-rate professionals, but they value the process and seem to have advanced degrees in protecting spirit along the way. That starts with founder Louise Hay, of course; and for me it began with Reid Tracy, the Hay House CEO.

When my husband and I first met with Reid, I believe it was the first time I have ever been in an executive's office with no phones going off, no assistants bringing in bogus memos, no mobile devices within reach, and no monitoring of computer screens. They walk their talk over there, and it was in the integrity of that moment that I knew it was a good fit. Thanks for being present, Reid, and for launching me into orbit. Shannon Littrell, my editor, despite being much younger than me, has mothered me in this process, leaving me alone so that I could stand on my own, but gently correcting and redirecting without any shame or blame. My gratitude to Shannon and the entire team for being enthusiastic and lovely to work with.

If you're an author and you were born under a lucky star, you get to be represented by Jan Miller. This woman redefines living without limits and elevates her profession to an art. They say she has a great eye for talent, and I can tell you that's true with her staff. Lacy Lalene Lynch (I loved her from the get-go with that name) is an arrow shooting directly toward success, always. Thank you, Lacy, for your business savvy, your decency, your ambition, and your commitment to your own growth, which I always found inspiring. You and the team at DuPree Miller have helped many authors connect the dots between the message and the marketplace. I'm so happy to be one of them.

Lacy connected me with Michele Mastriciani, and when I talk about a sanity sanctuary, this is what I mean. Michele, thank you for giving me a place to exhale, knowing that with your skillful guidance, even with my ADD and OCD tendencies, I could make sense of all the random ideas roaming the halls of my brain! Your editorial support was invaluable, besides the fact that you're just a really great person.

Speaking of great . . . that's what Fabio Storti is in every sense of the word for jumping on this train even as it was speeding down the track, adding his gifts and talents. Thank you for being so cool to work with, Fabio!

Many of my Girlfriend Goddess Gurus and dispensers of kitchen-table wisdom are mentioned in these pages, along with the families and teams from Leeza's Place and Leeza's Care Connection. These are sources of outrageous good fortune in my life. I am blessed beyond belief with my biological family from South Carolina and my logical family of choice.

Finally, my biggest hug goes to you, the person reading this page. However you got this book, whatever the reason, I know that we are now part of the same conversation, so let's move it forward . . . ever forward.

ABOUT THE AUTHOR

She has been called a social entrepreneur, the voice of the caregiver, product maven, and broadcast star; but if you ask Leeza Gibbons what she does, she'll simply answer, "I'm a storyteller." From television news journalist and host to producer and businesswoman, Leeza has been entering America's living rooms for over 30 years. She currently is cohost and executive producer of the syndicated nightly news program *America Now* and host of the weekly TV news show *My Generation* on PBS. Leeza is one of the best-known and well-loved TV icons still on the air and at the top of her game. Her recognizability, relatability, and reputation began on the national scene as an anchor and reporter on *Entertainment Tonight,* which she used as a platform to build an international radio presence and direct response business that created the Sheer Cover mineral makeup brand as well as several other beauty products.

Gibbons has a star on Hollywood's fabled Walk of Fame, but she is most proud of being a wife to Steven and mom to "three of the planet's most amazing kids." Two of them grew up on the Paramount lot, where she served as the host and executive producer of her award-winning daytime talk show, *Leeza*, which aired from 1994 to 2000 and garnered 27 Emmy Award nominations, winning three. Gibbons went on to become the managing editor and host of the TV show *Extra* until she left in 2002 to form her nonprofit organization, the Leeza Gibbons Memory Foundation, a 501(c)(3), and its signature programs, Leeza's Place and Leeza's Care Connection, which offer free services to family members who care for a sick or dying loved one.

Her passion for health advocacy began with her mother's and grandmother's journeys through Alzheimer's disease. She says, "After the two strongest women in my life fell prey to the thief of memory called Alzheimer's disease, I created what we wished we had . . . a place to get support, help, and hope for our family's challenging journey." Since then Gibbons has found ways to honor her mother's legacy through the website **AlzheimersDisease.com** and many other platforms, including serving as Governor Arnold Schwarzenegger's appointee to California's board that oversees the California Institute for Regenerative Medicine.

A recognized thought leader in the field, she wrote a book about her personal experience called *Take Your Oxygen First: Protecting Your Health and Happiness while Caring for a Loved One with Memory Loss*, which was named one of the best consumer health books in the marketplace by *Library Journal*.

More recently, Gibbons has developed two lines of scrapbook products called *Wishes and Dreams* and *All about Me* to underscore the importance of memories and the value of artistic expression to help create the life of your dreams.

With decades of speaking directly to women about "what's on their minds and what's in their hearts," Gibbons has become a trusted source for tips on everything from how to get ahead in business to lengthening your lashes and jump-starting your love life. Her philosophy is "Know Where You're Going, Look Good When You Get There" and her message is for anyone who wants to claim their future by taking control of today.

"I entered my second act by appearing on *Dancing with the Stars*," Gibbons says. "In life, just as it was for me on the show, sometimes you forget your steps and your music is bound to change." Now she shares what she calls her "Life Lessons at the Halfway Point" through speeches and appearances where audiences learn that if life is a test, Leeza can help you cram for the final!

Hay House Titles of Related Interest

YOU CAN HEAL YOUR LIFE, the movie,
starring Louise L. Hay & Friends
(available as a 1-DVD program and an expanded 2-DVD set)
Watch the trailer at: **www.LouiseHayMovie.com**

THE SHIFT, the movie,
starring Dr. Wayne W. Dyer
(available as a 1-DVD program and an expanded 2-DVD set)
Watch the trailer at: **www.DyerMovie.com**

✦✦✦

THE AGE OF MIRACLES: Embracing the New Midlife,
by Marianne Williamson

*THE ART OF EXTREME SELF-CARE: Transform Your Life
One Month at a Time,* by Cheryl Richardson

*COMPLEXION PERFECTION!: Your Ultimate Guide to Beautiful Skin
by Hollywood's Leading Skin Health Expert,* by Kate Somerville

THE HEALING POWER OF WATER, by Masaru Emoto

*SECRETS OF MEDITATION: A Practical Guide to Inner Peace
and Personal Transformation,* by davidji

WISHES FOR A MOTHER'S HEART: Words of Inspiration, Love, and Support,
by Tricia LaVoice and Barbara Lazaroff

WISHES FULFILLED: Mastering the Art of Manifesting,
by Dr. Wayne W. Dyer

All of the above are available at your local bookstore,
or may be ordered by contacting Hay House (see next page).

✦✦✦

We hope you enjoyed this Hay House book. If you'd like
to receive our online catalog featuring additional information
on Hay House books and products, or if you'd like to find out
more about the Hay Foundation, please contact:

Hay House, Inc., P.O. Box 5100, Carlsbad, CA 92018-5100
(760) 431-7695 or (800) 654-5126
(760) 431-6948 (fax) or (800) 650-5115 (fax)
www.hayhouse.com® • **www.hayfoundation.org**

Published and distributed in Australia by: Hay House Australia Pty. Ltd.,
18/36 Ralph St., Alexandria NSW 2015 • *Phone:* 612-9669-4299
Fax: 612-9669-4144 • www.hayhouse.com.au

Published and distributed in the United Kingdom by: Hay House UK, Ltd.,
292B Kensal Rd., London W10 5BE • *Phone:* 44-20-8962-1230
Fax: 44-20-8962-1239 • www.hayhouse.co.uk

Published and distributed in the Republic of South Africa by:
Hay House SA (Pty), Ltd., P.O. Box 990, Witkoppen 2068
Phone/Fax: 27-11-467-8904 • www.hayhouse.co.za

Published in India by: Hay House Publishers India, Muskaan Complex,
Plot No. 3, B-2, Vasant Kunj, New Delhi 110 070 • *Phone:* 91-11-4176-1620
Fax: 91-11-4176-1630 • www.hayhouse.co.in

Distributed in Canada by: Raincoast, 9050 Shaughnessy St.,
Vancouver, B.C. V6P 6E5 • *Phone:* (604) 323-7100 • *Fax:* (604) 323-2600
www.raincoast.com

Take Your Soul on a Vacation

Visit **www.HealYourLife.com®** to regroup, recharge,
and reconnect with your own magnificence.
Featuring blogs, mind-body-spirit news, and life-changing
wisdom from Louise Hay and friends.

Visit **www.HealYourLife.com** today!

WE ARE GROWING AND LEARNING . . .
REACHING FOR MORE.

WE BELONG TO A SISTERHOOD OF WOMEN WHO ARE
ALWAYS EVOLVING.

WE RELY ON OUR ROOTS AND WINGS, WHICH KEEP US
GROUNDED IN OUR STRENGTH AND ALLOW US OUR
FLIGHTS OF FANCY.

WE HONOR OUR PAST AND FUEL OUR FUTURE WITH
LIMITLESS EXPECTATIONS.

WE ARE FIERCE AND FEARLESS AND LIKE THE DRAGONFLY,
CAN SEE OURSELVES IN A WHOLE NEW LIGHT WITH 360
DEGREE VISION!